THE COMPLETE SPEAKER

An Introduction to Public Speaking, Third Edition

THE COMPLETE SPEAKER

An Introduction to Public Speaking, Third Edition

Brent D. Peterson,
Brigham Young University

Eric G. Stephan,
Brigham Young University

Noel D. White,
The Noel White Group

West Publishing Company

St. Paul   New York   Los Angeles   San Francisco

Cover Art: Lee Sievers
Copyediting: Marilynn Taylor
Indexing: Terry Casey
Composition: Parkwood Composition

A list of photo credits follows the index.

WEST'S COMMITMENT TO THE ENVIRONMENT

In 1906, West Publishing Company began recycling materials left over from the production of books. This began a tradition of efficient and responsible use of resources. Today, up to 95 percent of our legal books and 70 percent of our college texts are printed on recycled, acid-free stock. West also recycles nearly 22 million pounds of scrap paper annually—the equivalent of 181,717 trees. Since the 1960s, West has devised ways to capture and recycle waste inks, solvents, oils, and vapors created in the printing process. We also recycle plastics of all kinds, wood, glass, corrugated cardboard, and batteries, and have eliminated the use of styrofoam book packaging. We at West are proud of the longevity and the scope of our commitment to the environment.

Library of Congress Cataloging-in-Publication Data

Peterson, Brent D.
    The Complete Speaker: An Introduction to Public Speaking /
Brent D. Peterson, Eric G. Stephan, Noel D. White. — 3rd ed.
        p. cm.
    Rev. ed. of: Speak easy. 2nd ed. ©1984.
    Includes index.
    ISBN 0-314-93439-1 (soft)
    1. Public speaking. I. Stephan, Eric G.   II. White, Noel D.
III. Peterson, Brent D. Speak easy. IV. Title.
PN4121.P43 1992
808.5'1—dc20   91-41228
                              ∞   CIP

CONTENTS

PART II
PLANNING, PREPARING, AND PRESENTING 51

CHAPTER 3
SELECTING A TOPIC AND A PURPOSE 53

CHAPTER 6
DELIVERING YOUR IDEAS 139

PART III
SPEAKING WITH A PURPOSE 179

▰▰ CHAPTER 9
SPECIAL SPEAKING OCCASIONS 239

CHAPTER 10
SPEAKING IN SMALL GROUPS AND CONFERENCES 257

PREFACE

As we complete this third edition, we continue to feel strongly that this is not just another book about giving a speech but a book about speaking in public.

1. The text follows our conviction that the key to effective speaking is (a) getting the listener's attention, (b) keeping the listener interested and involved, and (c) stimulating a favorable response in the listener.

2. Further, we take the position that the roots of effective speaking exist in everyday conversing skills. Everyone already has a substantial experience base for speaking. In other words, public speaking instruction should not be seen as being at the opposite end of the communication continuum from two-person/interpersonal interaction. Public speaking principles evolve and can be best understood by examining the principles of interpersonal exchanges and transactions.

3. The reader will find the text to be designed, organized, and illustrated to parallel what an effective presentation should be. This is a do-as-I-do, not a do-as-I-say, book. The text is simple, to the point, and highly illustrative—a speech should be no less.

If you will take a moment to look over the table of contents and then glance through the pages, you will see that the book does not just talk about public speaking but rather models what it is teaching.

As speech-communication teachers, we have often discussed with each other what principles of traditional public speaking we actually use in our own professional lives. We discovered that mainly we adapt to the audience, develop the speech around a specific purpose or point, use plenty of examples and visual materials, and are enthusiastic about what we say.

We also noted that some of our personal discoveries regarding effective speaking do not appear consistently in other available texts. What do you do if your audience isn't responding after you have finished your introduction? How do you discover your own speaking style, rather than just mimic someone else's? Why are some of the more effective speakers today using an informal delivery? How can speakers make themselves more credible as they speak?

We embrace the idea that public speaking cannot be separated or taught apart from everyday talking, conversing, making a point in a meeting, or answering or asking a question in class. The roots of public speaking are in our everyday interactions; basic speaking skills exist in social exchanges. And we strongly believe that how you say it can be as important as what you say.

Our own research suggests why, physiologically and psychologically, some traditional techniques for speaking work. For example, the functioning of the right and left brain hemispheres helps explain why and how general and specific statements, verbal and nonverbal elements, abstract and visual points must be combined in a presentation. The reasons certain speaking formats or styles are effective have a lot to do with how the brain processes information.

In this third edition, we have expanded the material on listening into a separate chapter. We also have enlarged the section on how to reduce speech anxiety. Various new topics have been included, such as "consider the speaking occasion," "using transitions," "the ethics of persuasion." Models of speeches, introductions, and conclusions have been updated, and sample speech outlines have been added. We feel that *Speak Easy* has evolved to *The Complete Speaker*.

In this book, we continue to take the position that the instructor is a *coach*. The instructor may not have the time to model every single principle; neither does a coach. Various coaches have different approaches and sometimes can train people to do the activity better than they can do it themselves. Many beginning public speakers allow anyone who has an opinion to be the coach. *Our belief is that the student can have only one coach at a time. In this case, it is the instructor.* In addition, the student has to be willing to try out new skills, even though doing so may be a bit uncomfortable. You should not expect high grades on every class presentation, but your reward will be that this course will make a difference in your life. More specifically, when you, the student, complete this book and the course, you will find greater confidence and ability in:

- getting and holding a listener's attention.
- responding to critical questions and comments.
- being specific and to the point.
- accepting and using constructive speaking criticism.
- examining your credibility as a message source.
- organizing information to obtain a specific speaking purpose.
- speaking up in meetings and public situations.
- influencing others' opinions and attitudes.
- giving presentations in small or large groups.
- speaking to inform on a controversial issue.

And if you become addicted to speaking, as we have, you may end up making a living by doing the very thing that scared you to death at one point.

For the benefit of those readers who would like a simple overview of the book, we should mention that the book is organized into three parts. The first, "Speaking with Others," includes an opening chapter, "Public Speaking and You." A speaking analysis test is offered here. Chapter 2, "The Process of Public Speaking: An Overview," focuses on listener-oriented speaking.

The second part, "Planning, Preparing, and Presenting the Speech," has four chapters. Chapter 3, "Selecting a Topic and a Purpose," emphasizes speaking about topics that interest you. Chapter 4, "Supporting and Illustrating Your Ideas," has a special section on visual supporting materials. Chapter 5, "Organizing Your Speech Information," and Chapter 6, "Delivering Your Ideas," emphasize how to present yourself and the material.

The third part, "Speaking with a Purpose," has six chapters. Chapter 7, "Informative Speaking," covers the basics of informative speaking, including giving instructions to others. Chapter 8, "Persuasive Speaking," focuses on key persuasive techniques that have practical application. Chapter 9, "Special Speaking Occasions," Chapter 10, "Speaking in Small Groups and Conferences," Chapter 11, "Listening Effectively," and Chapter 12, "Responding to Questions and Comments," deal with the special speaking situations in which we find ourselves. Chapter 13 concludes the book on a high note of personal challenge.

We have gone through the same steps and materials in preparing this book that we would in preparing to speak for a large audience.

We think the book reflects that practical flavor.

We recognize also that trying to develop a public speaking text that matches other fine texts in coverage and currency requires a magnificent effort. To compile a text that responds more fully to student requests for more understandable explanations of key topics and how to implement important concepts in real life would not have been possible without the assistance of many individuals.

We acknowledge the support of the following reviewers who spent many hours making this third edition a more "complete book":

Richard N. Armstrong
Wichita State University

Ronald L. Aungst
Sam Houston State University

Jack Bain
Michigan State University

Dale Davis
University of Texas, San Antonio

George O. Enell
California State University, Fullerton

Elaine Baer Holliday
National University

Beverly Christofferson
Western Iowa Tech Community College

Susan Doyle
Prince George's Community College

Walter E. Doyle
Tidewater Community College

Martha Kuchar
Illinois Technical College

Dorothy B. Moore
Fort Lauderdale College

Beatrice D. O'Connor
Nassau Community College

Gary L. Robertson
El Camino College

Judy Santacaterina
Northern Illinois University

Milda Steinbrecher
Univerwity of Wisconsin, Oshkosh

Margaret Taylor
Orange Coast College

   We would also like to thank our editors, Clyde Perlee, Denise
Simon, Beth Kennedy, and the staff at West for their direction and
patience in bringing this book into a form that makes it appealing
in today's marketplace.
   And finally, for their daily support and kindness to us, we express
our deepest love to our splendid wives, Arlene Peterson, Sandra Stephan, and Judy White, and to all of our most remarkable children.

NOTE TO THE READER: If you read the foregoing material, you probably have a
better understanding of the writers, the book, and the subject of public speaking.
In fact, you may even feel a bit warm and encouraged about some of the possibilities for being more effective and comfortable when speaking. At any rate, congratulations for reading this first.

I

SPEAKING WITH OTHERS

Herein lies the tragedy of the age: not that men are poor—all men know something of poverty; not that men are wicked—who is good? Not that men are ignorant—what is truth? Nay, but that men know so little of men.

William E. B. DuBois

1
PUBLIC SPEAKING AND YOU

In this chapter, you will test your knowledge of public speaking concepts and learn how extensively public speaking is being used in the United States today. You will also learn some valuable tips for turning your everyday conversing skills into effective public speaking skills.

Chapter Content

- **Speaking: Common Misconceptions**
  Inventory of Public Speaking
- **Who Is Speaking?**
- **Things to Learn about Speaking Well**
- **What You Now Know**
- **What to Do to Learn More**

SPEAKING: COMMON MISCONCEPTIONS

You may have noticed by now a familiar experience related to speaking publicly. We tend to be "experts" in critiquing how others could have *obviously* improved their speaking effectiveness. This spectator expertise has been called "armchair quarterbacking" in relation to viewing football games. This confidence, which often comes in retrospect, tends to diminish and turn into outright humbleness when we are doing the speaking. Questions without apparent answers pop up uninvited in our mind. What would be the best approach to the subject? How should I organize what I want to say? For that matter, what do I want to say? Why am I so nervous? Does everyone else go through what I am going through?

Actually, most of us talk so much and have been talking so long that we fail to notice on the conscious level when we do it well and when we do it poorly. Somehow, we have come to believe that giving a talk is completely different from talking with others. This is in fact not true. Only minor differences in technique exist between talking and "giving a talk." In fact, we are likely to forget just how much time we spend giving talks or mini-speeches and expressing our opinions with others.

Before proceeding with the chapter, we want to give you an opportunity to assess your working knowledge of public speaking concepts. Complete the following Public Speaking Inventory to see how well you commonly sense what might be considered, upon the completion of this book, as speaking common sense.

Inventory of Public Speaking

Circle the response that you believe is *most* correct.

1. Delivery is more important in persuasive speaking than it is in informative speaking.

True   False

2. Most public speaking is informative.

True   False

AVERAGE OF STUDENT ANSWERS
TO THE PUBLIC SPEAKING SELF-EVALUATION

Present Knowledge of:											Priority Ranking
Listening	1	2	3	4	5	6	⑦	8	9	10	9
Informative speaking	1	2	3	4	⑤	6	7	8	9	10	5
Persuasive speaking	1	2	3	4	⑤	6	7	8	9	10	6
Audiovisual aids	1	2	3	④	5	6	7	8	9	10	11
Outlines	1	2	3	④	5	6	7	8	9	10	14
Introductions	1	2	3	4	5	6	⑦	8	9	10	8
Developing the body	1	2	3	4	5	⑥	7	8	9	10	2
Conclusions	1	2	3	4	5	⑥	7	8	9	10	10
Transitions	1	2	3	④	5	6	7	8	9	10	17
Holding audience attention	1	2	3	4	⑤	6	7	8	9	10	1
Eye contact	1	2	3	4	5	6	7	⑧	9	10	7
Bodily action	1	2	3	④	5	6	7	8	9	10	13
Gestures	1	2	3	4	⑤	6	7	8	9	10	12
Vocal inflection	1	2	3	④	5	6	7	8	9	10	15
Minimizing stage fright	1	2	3	④	5	6	7	8	9	10	4
Emotional appeals	1	2	③	4	5	6	7	8	9	10	18
Rate of delivery	1	2	③	4	5	6	7	8	9	10	19
Anatomy of vocal mechanisms	1	2	③	4	5	6	7	8	9	10	16
Organization of total speech	1	2	3	4	⑤	6	7	8	9	10	3

Students reported the least amount of knowledge concerning emotional appeals (3), rate of delivery (3), and anatomy of vocal mechanisms (3). They knew only slightly more about audiovisual aids (4), outlines (4), transitions (4), inflection (4), and minimizing stage fright (4). They knew the most about eye contact (8) and just slightly less about listening (7) and introductions (7). But look at how they ranked on items of most importance—almost everyone ranked the ability to hold the attention of the audience as the most important ability. The other items they felt to be of most importance in effective public speaking were: developing the body of the speech (2), organization (3), minimizing stage fright (4), informative speaking (5), persuasive speaking (6), eye contact (7), and introductions (8). Thus, what students enrolling in a public-speaking class want to learn is, once again:

▮ how to prepare a message (introductions, organization, and developing the body)

▮ how to feel confident before an audience (minimizing stage fright)

▮ how to hold the attention of an audience and win a favorable response (persuasive and informative speaking, and eye contact)

We have also asked people who take our introductory public speaking class: "What do you hope to gain from this course? List any particular goals, interests, or problems you wish." A typical response appears here:

> I would really like to become a dynamic speaker!!! I would like to be able to select interesting topics and present my message in such a way that people will truly listen and learn. Nerves and emotions are a problem to me. It would sure be nice to enlarge my vocabulary and add some "spice" to my speech but on the other hand, not be a "show-boat." Being able to talk to everyone, from tiny tot to senior citizen and also listening to them is important to me. I guess, just being able to effectively communicate with people is my main objective.

When participants complete the beginning speech course, we ask them what they gained from the course. Some sample responses follow:

I always felt that I had important ideas but no way to communicate them to people in a natural and honest way. I learned from this course skills necessary to accomplish my goal. I recently ran for the local school board and lost; however, as a result I was asked to serve on an influential study and planning committee.

I took this speech class because I have to teach this year and never felt I could really keep student attention. I'm impressed! My new ability to organize and illustrate ideas and speak in an enthusiastic way has changed my whole feeling about being a successful teacher.

I have been married twice and worked for the government 15 years on overages, shortages, damage shortages, and other transportational discrepancies. Better speaking and more confidence in presenting my ideas enabled me to change to higher pay and achieve more recognition.

It is often said that speakers are not born, they are made and that a speech communication course will not solve a personality problem. Interestingly, however, we all know people who seem to be "born" with a great natural ability to communicate and who develop quite nicely without a great deal of coaching. And yes, some minor personality problems can be overcome through a good course in effective speaking. What, however, is probably most discouraging to students are the lists of "things you must be" in order to be an effective speaker. For example, it has been stated that you must have knowledge, integrity, confidence, humbleness, self-esteem, responsiveness, communication skills, credibility, willingness, poise, fluency, sensitivity, organizational ability, and so on. Furthermore, you should be at once peaceful and forceful, simple and grand, listener and speaker, gentle and strong, creative yet thoroughly outlined. In short, it would be most helpful if you wear blue tights and an undershirt with an S on the front, if you speak faster than a speeding bullet, if you have vocal qualities more powerful than a locomotive, and if your voice can project over large audiences with a single resonating bound. Unfortunately, most of us will never have all these superhuman speaking skills. *Fortunately, we won't need to.*

"As I was saying . . ."

THE SATURDAY EVENING POST

We are concerned that you don't become overwhelmed by complex sets of instructions on speaking well and that you do have great confidence in the many natural speaking abilities you already possess and use everyday. We all have things to say, so the important thing is to learn to say them well—to change our talking into successful speaking.

Speaking Excellence

Secrets from a Speech Consultant: How to Be a Super Speaker

Sooner or later, there comes a time when we're called upon to address an audience. Whether we are making a presentation at a sales meeting or addressing the garden club on how to grow roses, we want to come across in the best possible way. Here are some valuable tips on how to do it.

From the moment Charlotte Hardy got up from the dais and approached the lectern she did everything wrong. The 400 PTA members stared at her expectantly, but Charlotte, her eyes on the floor, could not have looked more terror-stricken had she been on her way to the guillotine. When she reached the lectern she realized she was too short for it and would look ridiculous to the audience. She spoke in a soft, apologetic voice, stared at the far wall and tried to get through her speech as quickly as possible. After 35 minutes, during 33 of which the members of the audience shifted restlessly in their seats, Charlotte retreated from the podium to a smattering of polite applause.

Charlotte has everything to learn about presenting herself and her ideas to an audience. Had she consulted Dorothy Sarnoff, she would have picked up all she needed to know in just six hours. Ms. Sarnoff is the author of *Speech Can Change Your*

Life and founder of Speech Dynamics, a New York-based program that teaches people in all professions and levels of society how to give a speech, make a board presentation, appear on a television talk show or succeed with any communications-related pursuit. Her clients include diplomats, senior executives of major corporations, and editors from the nation's top magazines. In addition to the private, intensive courses she gives in New York and the seminars she leads around the world, Ms. Sarnoff has just completed a library of 20 cassette tapes for speech improvement. Included are tapes on overcoming nervousness, how to chair a meeting, being a better conversationalist, and even one on how to lose a New York accent.

Ms. Sarnoff, the vivacious, model-thin former Broadway singer of *The King and I* fame, is an expert in treating jittery speakers. Why, we asked, are most people so deathly afraid of getting up in front of other people to speak? "They're simply worried about looking ridiculous to others," she says. "But there are two kinds of nervousness. One is what my friend Gwen Verdon calls 'racehorse' nervousness, which is the kind that makes you high and gives sparkle to your performance. It's positive. The other kind is negative. It fills you with anxiety and literally cramps your style. It's this nervousness which you must learn to overcome." In her Speech Dynamics course Ms. Sarnoff's clients learn how to prepare their speeches and present themselves with authority and confidence. And no one, she asserts, is ever nervous after the fourth hour.

Here, Ms. Sarnoff offers some pertinent hints and techniques on speech-giving, so that you and Charlotte Hardy will be exciting, persuasive, and relaxed the next time you confront an audience.

Preparation

■ Make sure your speech is composed in "spoken" rather than "written" language. It should sound as if it's just conversation enlarged rather than an academic essay.

■ Keep it short. "Anything over 20 minutes is too long," cautions Ms. Sarnoff. "Edit, edit, edit! You can communicate a great deal of information in a very short time."

■ Do not start out with "It's a privilege to be here." Always begin with something that will relax you and your audience—a light touch, something local, an anecdote perhaps. In the body of the speech, ask questions, give illustrations, examples, things that involve the listeners and relate to their lives.

■ Be descriptive. Use images that the listener can see in his mind's eye.

■ End with something memorable—a quote, a startling fact, a call to action.

■ When you type your speech (or write it by hand) CAPITAL-IZE ALL THE LETTERS and triple-space the lines. Each line should contain one phrase spoken as you would normally speak it with one exhalation of breath, not necessarily a whole sentence. Then mark the phrases for emphasis, color, pauses, and pace. In this form your speech will be very easy for your eye to scan.

Familiarization
Having prepared yourself, you must now familiarize yourself with your material. "If you memorize your speech you lack luster," says Ms. Sarnoff. "If you read, you lack luster. Make sure those lines are in your system, not just in your head. You should be familiar enough with your phrased speech for your eyes to be up 90 percent of the time, only looking down long enough to key another phrase in your mind."

■ Rehearse your speech aloud on your feet at least six times as though you were in the real-life situation.

■ Guard against speaking in a monotone, and also make sure the pace isn't draggy. Nothing will put an audience to sleep faster than a droner. Your voice should come not from your throat, which will give a soft, wispy sound, but rather from below your solar plexus. At Speech Dynamics, clients are given an exercise to make their voices come out as full and rich as possible: Press the palms of your hands tightly together in a steeple position at chest level, elbows straight out to the side. This causes isometric pressure which tightens the diaphragm. After holding the press position for three seconds, let out your breath in a long sh-h-h-h-h sound. This is the effort you should use to speak every line.

▪ Give the last rehearsal of your speech an hour or two before you go on. If you can, use a tape recorder to check your delivery for pacing and energy.

▪ If there is to be question-and-answer period after your speech, quiz yourself on the most awful, embarrassing questions that you could be asked, and rehearse an answer for them. Anticipate and prepare.

▪ Several hours before you speak, visit the room where you will be appearing. Familiarize yourself with the setup. Check out the lectern and make sure it is the right height for you—the bottom of your rib-cage upward should be visible to the audience. Anything less or more can look silly. If you are short, make sure a "riser" for the podium is available. If you are too tall, requisition a lectern "wedge.,"

▪ Get to know the engineer in charge of the room. Learn his name, so that should anything go wrong while you are speaking—the room gets too hot, the microphone shrieks—you'll still be in control. Instead of looking helplessly around, you can calmly say, "John, could you please adjust the mike?" Bend the microphone toward you, so that you won't have to lean toward it.

▪ If you really want to be thorough, check the lighting. Take out a pocket mirror and see what the lights are doing to your face. If your eyes look like two black holes, or your face drawn and haggard, request "three-quarter" lighting so you can be seen clearly. Complete control is the name of the game.

Presentation
According to Dorothy Sarnoff, all message givers—speakers, announcers, TV-talk-show guests—should give out three positive "vibes." First is the vibe of joy—"I'm glad I'm here." Then there is the vibe of concern and interest in the audience—"I'm glad you're here." And finally the vibe of authority—"I know that I know." Before you approach the lectern, repeat this "mantra" to yourself: "I'm glad I'm here. I'm glad you're here. I know that I know." This is what's known as psyching yourself up.

■ Go to the podium saying to yourself, "I *love* that audience," advises Ms. Sarnoff. "You have the ability to trigger the response that you want. If you speak out of love, and not fear, your audience will respond positively."

■ Stand with your chest up and your weight evenly on the balls of both feet. If you stand on one foot or lean on an elbow, you will lose your look of authority. You whole style should be pleasantly assertive, and the way you hold yourself is an important part of your projection.

■ Do *not* look at just one person, do *not* look at the wall and do *not* look at hairlines. Instead, look *directly* into the eyes of the people in the audience as you speak. Glance from one to the other, linger for an instant to give each listener the impression that you wish you could speak only to him or her. You can judge the reception of your speech from the eyes of your listeners and act accordingly. Are the eyes glazed? Then accelerate your speech, animate your talk. There should be no unknowns by the time you step up to face your audience. Everything has been taken care of. You know the audience, your speech, the room, the engineer, yourself. There is nothing that should go wrong, no way that you can come across as ridiculous. You are well prepared and in control. Enjoy the moment. The times when you're the center of attention with a captive audience are probably too rare; make the most of it.

SOURCE: Reprinted from Nov. 1976 issue of *Family Circle* Magazine. © 1976 THE FAMILY CIRCLE, INC.

Opportunities for speaking surround us. The better prepared we are to speak, the happier we feel during those speaking moments. And the more that we improve our speaking, the more our opportunities for better living increase.

We all have special talents and attributes. Calvin Taylor, a creative-talent researcher for the last several decades, says that in a group of 5,000 people, one person can do at least one thing better than anyone else in the group; and in some special way of thinking about something or doing something, each person is literally a genius! Our university communication and self-concept research suggests that each one of us has the ability to become rather successful at something—even speaking. About the only important question that remains is how serious we are about changing our talking into successful speaking.

To continue on with our program for quick growth in public speaking: Review the suggestions on the process of public speaking (Chapter Two) and see if you can find your own best speaking style. Learn about selecting a topic and a purpose (Chapter Three), supporting and illustrating your ideas (Chapter Four), organizing your speech information (Chapter Five); and delivering your ideas (Chapter Six). Then sharpen your skills for informing (Chapter Seven), persuading (Chapter Eight), speaking on special occasions (Chapter Nine), and speaking in small groups (Chapter Ten). Learn to have fun by listening, responding and interacting more easily with your audience (Chapters Eleven and Twelve). Then reflect on the course we have put together: Tough but exhilarating, hard work but observable results, common sense but not always commonly sensed (Chapter Thirteen). We spend so much of our time talking we might as well learn to have more fun doing it.

If all my talents and powers were to be taken from me by some inscrutable Providence, and I had my choice of keeping but one, I would unhesitatingly ask to be allowed to keep the Power of Speaking, for through it, I would quickly recover all the rest.
DANIEL
WEBSTER

Have great confidence in your many natural speaking talents.

What You Now Know

We actually do more speaking in our daily lives than we suspect. Speaking ranges from informal conversation to formal public speech. We are all aware of what public speaking is, though we read to have more knowledge of the various elements in the process in order to be more effective. This book is a planned program for helping you accomplish your goal of becoming a more effective speaker.

What to Do to Learn More

Speaking Log for a Day

Design a log for recording every separate situation where you talk to others (express your opinion, make a comment in a class, interact in a conversation, tell someone how to do something, describe a recent movie, etc.) Look at your results:

1. Do you do one kind of speaking more than others?

2. Do you feel there is enough variety and challenge to you in the kinds of everyday speaking you do? If not, how could you improve?

3. Do you consider yourself to be more of an extrovert or more of an introvert? Are you comfortable with this? What will you do to improve?

Compare your results with other members of the class.

1. Could you predict what specific individuals have in their log results, based on your observation of them in class?

2. Did the results of a particular class member's speaking log surprise you? Why or why not?

Classroom Communicators

1. Make it a personal project to observe students who participate in the classes you are in. Pay particular attention to:
a. The questions asked.
b. How an opinion is stated.
c. How a person disagrees subtly or openly with another.

2. Look at classroom participation in relation to the instructor's communication style. How does the instructor respond to:
a. Questions of inquiry?
b. Questions that challenge the instructor's points of view?
c. Various class members discussing a point?

2
THE PROCESS OF PUBLIC SPEAKING: AN OVERVIEW

After studying this chapter, you will understand the process of public speaking, as well as the key elements involved in giving effective speeches. You will learn several approaches to reducing your speech anxiety and will be encouraged to find your own speaking style.

Chapter Content

▼◢ THE PROCESS OF PUBLIC SPEAKING

A simplistic way of viewing the process of public speaking has been presented in several other texts. Speaking is said to be a stimulus-and-response process. The speaker offers the *stimulus* (message) and the audience *responds* (feedback). This perspective can be graphically represented as:

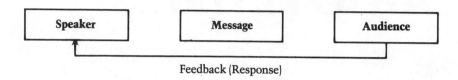

The focus of this perspective usually is on what the speaker says (content). The speaker is considered the primary entity in the event. The audience may be viewed as a group whose role is to respectfully attend to the message. The process that includes speaking and feedback is part of a start-stop process. The speaker talks and the audience listens. The speaker stops talking. The people in the audience, through questions or comments, give feedback (responses) to the speaker about how they are perceiving the message.

The same communication book that describes public speaking as a start-stop process may, however, label two people conversing as interpersonal communication and offer a transactional perspective as a description of the process taking place between the two. A transactional process is one where simultaneous encoding and decoding and sending and receiving are taking place on multiple levels, with both individuals experiencing changes in their perceptions to some degree. The diagram at the top of page 29 depicts the key factors of the transactional perspective.

We believe that what takes place in the process of public speaking is more accurately described from the transactional perspective. The speaker and each individual listener are in fact simultaneously encoding cues and decoding cues while sending and receiving on both verbal and nonverbal levels. We do not believe that the speaker encodes a message and then sends it via air compressions (words)

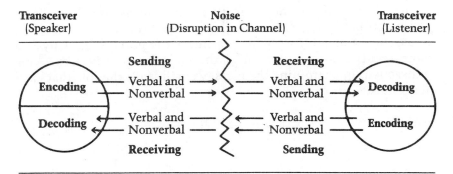

Encoding: *ideation; mentally creating the message.*
Decoding: *giving meaning; interpreting the received signals.*
Sending and receiving: *a physical activity involving signals*
(air compressions and light refractions).

and light refractions (gestures and movement) while the receiver patiently waits to receive the signals and then decode them. We hold that the speaker and all the individual listeners are involved simultaneously in one-to-one transactions. The speaker personalizes the message with first one listener, then another, then another, and so on.

You may be asking, "What difference does all this about stimulus-response versus transactional communication make?" It makes a tremendous difference in terms of the speaking skills the speaker thinks are available and how the speaker reacts to the listeners. Take eye contact, for example. A speaker who views public speaking as a stimulus-response (start-stop) process will usually scan the listeners as a whole, letting his or her eyes take in large anonymous sections of the audience at once. He or she is caught up in sending the message at this point. The speaker does not really see many individual behaviors or facial expressions among the listeners. The speaker may perceive the audience shifting in their chairs or making audible groans, if on a large scale. On the other hand, a speaker operating from the transactional perspective will tend to practice the skill of individualizing eye contact with the single listener for a second or two, then shifting to another section of the audience and establishing individual and momentary (personalized) eye contact with another listener, and so on throughout the speaking.

There are several other direct implications from viewing public speaking as a transaction similar to conversing, but we will, for now, let our argument stand or fall on the brief example we have presented.

Though we believe most effective public speaking follows from a transactional perspective (whether the speaker knows it is called transactional or not), we will present for the purpose of analysis a more traditional examination of the key elements in a speaking transaction. In examining the parts, we will learn the role that each plays in the process.

Key Elements of Public Speaking

- Speaker

- Message

- Delivery

- Listener(s)

- Feedback

- Situation

The Speaker

Your success with the listeners depends heavily on what they think about you. If the listeners feel that:

- you know what you are talking about (are competent)

- you can be trusted (have integrity)

- you are friendly (sociable)

- you are composed (emotionally stable)

- you are outgoing (dynamic)

- you have their best interest at heart (have helpful intentions)

then they will listen more attentively to you and more readily accept what you have to say.

It is imperative that your listeners think well of you the speaker. Traditionally, Aristotle called these characteristics of the speaker "ethos" and said they constituted "ethical proof." Today, we call these same qualities "source-credibility factors." Now, as well as in the past, researchers and practitioners in communication recognize the tremendous influence that these characteristics have on an audience. Successful speakers seem to have pertinent information and experience about their subject matter, are reputed to be reliable, seem friendly and cooperative, appear to be devoid of excessive fear and fidgeting, are very much alive and talkative, and appear to have helpful rather than selfish motives. Don't lose your audience by failing to consider these important speaker qualities.

The Message

The message as delivered is a product of the encoding, transforming ideas and feelings into words, that takes place before the speech, and also the encoding that accompanies the actual speaking. The topic and the listeners who will make up your audience help focus your encoding process. Its useful to learn some words that are specifically descriptive about your subject matter.

Although you may be assigned a subject to speak about, you usually have the task of deciding what you are going to say about the given topic. Focusing on what you want to say is an easier task once you decide what your specific purpose is: What do you want to accomplish with your audience? What is your main objective in speaking? Then it is important for you to visualize and analyze your listeners. What are *their* problems and questions? What can you say that will be particularly rewarding to this audience? After careful consideration of how to best help your listeners, select ideas with which you are familiar or can quickly get information about so that you can speak from experience and with authority. Also, find something that excites you and that you really want to share with others. No speaking gimmicks can hide a lack of enthusiasm for an idea. For example, given the topic "The Value of a College Education,"

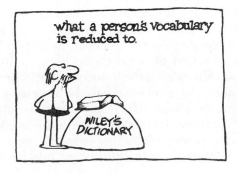

you might focus on one or more of the following ideas that really interest you:

■ College as a place to try out new social skills

■ College as a place to learn how to learn

■ College as a place to learn to adjust quickly to different "supervisors" and the standards they require—valuable adaptive skills for future jobs

■ College as income-generating—compare the average annual income of a college graduate with the average annual income of a nongraduate

We remember a speaker who was invited to speak to a very fussy group of teenagers seven times in succession because he kept selecting topics that fit their needs and that he was excited about sharing. For instance, one evening he spoke about "love and parking." Another time he talked of "prestige and smoking." Take time to consider your specific audience, and search until you find ideas that you feel excited about sharing.

Rhetoric is an art, not a science.
ISOCRATES

Message Supports (That Prove or Illustrate)

A message becomes meaningful and gains power when it is well supported. A vivid, firsthand experience is usually much more effective than a vague generalization. Even in a very short talk a speaker can include a visual aid, a quotation, a statistic, a comparison or analogy, or a specific example.

For example, a college student started his three-minute talk by holding up a pen and asking the audience to estimate its value. The small class responded with prices ranging from twenty-nine cents to three-and-a-half dollars. He then held up an ordinary lead pencil and asked his listeners to estimate the value of the pencil. Again, they responded with guesses, ranging from about four cents to seventy-nine cents. He next pointed out that they had all estimated the value of the pen and pencil in terms of dollars and cents, rather than in terms of what could be accomplished with the pen and pencil. After using these simple supporting materials to involve his audience, the student continued to give a most effective speech.

More detail on using support material is presented in Chapter Five. For now, let's remember that a speaker can also get attention and hold interest by using suspense, presenting a novel idea, identifying conflict, using humor, or self-disclosing to the listeners. So

THE SATURDAY EVENING POST

"I'm not going to bore you with a lot of words. . . ."

don't be caught speaking without message supports to help develop
your ideas.

Message Organizing

Listeners like a speaker who begins quickly, marches forward steadily, and stops with a minute to spare. You will feel more secure as
a speaker when you know that one idea will lead to the next in an
orderly manner. Speaking material must be organized so that the
main points are distinct and clear. The simplest organization consists of introducing an idea, developing the idea with supporting
details, and concluding the idea. Alan H. Monroe, a speech teacher,
offers one of the easiest and most effective plans for organizing a
short talk; he calls it the "one-point plan." In this plan, the speaker
begins the talk with a brief story, example, illustration, quotation,
testimony, or statistic, which has a point. Then the speaker states
the point. Next, another short illustration, quotation, testimony, or

Curtsey while
you're thinking
what to say. It
saves time.
LEWIS CARROLL
Through the
Looking-Glass

Voice and assur-
ance are neces-
sary to success in
oratory.
ISOCRATES

story that has the same moral or point is added. Finally, the speaker simply repeats the point and sits down! For instance, a speaker might start with a brief story about the happiness Albert Schweitzer received from rendering humanitarian service; state the idea that service brings joy; read a quotation from Schweitzer supporting the idea that service brings joy; and conclude by stating once again that service brings joy. This is a speech plan that is deceptively simple, yet effective. Remember, start right off with a good idea, develop it quickly, and stop on time! Be organized.

To follow these message-development steps does not take special talent or great intelligence, but it does mean you must look at each principle to see whether you are attending to the items that make great speaking great. Ask yourself these questions: Have I selected a subject I am interested in? Do I have a specific purpose? Am I using a variety of materials in my talk to make it interesting to the listener? Is my material organized?

Good speakers create an attentive, listening audience.

Exciting speakers select their messages carefully, speak with a purpose, use a variety of ways of illustrating their messages, and organize simply. But what happens when a speaker pays little attention to these message components?

First, the listeners become bored because the speaker talks about a subject with which they are familiar and develops it in a worn-out way—the same old thing in the same old dry way. Second, the audience is left hopelessly adrift because the speaker didn't plan for any end result. The speaker simply strings a number of ideas together and hopes the listeners will do something about them. But, alas, the listeners change very little. Third, the audience usually becomes quickly disinterested and disbelieving when the speaker does nothing to prove or illustrate a point. The speaker assumes that his or her word is the final proof and understanding of the subject. Fourth, the audience becomes confused and rapidly forgets what the speaker is saying because ideas are not related.

Now, what can be done about changing the things that bother listeners about the "puts me asleep" speaker? The next part of this chapter will present suggestions and helps so you will not be a "puts me asleep" speaker. A speaker's delivery of a speech can be an asset or a hindrance.

The Delivery

Remember, listeners are not passive receptacles for your words. They are actively involved in the process of encoding and decoding and sending and receiving at the same time you are speaking. Listeners perceive, to some degree, both *what* is said and *how* it is said. When you do present a speech, *feel* what you are saying while you say it. Keep the ideas fresh, and speak with energy and conviction, allowing your voice and body to react to the importance of your ideas. Audiences quickly lose interest in a speaker who doesn't get into his or her speech enough to portray much vocal and physical activity. And, perhaps most important, focus your attention on the audience. When you step up to a counter and ask for a chocolate ice cream cone, do you worry about your hands or what your knees are doing? Usually not. You focus your attention on the clerk to be sure you are understood correctly.

As you consider the delivery of your speech, four options or modes of presentation are available to you:

- *Manuscript:* write it out word for word and read it.
- *Memorize:* deliver it from memory.

It takes two to speak the truth— one to speak, and another to hear.
HENRY DAVID THOREAU

■ *Impromptu:* speak on the spur of the moment without any specific preparation.

■ *Extemporaneous:* carefully select, organize, and outline your ideas, but allow the specific words and sentences to form themselves anew at the moment of delivery.

The extemporaneous method of delivery is preferred for most situations because it gives us some of the security of specific preparation yet a good deal of flexibility, allowing us to focus on the listeners. In this method, the speaker relies on notes, rather than a manuscript or a memorized speech. A few notes together with a stimulating delivery should make speaking an enjoyable experience.

We do suggest that you practice speaking, especially when you use extemporaneous delivery. However, we do not mean you only practice the speech aloud. Running through the speech in your mind will be of great benefit when you speak later on. A combination of mental and physical practice will give you the greatest preparation. You should also time the whole speech to make sure that you are speaking within the time limit. You may want to try out your ideas on friends. Use their comprehension and response to your subject to help you formally organize and present what you want to say.

The Listeners

The ability of a speaker to help the listeners understand a complex idea or to change their beliefs about a matter seems to depend on the speaker's analysis of the listeners' present interests, values, and experiences. To communicate effectively, we must fire a message at a defined target—we must begin where the listeners generally are. To speak of choosing a career to a group of second graders misses the target. Or attempting to persuade someone to change a March of Dimes contribution from five to fifty dollars per year, without first estimating the income or values system of the listener, might prove futile.

In analyzing the listeners, you must consider how they feel about your subject, what they already know about it, and how they perceive you and your credibility. From the moment you accept an opportunity to speak, you should begin to assess the audience. Such information as the number of people who will be present; whether they will be male or female or both; their average age; their edu-

THE SATURDAY EVENING POST

"Let's face it, Ralph, you're not as popular as we thought!"

cational, occupational, and ethnic backgrounds; and their knowledge about your subject can help you meet them where they are. *Remember, speeches are prepared for listeners, not for* **speakers.** *A speaker must adjust the content of the speech to the listeners for maximum effectiveness. Find out all you can about your audience before you develop your speech.*

Feedback

The reaction (verbal and nonverbal) of the listeners during and after the speech is feedback. Feedback enables speakers to know whether they are being understood, heard, or even seen. An effective speaker uses feedback to monitor the communication effort. He or she watches the listeners to see whether they are getting the point. If the speaker notices that the audience is losing interest or becoming disturbed, she or he can alter the delivery of the message or modify the message so that it becomes more stimulating or acceptable. Listeners' responses fed back to the speaker thus influence the way the speaker will adjust the message while speaking.

As speakers, we want to be aware of the maximum amount of feedback that our speaking situation will allow. The better we monitor feedback from individual listeners or the audience as a whole, the better we can adapt how and what we planned to say to produce the results we intend. Unquestionably, feedback is essential for improvement in learning to speak effectively. Speakers who use this communication element are considered to be sensitive and good at understanding human relations.

Situation

Obviously, a speaker will do things a little differently when presenting a project in a marketing class than when presenting an advertising proposal to a financial corporation. Almost as important as analyzing the audience is reviewing the situation or the occasion where you will be speaking. Surprises for the speaker arriving on the scene have been known to cause distress for both the speaker and the listeners. A mismatch between the speaker's preparation and the speaking occasion is one of those "rhetorical nightmares" that can be avoided if you take a moment to find out about the physical setting for your speech, the nature of the gathering, and the time limits. Thus, ask about the location, sound system, lighting, room, seating, lectern, distractions, and so on.

Ask also about the purpose of the meeting and the social setting in which the speech is to take place. Consider what expectations the occasion engenders in the minds of the listeners. Be sure to clearly understand what part you are playing in the total program. And, finally, be keenly aware of the amount of time given to your presentation. Quite often, speakers do a poor job because they have prepared too much material for a limited amount of time.

 REDUCING SPEAKING ANXIETY

Just in case you still fee uneasy or nervous about getting up in front of an audience—join us and thousands of others! You are definitely not alone!

One of the most frequent requests among students taking speech classes is for help in controlling or overcoming this tension when they communicate. Their self-evaluations contain such statements as:

▮   When I get up to give a talk, I'm so nervous I forget the things I'm going to say. My mouth gets so dry, it's hard to talk.

▮   Many times when I speak in front of people, I get embarrassed. It's hard for me to open up and express my feelings.

▮   I stumble over words and speak too fast. I fidget and can't make good eye contact.

▮   I get really self-conscious in front of groups. The larger the group, the more I worry.

The causes of speech anxiety are varied and complex. It is clear that those who have low self-esteem are apprehensive about speaking in front of people. They experience a fear of failure and of being negatively judged by those who listen. Yet even students with a positive feeling about themselves experience anxiety and tension. Professional speakers often complain of prespeaking jitters. So first and last, being nervous or tense about speaking appears both normal and a natural state of emotional arousal to ensure energy for the occasion. Similar emotional states precede and are useful in athletic competition. However, in speaking or in athletic competition, excessive anxiety may be described as that additional emotional arousal beyond the degree needed for alertness and energy in the activity. It is this excessive emotional arousal that becomes dysfunctional.

Although the causes of speaking tension may be complex, helpful solutions have been developed and are being used with some exceptional results. Let us suggest three ways you might decrease or control anxiety about speaking in public: practice among friends, use positive imagery, and control your breathing.

Our first solution, and perhaps the most important, is that you learn to overcome excessive anxiety by speaking more often in informal settings. One reason new speakers are fearful is that they are required to address groups before they have learned to speak to two or three individuals. They must address strangers when they are nervous even among friends. Speakers also experience more anxiety if they are not fully prepared and organized for speaking to a group.

We can overcome these obstacles in the following way: 1) Choose a subject of great importance, one that you can be excited about and *want* to share with someone. 2) Then prepare a little speech for your family or friends. As you collect ideas and support them, organize them as suggested earlier. This may seem a little difficult at first, but if you are serious about overcoming a fear of speaking in public, you will be pleased with the results. 3) As your ideas develop, try them out on your friends and family. Take advantage of relaxed and informal situations to share one of your ideas and to ask a question or two. There is something about a good question that helps dissolve fears. The pressure to communicate is lifted from your shoulders and placed on the listener; and yet the listener is often flattered that you consider him or her a resource and is happy to answer your question. Find out what your ideas mean to others. If your first insights were shallow, enlarge them and adjust them to your listeners. 4) Then try sharing your ideas again, only in a larger group or in a classroom. Notice the increased confidence you feel in hearing yourself speak your ideas and in receiving responses from your listeners. These informal opportunities for mini-speeches are your best preparation for a large audience—so speak as often as you can to gain experience and confidence. You will find your fear of speaking will turn to simple tension or nervousness as you gain more experience. And nervous energy can be used positively in speaking.

Our second suggestion for overcoming excessive anxiety has to do with a simple relaxation technique using imagery. This approach to reducing fear involves receiving information from your body about functions that are normally autonomic and nondiscernible. If a body process can be monitored and fed back to the conscious mind, it can be controlled.

Whenever we experience tension or fear, our body responds by restricting the flow of blood to the extremities and by increasing the flow to the heart, vital organs, and the brain. Our heartbeat increases, our respiration rate changes and our hands get cold.

When you feel your hands getting cold as you prepare to speak, or feel "butterflies in your stomach," use that feedback from your body as a sign to relax. Think of warming your hands and being relaxed. Words won't do. You must *see* pictures of warm, beautiful places. Imagine yourself on a warm beach in the sunshine or in a peaceful meadow on a summer day. If you see such pictures vividly, the autonomic nervous system will respond accordingly. Physiologically, it's the same as being there. Now, as you relax and focus your mind away from the concern of speaking, see yourself as a successful speaker. Watch yourself deliver a great speech and visualize a tremendous response of appreciation from the audience. After relaxing with pleasant and successful images for a few minutes, you will notice your body and mind becoming more comfortable and at ease. Your hands will warm and your heart will slow down. We use sophisticated biofeedback equipment to demonstrate to students that this relaxation technique works. But you don't need the equipment. If you experience "being there" in your mind, if you think in pictures, you will relax and become less fearful when you engage in public speaking.

The third approach to reducing speaking anxiety is a breathing technique. Breathing is a central focus in various types of relaxation methods, including forms of yoga. The key idea is that modifications in the breathing patterns associated with fear, stress, anxiety, and tension have direct effects on physiology and levels of emotional arousal. We describe the technique here in abbreviated fashion.

First, sit in a firm chair that supports the body in an erect position. Place both feet flat on the floor and "center" your body in the chair so that you are comfortable yet erect (no slouching). Fold your hands in your lap or place them lightly on your upper legs. Begin taking deep breaths through your nose while extending your stomach. Push your stomach out in "beer belly" fashion as the air comes into your lungs. Your shoulders should be allowed to rise and possibly go back a bit. Take each deep inward breath through the nose slowly and methodically. You may find it comfortable to take five seconds to draw this deep breath in completely.

At the end of the intake phase, pause one or two seconds and just let the air escape naturally, as if you were letting it out of a balloon. You will find that the shoulders will fall and the extended stomach will come back in if you let go, thus forcing a deep exhalation of used air. Do this inhalation-exhalation ten times while concentrating on the sound of the air going in and out of your nose, the cool sensation of the incoming air in the moist part of the nose, and the warm sensation of the body-heated, outgoing air.

If you complete this breathing technique with full concentration, you will modify your body physiology and your level of emotional arousal.

Many experienced speech instructors encourage their students to engage in self-talk and self-affirmations before presenting a speech. For example, tell yourself that you have prepared a useful idea to present and the audience will benefit from your effort. Instruct yourself to "relax and not be nervous." "I will only be speaking for a few minutes not forever." "This is going to be an opportunity to share some good ideas that will leave the audience in an appreciative mood."

During the speech, relax by focusing on the listeners. Make eye contact, smile, and move around a little. Using some note cards helps to remind you of the next idea to be presented.

After the speech, take the time to relax. Praise yourself for making a good effort. Review your presentation and note the things that went very well and anything that seemed a little weak. If you feel comfortable asking others about your presentation, then get feed-back on your content and delivery.

 ## FINDING YOUR OWN SPEAKING STYLE

If all the preceding insights have started to intimidate you and made you wonder whether you will ever keep everything straight, or, worse, if at this point you are learning the rules but are becoming an "unreal" speaking monster made of artificial gimmickry and everybody else's rules, please read "The Veep's 'Kentucky Windage'."

Good speaking is a simultaneous process. It involves both speakers and listeners.

Speaking Excellence

The Veep's "Kentucky Windage"

William J. Buchanan

The late Vice President Alben Barkley once told me a fascinating little story. . . .

I was a senior at the University of Louisville that February in 1949, and failing miserably in a public-speaking course. When I learned that the newly elected Vice President would address the annual Jefferson-Jackson Day Democratic gathering on the 26th, I badgered my father, a longtime friend of Barkley's, into getting me an invitation. Here, I realized, was an opportunity to study one of the great speakers of all time. . . .

"When I was about your age . . . a friend of mine down in Paducah asked me to go skeet shooting with him. I'd never shot skeet, but I was pretty good with a shotgun, so I obliged. On the first round I powdered twenty-one of twenty-five clay birds. 'Good shooting!' my friend said. 'But there are a few things you should watch.' He then showed me the 'proper' stance, how to sight with both eyes open, and a whole slew of other things absolutely guaranteed to improve my style.

"Well, my friend was an expert, so I practiced his way. Only problem was, as my style improved my score went down. One afternoon, after I succeeded in breaking only eight birds, I asked a young lady watching from the sidelines how my form looked.

" 'Your form's fine, Alben,' she said, 'But aren't you supposed to break *all* those little black things?' Typical female reply, I thought. But her words bothered me; I found myself repeating them over and over. Was I really trying to "break all those little black things'? Or was I more concerned with trying to imitate a prima ballerina?"

He paused and chuckled softly. "Well, I realized right then that I'd never be much of a ballerina. I could hardly wait for the next round. I discarded all the fancy frills and went back and used my best Kentucky Windage.[1] I beat my friend that round—and he never outshot me again."

Barkley leaned forward in his chair, and looked directly at me. "What had I done wrong?" He paused to let the question soak in. "I had ignored my natural abilities, traded a way that worked well for me for one that didn't because I was overly impressed with my friend's criticism.

"Now don't mistake me. Expert advice can be a blessing. But only when it's used to sharpen your own instincts and talents— never as a substitute for them."

The Vice President held out his hand and said, "Next time you get up to speak, remember, use a little Kentucky Windage."

On my way to class next morning I threw away my carefully prepared notes with the marginal references to "pause briefly" and "emphasize here." I knew that never again would I try to imitate someone else's formula for success. When my turn at the lectern came I made my point as simply as I could and sat down. The startled professor nodded his approval. I finished that semester in the top quarter of the class. . . .

SOURCE: Originally appeared in *Reader's Digest.* Copyright © 1968 by The Reader's Digest Assn., Inc.

[1]The term is derived from Kentucky frontiersmen's unique long-rifle shooting style: instead of relying solely on gunsights, they estimated wind conditions and offset aim accordingly. Among Kentucky hill people today, the expression means using one's own personal estimate and judgment in a situation as well as, and sometimes in spite of, precedent.

What You Now Know

Public speaking can be described as a transactional process of communication similar in some ways to interpersonal communication. Both speaker and listener(s) are involved in simultaneously encoding and decoding and sending and receiving on multiple levels (verbal and nonverbal), which results in both the speaker and listener(s) experiencing a change in their perceptions.

Prior to speaking, the speaker needs to examine his or her cred-ibility, analyze the audience, examine the nature of the situation, plan the message, choose and practice his or her best style of deliv-ery, and plan for monitoring and using audience feedback. The or-igin of any fear of speaking is in the mind of the speaker—the con-trol and elimination of this fear is thus the mental discipline the speaker puts into play prior to and during speaking.

What to Do to Learn More

Question: Is an Instructor's Lecture a Speech?

Analyze a lecture given by one of your teachers. Does it have all the elements of a speech? Would you consider it to be a speech?

Are some of your instructors better at one particular skill, such as adapting the material to the listeners or encouraging feedback, than others? Do you think this adapting is a conscious effort on the instructor's part?

Survey

Ask ten students outside of class these questions and write down their answers for use in class discussion.

1. What, if any, would be your fears of giving a public speech to a large group of students, instructors, and administrators on what you like and dislike about your school?

2. Would you be more nervous if you had to stand in front of a group to speak rather than sit down? Why or why not?

3. Would you find it easier to speak to a group of elementary school children than to a group of adults? Why or why not?

4. While speaking, would you rather the listeners interrupt you with their questions or wait until you finish your speech? Why?

5. If you had to speak to a local civic organization, what kind of delivery would you use?

a. Write out and read the speech

b. Memorize the speech

c. Speak from outline notes
Why?

Discussion Questions
Why do you think young children immediately focus more on the television set the moment a commercial comes on?

What material covered in this chapter would help you analyze a television commercial as a message planned to elicit a particular response from the viewer?

II
PLANNING, PREPARING, AND PRESENTING

Throughout history people have had an insatiable need to know. Unanswered questions stimulate research; research yields facts; and facts, when properly ordered and developed, yield understanding.

Rudolph F. Verderber

3
SELECTING A
TOPIC AND
A PURPOSE

In this chapter, you will learn how to select a topic that is interesting to you and
your audience. You will understand the
three general purposes of speaking and
how to select a specific purpose for your
speech. Finally, you will learn how to listen to other speakers to discover how
they give effective speeches.

Chapter Content

- Selecting a Speaking topic
- Speak about Things That Interest You
- Speak about Things That Interest the
  Audience:
- Audience Analysis
  - Consider the Occasion
- General Purpose of Your Topic
  - Informative Speaking
  - Persuasive Speaking
  - Entertainment Speaking
- Specific Purpose of Your Topic
- Learning from Other Speakers
- What You Now Know
- What to Do to Learn More

SELECTING A SPEAKING TOPIC

In many of our communicating situations, we are assigned a speaking topic. For example, if a friend asks us about a certain person he or she would like to date, we have in effect been assigned to speak about this person. If we are asked how to change a tire, or why we like our brand of television set, we have been given a topic we know something about so we can usually give plenty of details about how to change a tire or plenty of reasons why we like, or don't like, the quality of our set.

Thus, we have little difficulty responding or speaking in informal settings because the subject of our speech is often chosen for us, and we already know quite a bit about the subject. Also, since our listeners "assigned" the topic, we know they are interested in it. However, in a formal speaking situation, we often have to choose the subject, and we do not want to be embarrassed by selecting a topic that seems silly or unimportant to our audience. To help you over this hurdle, we would like to share our approach to selecting a topic on which to speak.

There are essentially four major questions to take into account when you are trying to select a speech topic:

1. Is the subject matter interesting to you?

2. Will the subject matter be interesting to the audience?

3. What general purpose are you trying to meet by giving the talk?

4. What is the specific purpose of your talk?

This chapter will be devoted to answering these four questions.

SPEAK ABOUT THINGS THAT INTEREST YOU

There is nothing more boring than speakers who talk about subjects they are not interested in. Speakers who speak about things they like can get excited and be very fascinating. For example, if you have just run the rapids of the Grand Canyon in a small boat, the experience will still be vivid and you will be able to speak with great detail and enthusiasm about floating the rapids. If a close friend has just died, you will be able to share details about the difficulty of adjusting to the loss of a friend. The experiences you have had will give you a special position from which to speak. What you say will be unique because no one else has experienced life exactly as you have.

So whenever possible, choose a real-life experience to speak about. This puts you in a position to speak about something you know well. Most speakers, when asked to make a presentation, run immediately to the library, a magazine, or a friend. We believe the best source of information you have is yourself and your life experiences. Trust your own ideas and your own experiences. Even when your talk is assigned, you can make it better by including information from the experiences you have had. Add to your own ideas with solid research. Examples, quotes, and evidence will make your speech much more believable and you as a speaker more credible.

To determine if a subject interests you, ask yourself if you would go to hear someone else talk about it. If a subject does not pop immediately to mind, ask yourself the following questions:

1. What skills do you have? What do you do well and maybe even better than most people? What unusual things have you done?

2. What is your background? Where have you lived? What people have you known? What have you experienced with other people as you have grown up?

3. What are your special interests? What would you like to learn more about? What would you like to achieve? What seems to get you excited?

4. What knowledge do you have? What do you know a lot about? What do you know more about than most other people?

5. What special experiences have you had? What unusual things have happened to you that an audience might enjoy hearing about?

After you determine if the subject is interesting and important to you, you must then determine if the subject is important to your listening audience.

The gift of speech . . . is not often accompanied by the power of thought.
SOMERSET MAUGHAM

THE BORN LOSER   **By Art Sansom**

Speaking Excellence

Speak about Yourself

A common concern facing speech students is what to talk about.
Outside of the classroom, topics are dictated by the audience,
the occasion, the speaker's qualifications, or special request.
Robert Redford, for example, is frequently asked to speak about
film making or environmental issues because he is well qualified
to discuss those topics.

In the classroom, most of your speech assignments will come
with a designated general purpose but not a specific topic. You
may for instance be asked to give a speech to inform using visual aids. The subject of the speech will be left up to you. Fortunately, most of us know quite a bit about something. And all of
us would like to know more about certain subjects that interest
us. What you know and what you would like to know more about
may be great topics for your speeches.

We spend a good deal of our time talking about ourselves and
subjects in which we are interested. It makes good sense to begin by speaking about an event, idea, or experience that you
have felt, seen, and understand. One student told about his experience of catching shoplifters while employed in a grocery
store for three years. Another student who rebuilt car engines for

a living told about the strongest and weakest engines in U.S. automobiles. Still another student told about her experience of trying to become a registered nurse. These students gave exceptionally good presentations because they were speaking from first-hand experience and on a subject in which they were vitally interested.

Everyone has had some great experiences that are worth sharing with others. It isn't necessary to be an expert in anything, but it does help when you address large audiences to do a little additional reading on the subject so that the audience doesn't have to depend totally on your experience or opinion.

When you use your own knowledge and experience to address a large audience, select the most dramatic things to say that seem to fit the interests of the listeners. A police officer talked to a group of young people about the abuse of drugs in a major U.S. city. He described how a young man on cocaine sat in a room and stared at a parrot for twenty-four hours. The young man had to be placed in a rehabilitation center. After several years, he still thinks that he is a parrot and eats his food by pecking at it. The police officer added some outside research that showed that marijuana plants are becoming more potent and several drugs are now crossing the blood-brain barrier and producing irreversible damage. The speech he gave was startling, a little frightening, but most effective.

 ## SPEAK ABOUT THINGS THAT INTEREST THE AUDIENCE: AUDIENCE ANALYSIS

To be able to talk about things that are of interest to an audience, you must know the listeners who make up your audience. This necessitates evaluating the audience to determine their interests, needs, and concerns. To effectively evaluate your listeners, you need to gain data about them. You can then determine to what degree your topic fits your audience.

Be creative and turn your thinking cap on when evaluating an audience.

When evaluating an audience, you can learn many things, however, we suggest always starting your analysis with the following variables:

1. **Age.** It is not necessary to know the exact age of each audience member, but you should know the age range and average age of those who are present. The age characteristics of a group of students will obviously be considerably different from those of a Rotary Club.

2. **Gender.** Again, it does not matter that you know the exact number of males and females in the audience. However, if your audience is predominantly male or female you must adapt your subject to fit that characteristic of the audience.

3. **Occupation.** Is the audience mostly white-collar workers or blue-collar workers? Is it a mixture of both? Would the same topic interest an audience of physicians and an audience of lawyers? You must select a topic that will be understandable to people in the predominant occupations of the audience.

4. **Socioeconomic level.** Is your audience predominantly wealthy or predominantly poor? Do they come from a culturally deprived area? Are they high society?

5. **Educational level.** Do the members of the audience have an elementary, junior high, high school, or a college education?

6. **Audience opinion about the topic.** If you are speaking on a controversial subject, you may want to know the audience's attitude or point of view on that topic. Knowing whether they are pro or con may help you decide how to approach the subject.

7. **Audience opinion about you.** What does the audience know about you? Will they be expecting you to talk about a certain subject because you have recently been successful in some field of endeavor? If you are a young adult, is the audience expecting your point of view on an important matter?

Whenever you are asked to speak to an unfamiliar audience, question the individual who extended the invitation. Ask about the nature of the audience and their expectations and about past topics that were interesting to them.

◢◣ CONSIDER THE OCCASION

Another factor that you must analyze when selecting a topic or subject about which to speak is the occasion. Why are these people gathering together at this time and place to hear you speak? Is this a scheduled meeting of a college speech class or a religious gathering? Is this a regular meeting or a special occasion like a holiday? Or is there something else about the occasion that is unique? Is this a regular meeting where different speakers are invited each time, and now it is your turn? The key is to review the nature of the occasion and determine if there are any audience expectations that

A unique speaking occasion. What would such an occasion suggest about your speech?

need to be met in terms of a topic or the way a topic must be adapted to the situation.

Other questions that you must ask yourself are: What mood will the audience be in? Are you part of a program? What is the physical arrangement of the room or hall in which you will be speaking? How much time has been allocated to your presentation?

Think, for a moment, if the audience will be happy, possibly celebrating an event, or sad because of a death or other discouraging circumstance. Does the physical setting, room, lectern, microphone, and arrangement of chairs allow you to display visual aids, walk around, and use notes? Have you been to this particular setting before or asked someone about it so that you can make appropriate references at the beginning of your speech? Are you the first speaker or the last one? And finally, be sure to check the time limits of your speech. At a service club luncheon, the audience will leave to return to work whether you are finished speaking or not. It's amazing how a good speech can be ruined because your audience needs to be somewhere else before you planned to complete your presentation.

◤◣ GENERAL PURPOSE OF YOUR TOPIC

After determining whether you are interested in your topic and whether it fits your audience, determine the general purpose of your talk. The universal purpose of all speech is to win some kind of response. Most beginning speakers fail at this point because they do not consider what they want the audience to do as a result of their speech. Often, the speech becomes aimless and never reaches a target. It seems to us that the following are the major purposes of speaking:

1. **To present information**—to increase an audience's knowledge and understanding about an issue or process.

2. **To persuade**—to cause an audience to think or behave in a different manner.

3. **To entertain**—to cause a pleasurable response in an audience.

Some presentations include all three purposes, though one of these is usually the general (overall) purpose. Which of these purposes best fits your talk?

Informative Speaking

The purpose of informative speaking is simply to give the audience new information that is beneficial or interesting. How state government is organized, what the metric system is—these are examples of informative topics. In an informative speech, the main concern of the speaker is to help the audience learn and remember information. The best way to determine whether the speech has really met the purpose of informing an audience is to poll the listeners at the end of the speech to see what they now know about the subject.

**Informative
Speaking**

Persuasive Speaking

A persuasive speech is one that attempts to cause the audience to change its feelings or beliefs about something or to behave differently. Insurance salespeople use persuasive speech to get clients to purchase insurance. Football coaches give speeches at halftime to get the players to change their behavior and play differently. A mayor speaking about a new zoning procedure to the city council is giving a persuasive speech to get the council to adopt the new system. Each of these examples shows someone trying to get other people to change their opinions or behave in a different way. If you are trying to get someone to believe differently or behave differently, then the purpose of your speech is persuasive.

Persuasive Speaking

**Entertaining
Speaking**

Entertainment Speaking

The entertainment speech is simply to give the audience a good time. The speech may also inform and persuade, but its main purpose is to have the audience feel good, relax, and enjoy themselves. The entertainment speech is often used in after-dinner speaking situations.

A speaker with a clear purpose can aim a talk in a definite direction, gain audience interest, and save time. Decide early in your speech preparation what kind of response you would like to have from your listeners so that they do not leave saying, "It was an interesting talk, but what was the point?"

"The time has
come," the Wal-
rus said, "To talk
of many things:
Of shoes—and
ships—and seal-
ing-wax—Of cab-
bages—and kings.
. . ."

**LEWIS CARROLL
Through the
Looking-Glass**

SPECIFIC PURPOSE OF YOUR TOPIC

We have indicated that the general purposes of speaking are to inform, to persuade, and to entertain. However, to develop an effective speech you must strive to precisely form the general purpose into a specific purpose. The specific purpose should describe or indicate the exact type of response you expect or anticipate from your listening audience. It should state what you want the audience to know, feel, or do. A specific purpose should minimally do three things:

1. It should contain no more than one major or central idea.

2. It should be clear, concise, and to the point.

3. It should be stated in terms of what you want the audience to be able to do when you have finished speaking.

When the general purpose is **to inform,** some sample specific purposes might be: To have the audience know how to wax cross-country skis. To have the audience understand the methods of preparing natural foods. Or to have the audience understand the United Way organization.

When the general purpose is **to persuade,** some sample specific purposes might be: To get the audience to contribute to Muscular Dystrophy. To get the audience to accept the use of nuclear energy. Or to get the audience to donate more money to your university.

When the general purpose is **to entertain,** some sample specific purposes might be: To have the audience laugh by telling about your ineptness as a golfer. To have the listeners laugh at hearing themselves described as animals. Or to have the audience enjoy hearing about the difficulties associated with the fear of giving speeches.

The following examples help clarify the phrasing of general and specific purposes:

Topic:	Buying a car
General Purpose:	To inform
Specific Purpose:	To help my audience understand three essential steps in purchasing a car

Topic:	Buying a car
General Purpose:	To persuade
Specific Purpose:	To convince my audience that they should buy a late-model used car, rather than a new car

Topic:	Buying a car
General Purpose:	To entertain
Specific Purpose:	To have the audience laugh at my experience of how not to buy a car

◢◢◢ LEARNING FROM OTHER SPEAKERS

Listening to other people speak can help you learn a great deal about what to do, and what not to do, when working with your own topic and purpose. As you listen to other speakers, pay particular attention to how the speaker limits and adapts the topic and purpose to the particular listeners. You may find some presentations appear to be "canned" because the speaker does not adjust the content of the speech to the specific audience being addressed. Sometimes, students criticize teachers of large lecture classes of this shortsightedness. On the other hand, seasoned politicians are often polished at speaking from group to group using the same topic, general purpose, and specific purpose while adjusting and adapting the content to each particular audience's interests and concerns. Thus, each separate group of listeners feels the speech was personally developed with them in mind.

To learn from other speakers takes more than hearing. It takes more than just listening. To learn from other speakers, good and bad, requires being aware of how they start their speech and relate the topic to the audience. What do effective speakers do to hold audience interest and illustrate their ideas? Is the speaker's purpose clear, and did it achieve its goal? Why? How did the audience react to the speaker?

What You Now Know

Selecting an appropriate subject and purpose for your speech can best be accomplished by speaking on a topic you are interested in. Make the talk yours by drawing on your own experiences. Analyzing the characteristics, interests, and concerns of your listeners will allow you to adjust the material to them. Determining the general purpose of the speech (to inform, persuade, or entertain) is followed by formulating the specific purpose: the exact nature of the response you want from your audience. Applying your ability to listen to other speakers in one of the most direct ways to develop your own skills of limiting and adapting topics and speaking purposes to particular listeners.

What to Do to Learn More

Topic Inventory

STEP 1: Write down eight things (topics, issues, subject areas, activities, beliefs, interests, or any combination) that interest you. For the moment, do not be at all concerned about whether anyone is interested in them.

	Topics	Audience Ranking	My Ranking
1.			
2.			
3.			
4.			
5.			
6.			
7.			
8.			

STEP 2: Now rank the topics from 1, the one that interests you the most, to 8, the one that interests you the least.

STEP 3: Now set aside your interests. Look at the topics in Step 1 and guess which would be the most interesting to an audience similar to your speech-communication-class members. Now rank the topics again from 1 (the one that would interest the listeners the most) to 8, the one that would interest them the least.

STEP 4: You now have some rough data to use in selecting the speech topic you feel has the best chance of interesting you and your audience. How? Given the following example:

Topics	Audience Ranking	My Ranking
1. Abortion	7	8
2. Drugs	3	7
3. Sports-car racing	5	3
4. Surfing	2	6
5. Stained glass	8	4
6. Summer in Alaska	6	1
7. Advertising	1	5
8. Special education	4	2

You should choose special education because it has the lowest (and thus best) total score (6), along with the lowest "my ranking" (2). Given the premise that the speaker's interest in the topic ("my ranking") is more important to speech success than the audience's interest (audience ranking), you should choose special education rather than advertising, which also totals to 6 but has a "my ranking" of 5. Now choose a topic from step 1.

STEP 5: At this point, decide whether your general purpose will be to inform, persuade, or entertain. Finally, state clearly to yourself what specific response you want from your listeners.

4

SUPPORTING AND ILLUSTRATING YOUR IDEAS

After studying this chapter, you will know how to find information about your ideas. You will learn the various ways to support your ideas with verbal support materials, and you will also be able to use visual aids and equipment to create greater impact with your audience.

Chapter Content

◢◤ MAKING YOURSELF A MORE BELIEVABLE SPEAKER

If you are not an expert on alternative energy sources, what would be the main difference in the expression of your thoughts: (1) to a group of friends in the student center, (2) in a discussion in a science class, or (3) to a group of thirty or forty members of the chamber of commerce in your community who have gathered to hear you speak on the topic?

What would be the main difference in the following situations: (1) a student trying to talk a friend into buying his motorcycle, even though autumn has already arrived, (2) the same student attempting to sell the motorcycle to an unknown person who has phoned in response to a newspaper ad, and (3) the same student attempting to sell his motorcycle from the lot of a local Honda dealership, where the student is a part-time salesperson?

In both sets of circumstances, the main difference will most likely lie in the amount of supportive and illustrative materials the speaker uses. The closer the presentation of one's ideas comes to be what most people consider public speaking, the more use is usually made of these materials: testimony from experts, statistics, forms of reasoning, analogies, examples, and the like.

Why? The usual assumption of nonexpert speakers is that the credibility they lack as firsthand experts can be compensated for by demonstrating to listeners that they have become **secondary experts.** This is accomplished by quoting materials and facts that demonstrate a greater-than-average awareness of the subject.

We found an example of the credibility gap of a message source in *Reader's Digest,* where an unmarried person had written an article entitled "To Increase the Enjoyment of Sex in Marriage." Your authors had a bit of difficulty accepting the "expertness" of the article's recommendations of shoulds and should nots. Had the writer used surveys, interviews with married couples, or simply education in the field, his article would have been more credible to us as readers.

Similarly, picture yourself in a physician's office during a checkup. Your doctor is giving you advice about being out of shape and smoking too much. While he is talking, you happen to notice the roll of fat hanging four inches over his belt. As his voice wheezes, you look past him to a half-empty pack of cigarettes on his desk and an ashtray full of butts. Since this is a situation where one person is trying to influence the thoughts and actions of another (persuasion), the credibility (believability) of the source is even more important than in a strictly informative presentation—although, as we have just seen, it is significant there, too.

What does the title of the chapter, "Supporting and Illustrating Your Ideas," mean? In a communication sense, *to support* means to verify or to substantiate. In the same communication sense, *to illustrate* means to make clear, to shed light on. As you can see, there is an overlapping area between these two definitions. In the traditional approach, when you support your ideas, you back them up with facts, evidence, statistics, logical reasoning, expert testimony, and the like. When you illustrate your ideas, you paint a verbal picture with examples, stories, and specifics to help make your ideas live in the present. You create visual images for the minds of your listeners. You also may actually use visual or audio aids to be specific, clear, and interesting.

The key to using what we have called supporting and illustrating materials is in understanding the role they play in what we call the *basic message unit*. The basic message unit is made up of two elements: (*a*) a general statement followed by (*b*) a specific, either a supporting or illustrating, point (The order of *a* and *b* may be reversed.)

Example: Teachers forget what it is like to be a student studying for a major test (*general statement*). My instructor estimated that it would take only one or two hours to prepare for the test. It took me all evening to go through my notes. My roommate was up until 3:00 A.M. studying (*specific* illustrations).

Example: Hondas generally get the best gas mileage of any of the compact cars (*general statement*). A recent study conducted by the EPA rated the Honda Civic as having the best all-around gas mileage for compacts with ——m.p.g. city and ——m.p.g. country driving (*specific research evidence*).

You cannot deal with the most serious things in the world unless you understand the most amusing.
WINSTON CHURCHILL

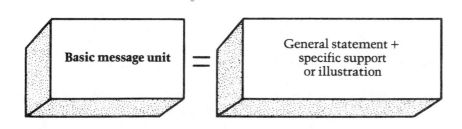

Since supportive and illustrative materials are absolutely necessary to you as a speaker, you need to know where to find materials related to the idea or topic you want to get across to others and how to keep track of them once they are found. Also, you should examine various kinds of verbal illustrative and supportive materials, as well as visual aids, that can be used in typical speeches to create interest in and prove your ideas.

FINDING INFORMATION ABOUT YOUR IDEAS

The more public and formal your speaking, the greater the variety of sources of materials you will want to research or investigate in preparing the content of your talk. Gathering material for speaking is like shooting film for a television commercial. An advertising agency takes about ten times as many feet of film as it will actually use in the commercial. The agency looks at all the film and selects just the parts that will best accomplish the objective. The selected parts are then spliced together. And the rough print is tested for the full effect and finally edited down to a polished version. This whole process is parallel to gathering and evaluating material for a speech.

Professional speakers usually gather two or three times more material than they will actually be able to use. This extra material does not go to waste, though. Often, speakers can work in additional information when answering questions and comments after the main part of the presentation is over.

There are several ways to locate information about your topic. The greater the variety of sources of information you look into, the more knowledge you will gain in your attempt to become a secondary expert.

Some traditional and unique sources of information are interviewing, surveying, structured observations, experimental manipulation, and the library.

> A fool uttereth all his mind.
> PROVERBS 29:11

Interviewing and Surveying

Interviewing campus or local professionals and experts can be an interesting way to gather information and materials. But be careful not to get so carried away with a particular source's information that the speech becomes one continuous reference to that expert. When you decide to interview or gather information on the same questions from many people, whether they are peers, voters, teachers, lawyers, married couples, or third graders, you are doing a survey. When you conduct a survey in order to gather information on a particular topic, do not be misled into believing that your information proves anything to be true or false. Your results may show a trend or tendency, but the survey would have to be done very scientifically to prove anything.

Surveys may take the form of printed questionnaires, face-to-face interviews, or telephone interviews. No matter what the surveying technique, you have to decide ahead of time how you will sample the people who represent the group about which you wish to discover something. You will also have to decide what questions will be asked of everyone and how you will ask the questions.

There are several different types of questions:

1. **Open questions:** How do you feel about artificial insemination of women? What do you think about the CIA scandal?

2. **Closed questions:** Do you like this course? Did you vote last year?

3. **Scaling questions:** How would you rate this class? Poor? Fair? Average? Good? Excellent?

4. **Multiple-choice questions:** How often do you openly argue with your spouse? _____ more than once a day. _____ About once a day. _____ Weekly. _____ Monthly. _____ Seldom. _____ Never.

5. **Directive questions:** Give me two reasons why you chose to attend this school.

Remember also that in face-to-face interviewing, you can ask a primary question, such as "How do you feel about the new tax increase?", and then follow it with a secondary question, such as "why do you feel that way?"

In designing your survey, allow your instructor to examine and comment on the questions and interview technique you plan to use.

Next, pretest the survey on about ten people who are not familiar with what you are doing. Ask them to complete the survey in the manner you plan. After they have finished, you will see where your survey has rough spots in wording, directions, completion time, and so on. Smooth out these problems, and you are ready to administer the survey to your chosen sample.

Structured Observations

The purpose of structured observations is to witness firsthand how people behave (respond) in a particular situation, to learn more than you know now. Structured observing requires that nothing be manipulated by you and that the people are not aware they are being observed. When people are aware that "something is going on," it affects what they do and what you end up observing. To keep track of the behaviors, you have to record them on a tally sheet, sometimes called a tracking instrument. A simple example is the following:

Objective: To observe door-opening behavior of male-female couples.

Procedure: Observe fifty couples approaching a closed door together and record which person opens the door.

RESULTS

Behavior	Total Number	Percentages
Male opened door	30	60%
Female opened door	12	24%
Both opened door together	8	16%

Experimental Manipulation

If you want to manipulate a situation to see how people will respond to a given stimulus, then you are setting up a mini-experiment. In most instances when you run an experiment, you need to record the behavior of people before you manipulate anything (structured observation) to see what the "baseline" behavior is. For example, you could observe the average length of time students spend talking with an interviewer who is doing a survey on some subject. You would record the results the interviewer had in this normal circumstance. Then you could ask the interviewer to avoid eye contact with the interviewees as much as possible for the same number of interviews as conducted in the baseline observation. You would record the results. Then you could ask the interviewer to have good eye contact with the same number of interviewees. And you would record the results.

In some instances you might not need a baseline to see what people's responses to an experimental manipulation will be, because what you are doing is straightforward and simple. For example, you may want to see who can get more students to fill out a questionnaire—a male in sloppy and dirty clothes, the same male in clean and casual clothes, or the same male in a suit and tie. In each type of clothing, the interviewer would approach twenty-five (or some other set number) subjects. And you would keep track of the results.

The Library

The library is the traditional place to locate books, articles, statistics, and other materials. You can use the encyclopedias for an overall view of your topic .The card catalogue will help you find books dealing with your subject. *The Reader's Guide to Periodical Literature* will lead you to articles on your topic or related topics in almost every published magazine in the United States. *The Statistical Abstract of the United States* will give you up-to-date statistics on a large range of subjects, from the number of women who are presidents of companies to the number of cars made in the United States last year. Best of all, almost every library is equipped with some type of computer-assisted retrieval system. With a subject name, article title, or author's name, it is quite simple to find large amounts of information in just a few minutes.

Before you begin your work in the library, find the reference librarian and ask for assistance. Don't overlook the deluge of popular magazines that surround us at the library as well as at home, work, school, and dentists' and doctors' offices.

A man should keep his little brain attic stocked with all the furniture that he is likely to use, and the rest he can put away in the lumber-room of his library, where he can get it if he wants it.
SIR ARTHUR CONAN DOYLE

RECORDING YOUR INFORMATION

One thing an experienced speaker learns is that all the interesting ideas and facts found in research are not automatically remembered once it comes time to prepare the talk. This is why taking notes and jotting down ideas are important. It is a waste of time and energy to consult a piece of material only to forget it two days later when planning the speech. Take more notes than you will possibly

need. Remember that the material will be refined and edited later.
Make one notecard for each source or major idea. Be sure to also
note the title, author(s), date, issue, and page numbers, in case you
need to consult the source again. Or sometimes a member of the
audience will ask for documentation of a source if it is questioned
or if that person is interested in a particular point. The information
can then be given from the card. A typical card might look like this:

> "The only records of the debates
> in the 'Federal Convention of 1787
> are the notes taken by individual
> delegates and published later."
>
> Farber and White, A History of the
> American Constitution, St. Paul,
> MN: West Publishing Company, 1990,
> page 92.

Keeping notecards of information is also an advantage when it
comes to organizing the talk. The notes can simply be arranged into
piles that will follow the opening, main body, and conclusion of the
speech. The notecards can also be organized so as to put ideas in
logical order. To add credibility to your information, mention the
source and page number of your information when using it in a
speech.

USING VERBAL SUPPORTIVE MATERIALS THAT PROVE YOUR POINT

Now that we have discussed ways of gathering material, you may be wondering, "What difference does it make what individual items of my potential information are called—factual examples, testimony, or analogy?" Secondly, you may be thinking, "If there is a gray area where supportive materials and illustrative materials overlap, why worry about whether the items I use are supportive or illustrative as long as they are effective?"

The answer to the first question is simple. We name the kinds of informational materials so you can analyze their use or absence in your speaking. Speakers tend to overuse favorite or habitual information types and ignore other types that could add more variety and interest to the speech. Maybe you can recall a persuasive speech where the speaker read one quote after another from supposed experts. How effective did you find this singular type of support in proving the point?

The answer to the second question ("Why worry about whether my material is supportive or illustrative?") is not as simple to answer. Illustrative and supportive materials are used to give a speech substance. They assist the speaker in developing the main points beyond abstract and general statements. When general statements of main points are given substance (specificity and vividness) by illustrative and supportive materials, we have what has been called the basic message unit in speaking.

In the literature on speaking, there is little consistent description of what is an illustrative material and what is a supportive material. Generally, supportive materials are used to prove, to offer evidence, to substantiate. Speakers rely on supportive materials to build their own credibility, especially if they are a secondary source, and to develop the credibility of the information. Illustrative materials are used to give concreteness, clarity, and interest.

Both illustrative and supportive materials are found in informative and persuasive speaking. However, primary use of supportive materials fits persuasive speaking better, whereas primary use of illustrative materials is more appropriate to informative speaking.

In summary, it is important to be able to label materials, to see patterns in their use or misuse. It is also important to realize whether your materials have to prove something or simply are meant to enlighten the listener. Now we are ready for a brief description of several supportive materials.

Reasoning

Reasoning is the ability to interrelate perceptions—to recognize or create patterns among these perceptions. Reasoning is a process of using words to emphasize relationships among the objects, events, or ideas for which the words stand. Three types of reasoning we use everyday are causal, inductive, and deductive.

Causal Reasoning

When something happens, we assume that it had a cause. We infer the cause even when we are not sure of it. "The high divorce rate is the result of too many early marriages." "The use of drugs by youth is a result of their loss of personal identity in a society of manufactured images and numbers." "Students with good grades have efficient study habits." Or "the football team lost the game because of too much 'night-before' partying."

In a similar sense, when we become aware of a process or event, we often speculate about what the end result will be. For example, your instructor comes to class without any materials except a pencil and note-pad, and you speculate that today, the class will be giving impromptu speeches. We reason from effect to inferred cause and from cause to what we think the effects will be.

Inductive Reasoning

This is reasoning from specific examples to a general conclusion. The speaker will try to prove that a general rule or conclusion is warranted because several specific instances occur in some relationship. For example, an observant student would be using inductive reasoning in concluding a quiz was in store today because every time the class has a quiz, the instructor, upon entering the room, does not establish eye contact with anyone, and today, the instructor has entered the room and not established eye contact with anyone. Inductive reasoning can be diagrammed like this:

■ FACT: My speech class required reading three textbooks,

■ FACT: and two significant research reports,

■ FACT: presenting eleven speeches,

■   FACT: and passing three major examinations.

■   CONCLUSION: This speech class is much too difficult.

Deductive Reasoning

This is reasoning from a generally accepted law or principle to a specific case, as in the example: "Divorced women are disappointed women. Mary is divorced, therefore, she is a disappointed woman." Other examples of deductive reasoning are: "Buicks are reliable cars. I bought a Buick, therefore I have a reliable car." Or, "Religious speeches given in Smith's communication class get As. Therefore, I'm going to give a religious speech so I can get an A."

Checkpoints

■   In causal reasoning, check to see whether there could be more than a single cause. Could the effects vary?

■   In inductive reasoning, it is important to decide whether the examples are typical or representative and sufficient in number.

■   In deductive reasoning, it is important to examine the factual basis for the "law" or "principle."

Testimony

Opinions and conclusions taken from others can add weight to the point you are trying to put forth if the audience makes the connection between your ideas and the ideas of other people. There are two commonly accepted kinds of testimony: expert testimony and peer testimony.

Expert Testimony

This is called for when the experience, knowledge, or insight of highly qualified people will be accepted as believable because of the complexity or sophistication of the material. For example, a ballistics expert is called into a trial to testify regarding the matchup between a bullet and a gun used in a crime. However, a problem in expert testimony can arise when "experts" claiming to be right are found on both sides of the topic.

Peer Testimony

This kind of testimony is helpful because listeners are interested in the opinions of people like themselves. Conducting a survey is a good way to arrive at peer or lay testimony. Various television commercials have used this technique to sell products. We hear Bertha Grogen's advice on everything from cars to personal hygiene products because Bertha is one of us, a common, everyday American with an opinion.

Checkpoints

■ Choose the expert who is a credible source to your listeners, not necessarily the most credible source to you.

■ Be aware of the expert's obvious biases (a biologist may not be seen as an objective expert if working for an environmental protection group).

■ If your only expert is unknown to your audience, present the expert's credentials to the audience before giving his or her opinion.

Quantifying and Using Statistics

When figures (numbers) are used to show relationships between specific items, we call these statistics. Statistics are numerical summaries of facts. They can be effective proof if they are (1) understood by the listener, (2) meaningful to the listener, and (3) related to the point being made. For example, instead of saying "55,000 people are killed in needless traffic accidents every year," you could bring that large, abstract figure down to earth by adding, "that means one person dies in traffic accidents every ten minutes of every day." An example involving billions of dollars could be made more vivid by your stating that it would take a sixty-story pile of hundred-dollar bills to add up to a billion dollars.

The common reaction to the suggestion that a speaker use numbers or statistics to support (prove) or illustrate (add interest and concreteness) to the presentation is "Numbers can be so confusing." This is correct if they are not used well. If you use many figures or comparisons, they should be put on visual aids. But if you want to make a single point that involves numbers or statistics, you can do this effectively by relating the numbers to something concrete and easily visualized. (This is similar to an analogy.) For example, "It is roughly 240,000 miles from the earth to the moon. Comparatively, that means if the earth were this softball (hold up softball) the moon would be about the size of this golf ball (hold up golf ball in other hand). Another example would be "The moon is

240,000 miles from the earth. This means that if you started driving your car toward the moon at 55 miles per hour and you could continue without stopping, you would get there in 182 days."

The use of calculators can be fun in figuring costs, time lost, and percentages, to add interest to a topic. The results can be unique to a listener who has never stopped to think about the idea in that way. An example could be figuring how many years of a lifetime a person spends sleeping: "If you sleep an average of eight hours a night for a life of seventy years, you will spend over twenty-three years sleeping. If you could get by with only six hours of sleep per night instead of eight, you would have over five and one-half more years awake to be active in your life." Or: "A person who drinks at least one six-pack of beer a week will drink about 1560 six-packs of beer in a thirty-year span. At $3.95 per six-pack, that would be close to $6,162. If that same person also smoked a pack of cigarettes every day for thirty years, the total amount spent would come to approximately $24,000. Now, if that person put the $19.70 per week for beer and cigarettes in a savings account in the bank each week, at 6 percent interest compounded quarterly, the person would have approximately $84,843 after thirty years."

Another interesting point the calculator can help you illustrate relates to the present interest in exercising. For example, "When they say we can add five years onto our life by exercising one hour per day, we forget that one hour is one less hour we have to do other things. When you figure this out for fifty years of exercising, we will spend two years of our life just to add five years on. That appears to be a net gain of only three years, not five."

The calculator can assist you in discovering all kinds of interesting figures to use in your presentations. To pursue the use of numbers and statistics further, you can go to your library and examine *Facts on File, The Statistical Abstract of the United States,* and other similar source books.

People are also becoming more aware of the use of statistics to produce false "truths." Nine out of ten doctors may recommend Gag toothpaste, but they may also have recommended three or four other brands along with Gag. Statistics must be analyzed. To do this, use the following checkpoints:

Checkpoints

■ Remember that listeners do not always trust figures.

■ Check to see whether statistics are complete or whether they are lifted out of context. ("Three out of four people said they like

Grit soap." You are not told that these statements were extracted from people after they were given free boxes of Grit in a store.)

■ Check for dated statistics.

■ Round off numbers when the decimals are not necessary; for example, 98.56 percent becomes 99 percent.

Factual Examples

The best factual examples are specific instances of an event, process, or incident that have been observed and documented by objective sources. Personal examples, though they may be factual, usually carry the bias of personal involvement or emotion. We suggest that the most potent factual examples are those which are recorded by noninvolved outside observers who do not add a personal bias to interpretation of the event. An innocent bystander who observes an accident is seen as an objective witness and is believed to be more factual than either of the two or more parties involved in the accident.

Materials we have described as helpful in illustrating can also be used in supporting (proving) a point. Specific instances, analogies, examples, and so on can be used in a persuasive manner and will give additional impact to your message.

To get a clear idea of what we mean by examples, look back over the pages you have read so far in this book. Look for the instances where we have said, "for example." These should give you an indication of what examples are and how to use them. There is a factual example about exercising in the middle of the preceding page.

Checkpoints

■ Examples should be explained vividly and specifically, rather than generally.

■ To aid in persuasive speaking, the example has to be believable.

Hypothetical Examples

Factual examples describe real experiences. Hypothetical examples describe imaginary or "what if" situations. A student used the following hypothetical example to illustrate the need for everyone to learn how to use the Heimlich maneuver:

> What if you are eating dinner with your family. Suddenly, your mother starts to choke. She didn't chew a piece of roast beef as she should, and it has lodged in her throat. Frantically, she pushes herself away from the table and starts to panic. It all happens so fast that you are not sure of what to do. Her face color is changing to blue. Her eyes meet yours and plead for help. You know that in a very few minutes, your mother will be beyond helping.
>
> Imagine how you are feeling. Your mother is struggling to stay alive, and you are unable to assist her. You thought this would never happen to you, and here it is happening.
>
> Even though this situation is hypothetical, choking does occur more frequently than you suppose. There is a solution to this problem and that's what we are going to learn more about in the next few minutes.

The speaker openly creates an example as fiction to make a point. Usually, the example is invented because a factual example is not readily available, the factual example is too complex to be explained in simple terms, or some of the details of the factual example are not suited to the purpose the speaker has in mind. As with other speaking materials, the hypothetical example can be used either to advance the clarity of comprehension or to convince the listener through emotional or logical means.

Checkpoints

■ In persuasive speaking, keep hypothetical examples to a minimum, as the listener knows they are fiction.

■ Keep the hypothetical example believable by avoiding exaggeration in description of numbers, amounts, size, frequency, and so on.

■ Add some further interest to the hypothetical example by giving names to people, places, and things in the example, then refer to the items by name, as if they might easily be real.

Personal Experience

Relating an **actual experience** you have had can be one of the most powerful methods of illustrating or supporting a point in the message. If you include when it happened and where it happened, along with what happened, the listener will "relive" the experience with you. Colorful words and concrete images will add to the interest.

This book is the result of a personal situation your authors experienced. The three of us were puffing our way around the Brigham Young University football practice field. Between gasps, we were musing that it was too bad that talking was not as good an exercise as jogging. As speech-communication teachers (notorious for our long-windedness in the classroom), we would surely be in top physical condition. We speculate that we could then write a book titled *Pumping Words* (a takeoff on Arnold Swartzenegger's movie *Pumping Iron*). After an attempted laugh from lungs that could not spare the air, we slowed to a walk, and this book began to take shape (much faster, by the way, than our bodies did).

Checkpoints

■ Describe the personal experience so your listeners can identify with you and what you did or thought.

■ If your personal experience is long (three or four minutes in length), build to a climax at the end.

Analogy

When you draw a **comparison** between a point you are attempting to make and an activity or situation with which the audience can readily identify, you are using an analogy. Many management-motivation and religious speakers use analogies to make their ideas clearer and more interesting. The process, for example, of managing a business may be compared to coaching a football team. When we wrote about gathering material for your speech, we compared it to shooting film for a television commercial. We were using an analogy.

Checkpoints

■ Listeners tend to judge analogies from the perspective of whether they appear to fit or make immediate sense in terms of the point at hand.

■ Analogies used in persuasive speaking cannot break down too easily; in other words, the analogy has to appear to parallel the point being made in both detail and the perspective of the situation.

VISUAL AIDS CREATE IMPACT IN SUPPORTING OR ILLUSTRATING

It has been estimated that more than 75 percent of the information we take in during the day or in any given situation comes in through our eyes. The film *Visual Aids*[1] states that we learn

- 3 percent through taste
- 3 percent through smell
- 6 percent through touch
- 13 percent through hearing
- 75 percent through sight

Examining the data from a different viewpoint, the Industrial Audio Visual Association[2] reports that we remember:

- 10 percent of what we read
- 20 percent of what we hear
- 30 percent of what we see
- 50 percent of what we see and hear
- 80 percent of what we say
- 90 percent of what we say as we act

It may be only recently that we have received scientific confirmation of these facts, but intuitively, we have known them for a long time. There is an ancient Chinese proverb that says: "I hear and I forget. I see and I remember. I do and I understand."

[1]BNA Communications Inc., 5615 Fishers Lane, Rockville, MD 20852.
[2]P.O. Box 656 Downtown Station, Chicago, IL 60690.

Another study by R. Benschofter[3] reports the influence of using sound and sight, separately or combined, as a teaching tool:

| | **Percent of Recall** | |
Methods of Instruction	3 hours later	3 days later
Telling, when used alone	70%	10%
Showing, when used alone	72%	20%
Combination of telling and showing	85%	65%

Taking into account that the average speaker talks at 125 to 130 words per minute and that our brains can think four or five times that fast allows us to understand why listeners get bored and disstracted. Now add to this that our language can be up to 60 percent redundant, and you have a clearer picture of why people tune out when presentations are totally verbal in content.

When speakers use visual aids, they "entertain" or focus the visual attention of the listeners on material related to the talk. Thus, the speakers have more influence over the total information pro-

Reinforcing a spoken message with a visual presentation not only helps entertain listeners but also enhances their ability to recall and understand the information.

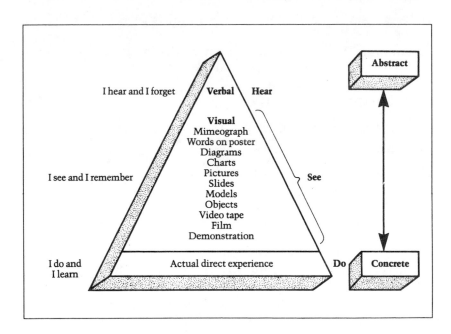

[3]"In-Service Training Aids," *Proceedings of Nebraska's In-Service Training Conference.* Omaha, 1974.

cessing of the listeners. It is common knowledge in the fields of education and speech communication that visual aids are helpful in the comprehension and recall of information. Visual aids can add interest and impact. In this sense, visual aids add greatly to the effects of persuasive messages. also, specific messages that can be supported by facts and figures are strengthened by visual materials that are consistent with the verbal aspects of the speech.

The old saying "Use a visual aid when you need to make a complex idea clear" should, in light of the evidence, give way to a saying such as "Use visual aids *whenever you want to enhance what you are saying.*"

Types of Visual Aids and Visual-Aid Equipment

The following types of visual aids are ways of presenting information visually. They are listed in order from the most static materials to the most active.

1. Mimeographed, dittoed, or Xeroxed handouts (color-coded or keyed for easy reference)

2. Samples of actual written materials

3. Lettered posters

4. Diagrams (bar graphs, pie charts, organizational diagrams)

5. Photographs (usually enlarged or projected on a screen)

6. Slides

7. Models (of objects, processes, etc.)

8. Actual objects

9. Videotapes

10. Films

11. Demonstrations

There are also other frequently used pieces of equipment that aid speakers in presenting visual materials to the audience:

1. Boards: magnetic board, flannel or felt board, hook and loop board (Velcro), metallic- or plastic-surfaced board, chalkboard

2. Flip chart

3. Overhead projector

4. Opaque projector

5. Slide projector

6. Videotape record and playback unit

7. Film: 16 mm, 8 mm

8. Computer-generated graphics

We will note some simple considerations for the use of each piece of equipment.

Boards

Stand to the side of a board as you write or display your materials. Write clearly and thickly with chalk or felt-tip marking pens (Magic Markers). Do not use thin-line "writing" felt-tip pens on visuals. Use key words only; do not put every single word down. Look at the audience after you write a word or phrase on the board. Also, after you look to see where you are pointing on a prepared visual, be sure to look at the audience as you talk. Do not get caught talking to the board or visual, rather than to the listeners. Try to carry on a little conversation while you are writing or pointing or putting up material. Not saying anything while you manipulate parts of a board can create an awkward silence that can ruin the pacing of your presentation. Finally, do not keep turning your head and looking at the visual aid—look ahead at your audience.

Flip Chart

This may be prepared in advance so that as you flip the pages up and over the top of the easel, each page appears already complete. The same guidelines for writing and pointing when using a board apply to using a flip chart. With a flip chart, though, you have to be careful that the felt-tip marker used for writing does not "bleed" through to the pages behind. It may be necessary to try out different marking pens until you find one that has ink that dries on contact.

Overhead Projector

This works on the principle that light passing through a clear or tinted plastic sheet on which there is printing or a picture will project the image on a screen or wall.

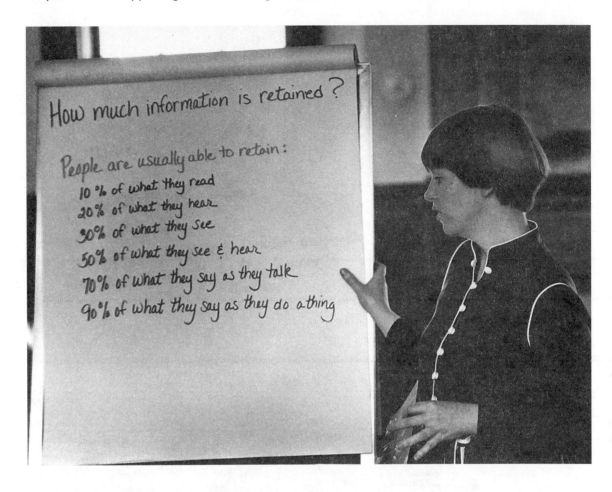

How much information is retained?

People are usually able to retain:
  10 % of what they read
  20% of what they hear
  30% of what they see
  50% of what they see & hear
  70% of what they say as they talk
  90% of what they say as they do a thing

Special transparent marking pens are available for writing or drawing on the plastic sheets used with overhead projectors. It is important to use these specially designed pens, especially if you are going to prepare your overhead visuals hours or days ahead of time. The ink from a regular felt-tip may go on the plastic properly, but it will evaporate over time. Many a speaker has used a felt-tip pen to draw overhead transparencies the night before the presentation only to wake up in the morning to find that half of the visuals have disappeared.

You should be careful as you talk not to stand in front of the light being projected to the screen. You also have to choose whether you are going to stand beside the overhead and face the audience while you talk or have someone run the overhead for you while you stand back by the screen with a pointer, again facing the audience.

Always stand to the side of the board as you discuss your materials.

Never stand in front of the light being projected to the screen.

    Be sure to rehearse with the overhead. Learn how to turn it off and on without looking for the switch. Locate the side the fan is on, because the fan could blow your notes or transparencies onto the floor during your presentation. Learn how to focus the overhead quickly. Once it is focused, put a piece of tape or chalk marks on the floor so you can quickly roll the overhead to the exact spot and the focus will already be set. Always have an extra bulb for your overhead projector or a backup projector in case the light burns out.

Positioning the overhead and the angle of projection is important for the audience to be able to view the screen. If the screen is the permanent kind that requires the overhead to be in the middle front part of the audience, you will want to arrange the seating so that the listeners sit on the sides and not in the middle.

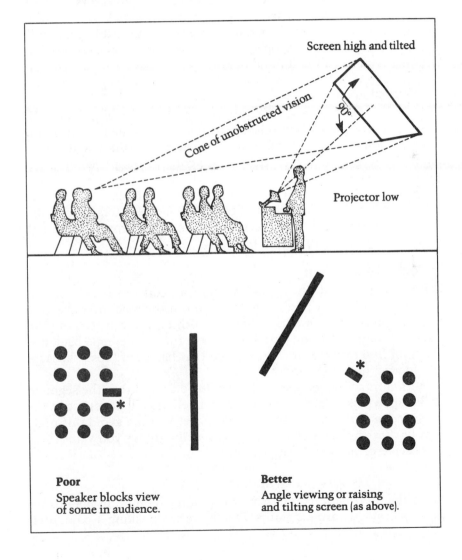

Overhead projection hints: Tilting the overhead screen (shown at the top) or placing it toward the corner of the room (shown below) reduces the possibility of the speaker and equipment blocking the vision of some viewers, as might be the case when the projector is located in front of the group (lower left).

Opaque Projector

This projector projects the actual image of a page in a book, a letter, or a diagram that is no bigger than twelve by twelve inches. Light does not pass through the printed page, as it does through overhead transparencies. Opaque projectors can enlarge and project original materials, but they are notoriously cumbersome and noisy machines to use and sometimes do not focus the complete picture at one time. It also is difficult to get the material into the machine straight and the right side up without considerable practice. Thin sheets have to be taped to cardboard to keep the fan from blowing them out of the machine. Also, because opaque projectors get very hot, materials covered with plastic coating will melt and wrinkle before your eyes. In some instances, highly combustible paper will start to smoke. However, opaque projectors allow you to show original material in full color and detail.

Slide Projector

The use of a slide projector requires that the order of points to be covered in the presentation be set firmly prior to the talk. Jumping back and forth between more than two adjacent slides is awkward to do. If there is an automatic advance cord for the projector and it will reach the screen, you can stand by the screen and face the audience while the slides are projected. This will allow you to have eye contact with the listeners. Speaker-audience interaction is difficult if the speaker has to stand behind the slide projector and talk to the backs of the listeners heads.

Videotape and Film

With videotape and film, it is important to edit to the precise sections desired so that there is no need to run the machines ahead or back to pick up segments. There is nothing more frustrating for listeners than to sit and watch a speaker run a videotape back and forth for five minutes to find a piece that has been "lost" because the footage notations are off.

With film and videotape, you need to be careful that the segment to be shown is not so engrossing in itself that listeners lose the perspective of the point that is being made. You can avoid this problem by "setting listeners up" for the specific things you want them to observe or notice in the segment.

Computer-Generated Graphics

With the increasing popularity of computers comes an abundance of graphics software programs. Don't overlook asking a computer-wise friend to show you a sample of the graphics that can be used to prepare visual materials. And check your library or school computer resources to see what is available for your use.

Guidelines to Visual Aid Design and Use

The two key guidelines for designing and using all visual aids are not readily observed today, even in some professional speaking situations. The reason is that speakers tend to design and use visual aids the way they see others doing them, rather than thinking through how the visual can sequentially and systematically aid their presentation. The two guidelines are:

■ visual aids must unfold with the speaking

■ visual aids should exploit the visualness of the medium

It is not difficult to find a speaker who has designed the visual aid as it would appear in a magazine or book. The complete working and diagramming is totally exposed for the viewer to read or see ahead of, during, or after the actual speech. Since the audience members can read or see the points much faster than the speaker can talk, the listener tunes out what the speaker is saying and focuses on the visual, then tunes the speaker back in again. If the visual is confusing or complex, the listener may tune the speaker out and stay with the visual long after the speaker has finished referring to it.

For greatest impact and effectiveness, the words of the speaker and the words or pictures on the visual should be absolutely synchronized. *The visual must unfold in front of the listeners' eyes and in exact synchronization with what the speaker is saying.*

What this means is that visuals, such as posters, flip charts, and boards, must utilize techniques that keep images covered or make images appear at the point of actual verbal reference. This is where creativity in covering and uncovering images and sticking images onto the board or poster will pay off.

This will take a different kind of thinking about the design and use of visual aids than you may be used to. For example, one of the authors attended a three-day banking conference. The closest thing to effective use of visual aids he observed was by a speaker who put a blank piece of paper across the bottom of an overhead transparency and moved the paper down to the next point every so often. Many times the sheet being used to mask the bottom lines of the visual was crooked on the screen. Our level of awareness regarding effective visual-aid design and use will not necessarily be enhanced by observing others. For some reason, there is a distinct gap between our academic knowledge regarding visual support materials and actual practice by teachers and professionals alike.

The second guideline, that visuals should exploit the visual medium, is also not easily observed in educational settings. Too often, the total content of the visual is words, words, words—so many words the speaker and listeners have to read them as they would a memo. A visual aid should be understandable and clear at a glance. This means words should not be the focus; images should be the focus. You often hear the adage, "A picture is worth a thousand words." We don't believe many people really listen to that statement.

Graphs and charts that are designed for written reports are *not* usually effective for oral presentations. Written reports can be studied and analyzed closely over time by the reader. This is not possible with visuals.

Design Features of Visual Aids

Other important items in designing visuals are the figure-ground relationships, the colors, the size, the type of lettering, the simplicity, and the use of graphics and abbreviations.

1. **Figure-ground relationships.** A picture needs to have a central figure or focus for the eye. The remaining portion of the picture supporting the central part should complement the focal point.

2. **Colors.** When color for the lettering or graphics is being chosen, creativity should come second to sound color combinations for ease of viewing. It is wise to avoid too many colors in one visual. Pastel or bright-colored posters look good with black lettering or graphics. White lettering shows up well on dark posters. Remember to avoid using poster paper whose color is too close to the color of the graphics.

3. **Size.** The poster, flip chart, or overhead projection should be large enough to be easily read. Plenty of empty space around the words and design is needed so that the item does not appear

crowded. Twenty-four by thirty-six inches is a good size to allow for graphics and empty space.

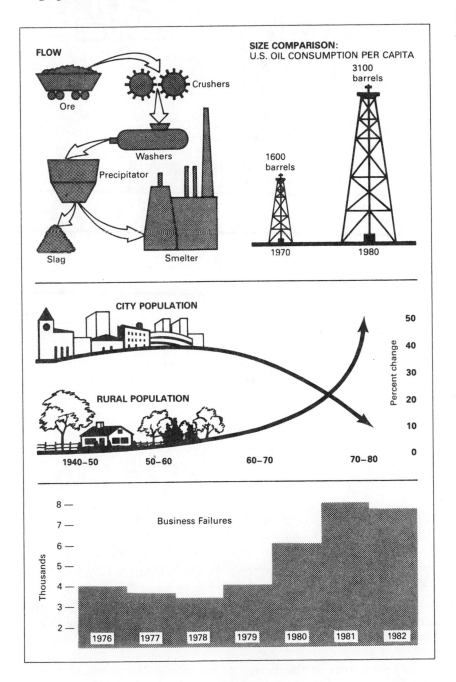

Note how visuals above use the visual medium more completely than the simple bar graph below.

Note how few words are needed to convey the facts because of the multiple visual cues the listener is given.

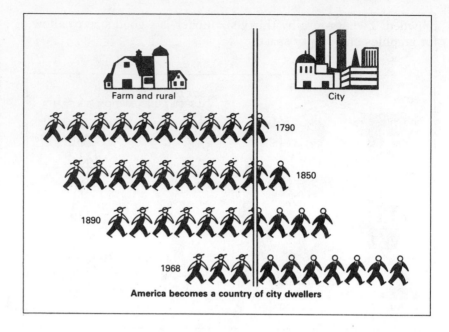

4. **Lettering.** The size of the lettering on the visual needs to be tested prior to the design of the visual. Trace a word from a stencil with a Magic Marker, and then put the paper up and step to the back of the room for a look. How well can you read the word? How well could you read a whole line of words that size? Lettering of less than an inch and a half is usually too small for an audience of more than fifteen people.

When choosing a lettering style from stencils, use roman or the style that looks most like block printing. Script, slanted letters, and fancy Gothic lettering are too difficult to read. If you plan to write on your visuals during the talk—PRINT.

5. **Simplicity.** Too many words, diagrams, or drawings are difficult for an audience to read. The listener should be able to catch the meaning of the visual at a glance. Limit yourself to key words, and use graphics to say what you want to say whenever possible.

6. **Graphics and Abbreviations.** Use arrows, silhouettes, lines, and accepted abbreviations for long words to save space and reading time.

Another aspect of the design of visual aids for presentations is whether the visual is completely prepared prior to the presentation,

Graphics
Should Be
Well-Spaced
and Easy
to Read

GRAPHICS
SHOULD BE
WELL-SPACED
AND EASY
TO READ

**Well prepared vis-
uals are usually
more effective and
professional.**

whether it is designed during the actual talk, or whether it is developed somewhere on a continuum between these two points.

1. The speaker completely prepares the visuals prior to the presentation. During the presentation, the speaker shows each visual and points to the appropriate part. Using various techniques, you can cover up sections of the visual so that the audience will not read ahead of your speaking.

2. The speaker underlines, circles, and/or checks off points on the visual with a marking pen. Or the speaker uses a partially completed visual with headings and roughed-in diagrams. During the talk, the speaker fills in missing parts with marking pens or prepared stick-on pieces. Or the speaker can design overhead transparencies so that one visual overlays on another and a progressive picture can be shown.

3. The speaker completely develops the visuals during the presentation. (This does not mean preparation has not taken place.) This is the most difficult approach, since visuals designed during the talk stand the greatest chance of being messy and incomplete. (Recall how some of your teachers use the chalkboard to develop their in-talk visuals.) When writing or drawing on flip charts or

Readability chart for determining size and thickness of letters for non-projected visuals. Size of lettering on projected visuals should be such that lettering is of adequate size when projected on screen. Make sure that thickness is proportional to height, that spacing between lines is about letter height, and that color *aids* readability, not fights it.

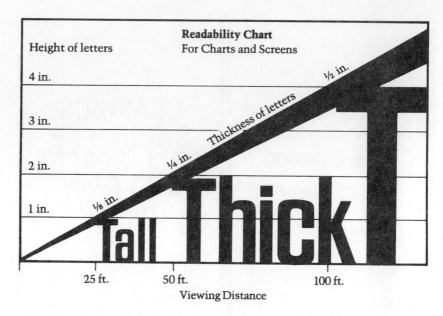

overhead transparencies, you must take care not to run the writing (printing) up or down hill. To prevent this, you can trace lightly with a pencil the outline of the words or figures prior to the presentation. During the talk, then, the light lines can be traced over with a marking pen.

Practice with Your Visuals Prior to your Presentation

As in rehearsals for the presentation of a play, you should "try out" the parts of your presentation that involve visual aids. Many times speakers just rehearse the verbal part of the speech. Practice when, how, and where you will use the aids. Pay attention to where you will place the visuals once you have referred to them. Become so familiar with the visual aids that you can point to a section accurately with just a brief glance at the visual.

Your rehearsal(s) should include practice in operating the equipment, locating backup bulbs, testing the electrical outlets, measuring the length of cord needed, and testing viewing angles. Know how the drapes close, and where the light switch is.

Before a play is performed for the public, there is a dress rehearsal. You, too, must have a dress rehearsal to put everything together.

THIS IS WHAT A GROUP OF YOUNGSTERS LOOKS LIKE WAITING FOR A SCHOOL BUS AT 5 A.M.

Double and triple sessions are as close to becoming realities in the Capistrano Unified School District as March 7.

On that day, you'll have the opportunity to vote YES on a school bond that will buy us six new schools, 70 badly needed portable classrooms and a number of long awaited district-wide improvements.

Or you can vote NO and start sending your children to school for 6 A.M. classes. Even the five-year-olds.

This kind of alternative isn't out of spite. It's out of desperation.

We've also got over-crowding, tent classrooms and extended days to look forward to.

Here's the situation. A combination of last year's bond defeat, current bursting-at-the-seams enrollment and a projected 1000 students more per year has driven California's fastest growing school district to its knees.

And with building costs increasing at the rate of 1% per month, things can only get worse.

We need your help. Desperately.

Please take the time to get out and vote YES March 7.

And help keep our kids' education out of the dark ages.

VOTE YES ON SCHOOL BONDS

Paid for by Bond Election Support Team. For additional information, call (714) 768-6978 or (714) 496-1215, between 8:00 A.M. and 4:30 P.M.

In some instances, words cannot convey the message, whereas a visual can convey it immediately and with impact (left).

At 55 mph this is what happens to a common honey bee when it hits your windshield.

Survivors wear seatbelts.

Sometimes a simple blend of an image and words has impact (above; facing page).

We have seen that in classroom speaking, the complete rehearsal makes the difference between a B presentation and an A presentation. The dress rehearsal adds the polish that is necessary for excellence.

Word of Caution
The visual is an *aid.* It should never become more important than the speaker it is aiding.

What You Now Know

Illustrative and supportive materials are used in speeches to give substance to the general points the speaker is making, forming what

It seems cocaine is in a class by itself. The upper middle class.

And in the Twin Cities you might be surprised to find out who's got the sweet tooth for nose candy.

Tonight on the *10 PM Report*, WCCO-TV's Mike Walcher investigates the local use of cocaine in a five part series entitled "The Rich Man's Drug." (It's a good title. A couple ounces of this stuff is worth a new car.)

Mike uncovers some startling facts. Like people snorting in Edina. North Oaks. Wayzata. All over suburbia. People who are local business leaders. Sound citizens.

How do these people get their cocaine? How much does it cost them? What are the physical and psychological side effects? What happens when it's mixed with other drugs? And how do the cops feel about these unconventional criminals?

Find out this week when the *10 PM Report* sticks its nose into cocaine.

Cocaine: The Rich Man's Drug
10 PM Report May 7-11

Perhaps the ultimate example of the design and use of a visual aid to convey a complex message in a simple manner can be seen daily on your television weather broadcast. Without the map and the graphics of the sun, clouds, rain drops, snowflakes, and high and low pressure lines, the average viewer would not be able to grasp the national weather. Can you imagine the weather person on your local television station standing erect, looking at the camera, and with no visual aid, attempting to verbally describe the national weather scene?

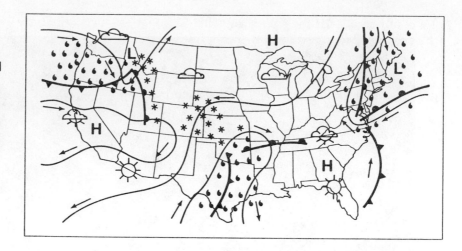

is called the basic message unit. Both illustrative and supportive materials can be used in combination in an informative speech or in a persuasive speech. However, heavy use of illustrative materials is more appropriate to an informative speech, whereas substantial use of supporting materials fits the needs of a persuasive speech better. Locating information on your chosen topic can be as creative as interviewing, surveying, observing, and experimenting and as traditional as library research.

Visual aids are used in informative and persuasive speeches to enhance the points being made. Visual aid must unfold in synchronization with the speaking. Visual aids should exploit the visual medium. The type of visuals used will depend on the time, resources, and equipment available to the speaker. Visuals should be designed with use of figure-ground relationships, color, size, bold lettering, and simplicity in mind. The effective use of visuals comes with practice.

What to Do to Learn More

TV versus Radio Commercials

Tape-record five radio commercials for national products and five

TV commercials for the same or similar national products. Analyze the commercials along the following lines:

1. Is there a difference between the use of illustrative versus supportive materials in the total group of commercials?

2. Examine the number of illustrative and supportive materials in radio versus TV commercials. Are there more, less, or about the same in the two mediums?

3. In the TV commercials, does the use of visuals meet the criteria given in this chapter?

Use of Supportive and Illustrative Materials in the Classroom

Observe the instructors' lectures in your various classes. When your instructor is attempting to prove a point or illuminate the advantage of a particular viewpoint, does he or she use more supportive or more illustrative materials? When your instructor is lecturing on a noncontroversial topic, are more illustrative or supportive materials used?

Visuals in Magazine Advertisements

Examine several magazine advertisements for their use of visuals.

1. Can you find definite figure-ground relationships?

2. Note the use of color, size, lettering, and spacing in the ads.

3. If there are people or activities in the ad, how is the product pointed out?

Making a Point

The next time you have difficulty giving instructions, directions, procedures, or explaining a complex point, sketch the main points in words on a diagram on a piece of paper for the listener. Also, draw a diagram of circles or boxes that includes all the factors you should take into consideration in studying for an examination. If you haven't thought about this before, your diagram may prove useful in the future.

5
ORGANIZING YOUR SPEECH INFORMATION

By starting with ordinary conversational patterns and building to a fully developed speech, you will learn how to organize your ideas in such a way that the audience will be able to comprehend and remember what you say. You will also learn how to increase the strength of the introduction, body, and conclusion of your speeches.

Chapter Content

◢◢◢ PROPER ORGANIZATION LEADS TO BETTER UNDERSTANDING

Everyone likes speakers who start well, continue on schedule, and quit on time. Also, speakers gain confidence when they know where they are going and how they are going to get there. A well-organized speech is easier for a speaker to give and for an audience to understand. In fact, the main purpose of organizing our ideas is to increase the possibility of having our information comprehended and retained by listeners.

◢◢◢

He must adapt his speeches to occasions and persons: His openings must be tactful, his statement of facts clear, his proof cogent, his rebuttals trenchant, and his perorations vehement. CICERO

Considerable research in theories and techniques of public speaking warns us, however, to be careful of how much emphasis we place on organizing a speech. Several studies indicate that the exact order of presenting main ideas has little relation to audience comprehension and attitude change. Other research shows that "well-structured" messages improve comprehension and that the addition of repetition and transitions further increases the amount of material comprehended and retained. The conclusion is that some organization of materials is superior to poor or no organization of the message. Our suggestion then is to organize but to organize simply. According to Gerald Kennedy, a Methodist preacher:

First, too many of us do not work on our preaching hard enough or long enough. The more gifted a man is, the more he is tempted to neglect his preparation. You listen to a man and he brings out an interesting point here or there, but there is no sense of solid structure. He makes too much of one point and too little of another. He milks an illustration dry, and what would have been effective if kept short and sharp loses its cutting edge and gets wearisome. Such a man circles back to something already dealt with and there is no sense of the inevitable, forward march of the thought.

Secondly, too many preachers fail to organize their material so that it is at once plain and clear. The people leave with a vague sense of something religious having been said, but the points which give a subject directness are either hopelessly smudged and muddled or they were never there in the first place. I have lectured on this, written about it, and discussed it at every opportunity, but it has done little good. So many preachers will not believe that their first responsibility is to be understood. I still have church members come up after the sermon and say, with a

"I would've left, too, but I'm the next speaker."

THE SATURDAY EVENING POST

kind of wonderment, "I understood you." To organize your material does not take special gifts and it does not demand any great intelligence. But it does demand the assumption that an involved and obscure style is not so much a sign of profundity of thought as of confusion of mind.[1]

Once you gain skill in ordering your ideas and settle on a method that works effectively for you, that same approach can be applied

1. From *While I'm on My Feet* by Gerald Kennedy, copyright© 1963 by Abingdon Press. Used by permission.

to writing articles and giving lessons, as well as to presenting speeches. Organizing ability is an extraordinarily valuable asset in effectively communicating your ideas to someone else.

TYPES OF ORGANIZATION

Conversational Organization

The simplest form of organization is used in everyday conversation. We make a point and give an illustration, or we give an illustration and make a point. For instance, someone dashes up to us and excitedly exclaims, "I'm the happiest person alive!" (That's the point.) "I lost fifteen pounds, John gave me this engagement ring, and we have set our wedding date!" (That's the illustration.) Or the sequence is reversed, with the illustration or example being given first, and the point being made immediately afterward. Diagrammatically, it looks like this:

I. I'm the happiest person alive
   A. I lost fifteen pounds
   B. I received an engagement ring
   C. We set our wedding date

   Or, if reversed:

   A. I lost fifteen pounds
   B. I received an engagement ring
   C. We set our wedding date
I. I'm the happiest person alive

This conversational pattern is the basis for every approach to organizing a speech. Let's expand and vary it to see what happens.

One-Point Organization

If we start a conversation or speech with a story, a quotation, or some statistics that have a moral or a point, and then we state the point and follow with other research, illustrations, and examples that support the point; and if we conclude with a rephrasing or eloquent statement of the point, we have organized our talk into a pattern popularized by a speech teacher named Alan H. Monroe. In outline form, it looks like this:

   A. Illustration or proof
I. Main idea
   B. Examples, quotations, research, stories, etc.
I. Restatement of main idea

This is a rather simple organizational plan that can be used for presenting a short speech that has just one main idea. Many writers cast brief newspaper and magazine articles into this pattern of organization.

Ho Hum! Organization

So far, we have followed a rational pattern for presenting a single main idea. Let's now examine the psychological aspects of organizing our ideas, so that we *feel* the "forward motion of thought," as well as think it.
   Another noted speech teacher and author, Richard Borden, felt that too often students were organizing speeches for themselves and not for the audience. He designed a speech plan that looks like this:

1. Ho hum!

2. Why bring that up?

3. For example . . .

4. So what?

Ho Hum!
The Borden plan can be used properly when the prospective speaker imagines that as he or she stands up to speak, the audience will collectively sigh in boredom "Ho hum!" The speaker must plan something to capture their attention:

■ Ask a series of questions that will stimulate thinking.

■ Quote an impressive statistic.

THE SATURDAY EVENING POST

■ Tell a humorous story that is relevant.

■ Make a provocative statement.

Why Bring That Up?

If the speaker starts well and gains the interest of the audience, he or she then imagines the audience asking, "Why are you bringing that up?" The successful speaker must say something that gives the audience a desire or reward for listening. All of us are a bit selfish, and before we do anything, we want to know: What's in it for me? and Why is this important to me?

■ Use illustrations to demonstrate the negative effects of not knowing more about the subject.

■ Suggest benefits to be gained by understanding the subject.

For Example . . .

If the speaker gains the attention of the listeners and successfully stimulates them to seek the rewards of continued listening, then they will invite him or her to go on—"For example?" "What?" "Get on with it." The organized speaker will then unfold the main ideas:

■ Give the main points and then three or four supporting points.

■ Explain, illustrate, prove, or demonstrate each supporting point.

■ Keep relating your ideas back to the main point and the importance of your subject.

So What?

As the speaker nears the end of the presentation, everyone will want to know: "So what?" The audience is really saying, "Okay, you caught my attention, got me involved in your ideas, and explained everything in an interesting way, but so what? What specifically do you want me to understand or do when I leave here?" The speaker will then point out the main idea and give the audience a suggestion for using the information in some beneficial way:

■ Present a challenge.

■ Give a small inducement.

■ State your own personal intention.

■ Summarize by using a final illustration.

Remember, earlier we suggested that once you gain some skill in introducing, ordering, and concluding your ideas, you can use that skill in writing, speaking, and teaching.

We can use conversational organization for very brief presentations, one-point organization for concise development of a single idea, and ho hum! organization to respond to the subtle requests that most audiences make to speakers.

Speaking Excellence

Learn How To Defend Yourself

Dan Stephan and Ron Heimberger

By combining the most powerful Shaolin-derived Kung Fu martial art principles with a superior teaching approach we are able to offer one of the most effective Martial Arts Personal Development Programs in the United States. Our approach is unique in that our students learn 25 correct principles that guide defensive action, enable clear thinking when being threatened and build the utmost confidence in one's natural abilities to contend with any type of aggression.

This program is based on a self-defense system that has been used to instruct military special forces in hand-to-hand combat, and teach self-defense to FBI agents, SWAT teams and police officers across the nation. Students learn the fastest and most powerful moves to neutralize an attacker no matter how big or strong the aggressor may be. The fundamentals of balance, flexibility, foundation strength, accuracy and body angles taught by demonstration, application, video clips, speed-building games, video taping, and homework assignments are easily remembered and can be used throughout life.

Along with learning correct martial art principles, our students are encouraged to work on effective corresponding behaviors such as commitment, politeness, and patience as well as to develop good eating, sleeping, and working habits.

Always, our emphasis is on helping students discover their own inate abilities and increase their confidence. Blind memorization of moves and techniques is no substitute for the power, speed and flexibility that come from understanding correct principles built upon our own natural instincts.

> Good martial arts can not be taught in a mass production manner. Controlled enrollment preserves the quality of instruction, allows personal time for each student, and greatly enhances the probability of success. Therefore, we would like to first enroll those students who want the best marshal arts instruction compressed in the shortest amount of time, and who are willing and even anxious to learn how to increase their confidence and ability to defend themselves.
>
> Courtesy of Wing Chun Kung Fu
> Council, OREM, Utah, 1991.
>
> In this announcement, the first paragraph gets our attention and states the subject. Paragraphs two, three, and four develop the subject with several unique main points. The final paragraph concludes with a suggested course of action.

INTRODUCTION, BODY, AND CONCLUSION ORGANIZATION (IBC)

Most experts in the speech profession agree that an important idea should be introduced, developed, and concluded. Plato suggested that in order for a speech to come alive, it must have a head, body, and tail. As you develop a plan for organizing your ideas, keep in mind this checklist:

1. Does my introduction get *attention,* help the listeners feel the *importance* of my ideas, and lead them to the *main subject* of my speech?

2. Does the body of my speech present *three or four main points* and clearly *illustrate* or *prove* each one in an interesting manner?

3. Does the conclusion review the main ideas, *tie everything back* to the main subject, and *motivate* my listeners to accept and use my ideas?

For an organizational plan capable of handling a main theme and several supporting points, as well as fulfilling the psychological needs of a listening audience, we recommend the following:

INTRODUCTION	**Attention** Your "attention getter" goes here.
	Importance The importance of your subject to the audience comes next. "Why should we listen?"
	Your Qualifications "Why should we listen to you?"
	Theme or Purpose What specifically are you going to explain or suggest that the listeners do?
BODY	**First main point** Illustrative or supportive materials
	Second main point Illustrative or supportive materials
	Third main point Illustrative or supportive materials
CONCLUSION	State what you want the audience to understand or do and end with a final summary, illustration, or application or your main theme.

Check whether the "attention" and "importance" ideas lead directly to a specific main theme. Then, examine each main point to determine whether it directly supports the main theme. Finally, determine whether the conclusion creates a strong final impact on the audience and actually concludes the main theme. If your answer is yes to each of these questions, you probably have a well-organized speech.

 ## THE BODY OF THE SPEECH

Usually, in preparing and organizing a speech, the speaker selects the main topic and develops the body of the speech first. Deciding

The organization of a speech is critical to effective delivery.

how to begin and end the speech is generally left until later in the preparation process.

The body of the speech must have valuable and interesting information. That information must be organized in such a way that it moves the speech along and at the same time makes sense. Most speech authorities agree that there are four basic ways of organizing the main ideas presented in the body of the speech: chronological or time sequence, space or geographical sequence, topical sequence, and logical sequence.

Chronological or Time Sequence

This pattern of organizing the main points in the body of the speech means that what you say moves forward or backward in time from

If art is a power reaching its end by a definite path, that is, by ordered methods, no one can doubt that there is such a method and order in good speaking.
QUINTILIAN

a specific point in time. In other words, you organize according to the time when the events occurred. This sequence works well when you are talking about a person's development, a scientific process, or how to do something, or you are reporting an experience of some sort. For example, a talk on hypnosis might be arranged into a discussion of its origin, present use, and future expectations. A report on how to prepare a speech might include: (1) selecting a subject, (2) gathering material, (3) organizing ideas, and (4) preparing the delivery. Presenting a talk on your trip around England could move chronologically from: "Our first impressions . . . later on we saw . . . And, finally, we discovered. . . ." Think about explaining the registration process at your school. You will probably pick the time pattern to organize your explanation.

Space or Geographical Sequence

The subject matter of your speech may divide more naturally into a spatial pattern. If, for example, you were describing the present state of education in the United States, you could talk about education in the northern, southern, eastern, and western states. You might talk about a university in terms of the peripheral, central, and core buildings. For explaining how to get to school or to the beach, you would probably use a space sequence. In using a space sequence, you compare one area of something with another area so that the audience moves systematically through the subject matter.

Topical Sequence

When the preceding patterns seem unsuitable for organizing the main ideas to be presented in the body of your speech, you could determine whether the main ideas fall into a "natural" sequence. For example, talking about university personnel might include a discussion of the administration, faculty, and student body; or you might talk about the effects of pornography on men, women, and children. If your speech seems to consist of three or four similar or related main ideas, the topical pattern is probably the best way to organize.

It is usually preferable to move from a less interesting idea to a more interesting one. If, however, your "topics" or main ideas are unequal in their strength for stimulating audience interest, you may want to put a stronger idea first, a strong idea second, and the strongest idea last. In this way, you avoid a presentation that concludes on an anticlimactic note. Consider, also, that if the subject matter is complex, it will be best to move from simpler ideas to more difficult ones, as when explaining a highly complicated skill or process.

To ensure a good speech, take time to consider the various ways to organize your message.

Causal Sequence

The causal pattern for arranging ideas involves moving from a cause to an effect or from a problem to a solution. As a speaker, you may wish to inform an audience of the effects of raising income taxes or relate the Gulf War to increased gasoline prices. In either case, you are informing your audience. The causal sequencing of ideas is more often and more easily used in persuasive speeches, when you take sides on an issue and present arguments in support of your position. "Yale locks are the best in the world because (1) they are made of U.S. steel, (2) they are burglarproof, and (3) they are easily installed." Following a causal order simply means to move from one point to another so that a position is defended with evidence and reasoning. Or an explanation is given of how a problem was solved or an effect followed a cause.

Whenever possible, use one of these patterns of organization because it will serve as a memory device to assist you and the audience in remembering the ideas presented in the speech. Our minds have already been programmed to think chronologically, spacially, topically, and logically. When we are well organized, it becomes easier for us to remember the order of ideas presented, and a minimum of notes are needed. If we then organize the ideas in the minds of the listeners, they also will have a better chance of remembering our main points.

Having devoted time to the body of the speech, we now need to consider more carefully the introduction and conclusion. Every good speech, whether long or short, must have a strong beginning and end. Many speakers devote so much time to their main ideas that they do not plan how to open and close a speech effectively. An effective speaker, as we have shown in our former examples of speech plans, gains attention quickly at the outset of the talk and wisely uses the conclusion to create a strong impact on the audience.

THE BORN LOSER   **By Art Sansom**

THE INTRODUCTION

Good introductions get audience attention, demonstrate the importance of the subject, and lead into the purpose of the presentation. We will now take a look at some popular ways to start a speech.

Your approach to the podium can be part of your introduction.

Reference to the Audience, Occasion, or Purpose of the Gathering

This approach tends to quickly unite speaker and audience. Even though the speaker is a stranger, he or she may soon become a friend by referring to something that is familiar to the audience. A certain informality and relaxation is present when the speaker associates with the mood of the audience and the nature of the occasion that brings them together. An excellent example is provided by William F. Eadie, professor of speech, when he delivered an address at the annual honors convocation at California State University at Northridge on May 8, 1989:

> I'm delighted to be able to address you today, because doing so fulfills a fantasy I suspect I share with most faculty: to speak in front of a group of students and know that they will be listening. And there's not even going to be a test!
>
> I don't say this to be demeaning. In fact, you wouldn't be here unless you had become expert listeners. Moreover, I suspect that you have learned to be critical listeners. But, as Robert Greenleaf has noted, there are plenty of people who are experts. There are also plenty of people who are critics. There are, however, too few responsible people. I'd like to take the next few minutes to investigate how we can move beyond "expert" and "critic" to become responsible listeners.[2]

Identifying with the audience by including yourself among them in terms of general interests, common problems, and similar backgrounds is one of the most popular ways to begin a speech. Referring to the occasion or purpose for which the audience has gathered also generates a common bond of interest between the speaker and the audience.

Direct Reference to the Topic

Probably the most common method of beginning a speech when time cannot be wasted or the audience is keenly interested is direct

---

[2]Vital Speeches 55 (July 15, 1989) 587

reference to the topic. Examples of the direct-reference approach sound like this:

> Today, I would like to examine some of the results of poor public-speaking techniques and make three suggestions for correcting the situation.
>
> Every day we engage in the decision-making process without knowing how to check our efficiency for making good decisions. I would like to explain an assessment instrument designed by Organizational Associates to measure our decision-making effectiveness.
>
> Religion is not the opium of a capitalistic society used to keep the poor from rebelling against the rich, and I will prove it?

The direct-reference approach assumes that the audience is ready to listen and does not need much "attention-getting" stimulation. Consequently, the introduction is brief and uses few words. If an audience needs to be warmed up, then this is not a good approach.

Rhetorical Questions

A speech may begin with a series of questions that the audience is not excepted to answer. The questions serve to stimulate the listeners' interest and lead them to the main topic of the speech. Jawaharlal Nehru, former prime minister of India, began a speech at the Asian Conference in 1947 in the following manner:

> Friends and fellow Asians, what has brought you here, men and women of Asia? Why have you come from the various countries of this mother continent of ours and gathered together in the ancient city of Delhi? Some of us, greatly daring, sent you invitations for this Conference and you gave a warm welcome to that invitation. And yet it was not merely the call from us but some deeper urge that brought you here.[3]

In a more provocative question approach, you might ask your audience "What would you do if you had just been informed of your mother's death?" or "What if you had just inherited $10,000? How would you invest it?"

[3]In Lewis Copeland, ed. *The World's Great Speeches,* 2nd ed. New York: Dover, 1958, p. 617.

Using a quotation is a good way to introduce your topic.

Humor, Stories, and Quotations

Using humor and/or beginning with stories and quotations are also helpful ways to win audience attention. But be sure, in each instance, that the humor, story, or quotation is connected to the main topic of your speech. To fail in this respect will only mislead the audience and label your introduction "gimmicky" instead of sincere. Notice the following use of humor in an introduction:

> You are right about teachers. If everything else fails, you become a teacher. Look at me. I came to this university ten years ago and applied for the job of elevator operator but was quickly fired because I couldn't learn the route!

In this case, the punch line might be funny, but where does it direct us? Are we to conclude that university faculty members indeed are fired from previous positions and that they are intolerably stupid? Humorous beginnings are effective if they are not misused.

The type of introduction you select must be brief, relevant, and attractive. For every minute of introduction, you should have about three or four minutes of body or development and at least a half minute for the conclusion. The introduction must clearly lead to the theme or topic of the speech. And, of course, any beginning needs to stimulate the listeners and put them in a "willingness to listen" frame of mind.

Examine the following introductions of speeches by a speech professor, a chief executive officer, and a lecturer and former U.S. senator.

Speaking Excellence

Bastille Day in the Oil Patch: When Passion Guides Energy Policy

By C. J. SILAS, Chairman and Chief Executive Officer, Phillips Petroleum Company, Delivered at the Houston Club, Houston, Texas, September 12, 1989

Thank you for inviting me to share my views. It's a privilege to address the members of Houston's oldest and largest business club . . . a club that has accomplished great things over the past ninety-five years.

Many of your members have achieved unparalleled success in business, politics—or both.

For example, we all know the oilman who in 1960 moved his business from West Texas to Houston and joined this very club.

His skills—and his heart for public service—led him to Austin.

Later, he served in other U.S. cities—and even on foreign shores—before settling into his current home on Pennsylvania Avenue.

I'm referring, of course, to George Bush.

With such great leaders coming out of the Houston Club, it's no exaggeration for me to say that all of us at at Phillips are proud of our association with you . . . with this city . . . and with the great state of Texas.

SOURCE: *Vital Speeches* 56 (January 1, 1990): 187.

Speaking Excellence

The Dynamic Teacher: Six Characteristics That Bring Energy, Vigor, and Force into the Classroom

By RICHARD L. WEAVER II, Professor,
Department of Interpersonal and Public
Communication, Bowling Green State University
Delivered to the Australian Communication
Association,
Melbourne, Australia,
July 11, 1990

The dynamic teacher is one who reveals energy, vigor, and force—the energy, vigor, and force that can bring about changes in students. It is Wilbert McKeachie, in his book *Teaching Tips,* in my opinion, one of the best books written on teaching, who says that changing students is *the* purpose of education.

Effective teaching is a topic that has been (and is) heavily and continually researched. I wonder . . . if there is so much published on the topic, why don't we have more examples of dynamic teachers? Of course, writing and researching doth not (necessarily) a good teacher make! But think about it for a moment, in all of your education, how many "dynamic teachers" did *you* have? I went to very good schools, including two "Big Ten" U.S. institutions, and I calculated that I had somewhere close to 125 teachers during my formal educational career. From my experience with them, I would say that fewer than five of those could be classified as dynamic teachers.

In addition, I have between thirty and thirty-five instructors working for me at Bowling Green State University each year, and I have the opportunity to visit many of these instructors in the classroom. Of those, one or two per year would likely be classified as, or, perhaps grow into, dynamic teachers. That is about 5 percent.

I don't have an answer to the question, "Why don't we have more examples of dynamic teachers?" Maybe it's true what they say about universities—that a university is a disorganized institution composed of individuals linked together by a common concern for coffee and car parking! I *am* concerned. I have been teaching for twenty-five years, and during that time I have written more than eighty-five articles in the area of, or related to, instructional communication. It is a topic to which I am closely attached; you could even say that it is a topic to which I am passionately attached!

Based on my teaching experience and some of what I have observed and read about education today, let me share three general conclusions about its status:

1. Education tends to be too narrow and specialized.

2. Education can be viewed as a "greenhouse" in which people fulfill their learning obligations usually in three to four years (in the case of higher education), and there is very little continuing education or sense of education as a lifelong process.

3. The quality of teaching is, in some instances, appalling. The techniques of teaching tend to be old fashioned, ineffective, and dull.

I wonder how closely these three relate to education in Australia? Whether or not they do, I think these three observations are closely linked. It seems to me that students are not being caught up in the excitement, the challenge, and the fun, even the passion, of education! And I think instructors are likely to be, for the most part at least, responsible. Not totally. But probably more responsible than any of us care to, or want to, admit.

What I want to do today is to outline what I consider to be the six essential characteristics of the dynamic teacher. In all cases, I assume the instructor, whoever he or she is, is competent in his or her discipline. Competency is, of course, absolutely essential, and I do not want to minimize its importance at any point. So, the display or *sound* knowledge is assumed and expected.

SOURCE: *Vital Speeches* 57 (October 15, 1990): 13.

Citizen Responsibility: Building an American Renaissance

By DANIEL J. EVANS, Public Leadership Fellow, University of Washington, Former U.S. Senator from Washington
Delivered as a Commencement Address, University of Washington,
Seattle, Washington,
June 9, 1990

It is an extraordinary pleasure to return to the University of Washington forty-two years after my own graduation. As a shy young engineering student, I didn't dream that this privilege would ever be mine.

Engineering courses seldom allowed me past frosh pond to the upper campus. While others were learning how to think great thoughts, we were learning to build great structures. I don't know what happened to those great thinkers, but my first job was as a designer of the Alaskan Way viaduct. It may not be beautiful, but at least it's utilitarian and necessary.

Since leaving the university, I've learned to value a liberal arts education. More accurately, I think I have discovered the joy of new ideas, new knowledge, and better understanding.

I've also struggled with my message for today. Should it be serious or funny? Challenging or comfortable? My wife said—compromise—"be mercifully short."

SOURCE: *Vital Speeches* 56 (August 1, 1990): 634.

Speaking Excellence

The Risk of Being Different: Stretch Yourself

**By SYDNEY H. SCHANBERG, Columnist and Associate Editor for *Newsday*
Delivered at Nazareth College,
Rochester, New York,
May 14, 1989**

Most important of all, you may never again have the freedom of options and the fire of spirit that you have now, at your age. You'll have plenty of time to become comfortable. But *now* is your moment to believe that you can ride the wind, to believe that everything is possible—for it is. I don't mean that every dream can be a reality, just that some dreams *are* possible—and that therefore it's worth trying.

I leave you with a quote from Winston Churchill, who was speaking about his own young years and speaking to all young people. He said: "You will make all kinds of mistakes, but as long as you are generous and true, and also fierce, you cannot hurt the world or even seriously distress her. She was made to be wooed and won by youth."

Thank you very much.

SOURCE: *Vital Speeches* 55 (September 1, 1989): 700.

Speaking Excellence

Hearing What We Ought To Hear: The Responsibility

By WILLIAM F. EADIE, Professor and Chairman, Department of Speech Communications Delivered to the Annual Honors Convocation at California State University, Northridge, California, May 8, 1989

Responsibility is one of those things that Robert Browning said must exceed our grasp, "else what's a heaven for?" And yet, I've found that my best moments with others have come when I'm willing to put aside hearing what I want to hear and move to hearing what I ought to hear. Like a lot of things, we can't be perfectly responsible, but that shouldn't keep us from trying. I invite you to join me on the road called Responsibility, and I wish you Godspeed on your journey.

SOURCE: *Vital Speeches* 55 (July 15, 1989): 587.

Speaking Excellence

The Future of Gambling: You Can Bet On It

By PHILIP G. SATRE, President and Chief Executive Officer,
Harrah's Hotels and Casinos
Delivered before The Commonwealth Club of California,
San Francisco, California,
November 3, 1989

Gambling has been with man for a very long time. It was certainly a gamble to set foot on the *Nina,* the *Pinta,* and the *Santa Maria* almost five hundred years ago . . . or on the Mayflower almost two centuries later.

   Americans have a philosophical drive, an instinct for achievement . . . and that includes taking risks. They have an inbred tendency, if you will, to gamble.

   It has been true in our frontier past. I think it is true in our entrepreneurial present.

   And I believe it will be equally instinctive in our high-tech, space-age future.

   As long as people strive for the charms of wealth . . . and try to avoid the pitfalls of poverty . . . the gamble to win will be a part of our makeup.

   It is part of our nature and part of our future.

   As luck will have it, gambling will be with us for a long time. You can bet on it!

SOURCE: *Vital Speeches* 56 (April 1, 1990): 367.

THE CONCLUSION

In our final efforts to keep our ideas organized and leave a good impression on the audience, we must consider how to conclude our speech. Your authors heard a former president of the United States end a magnificent speech so abruptly that the startled audience sat quietly until a senator rose to his feet and started applauding.

Some ways to conclude a speech so that audiences leave with a favorable impression, remember the speech longer, and are more persuaded to think as you do are demonstrated in the following examples, which use restatement of main topic, quotations, and various personal appeals.

President John F. Kennedy gave one of the most eloquent and remembered conclusions to a speech when he ended his 1961 inaugural address:

> And so, my fellow Americans: ask not what your country can do for you—ask what you can do for your country. My fellow citizens of the world: ask not what America will do for you but what together we can do for the freedom of man. Finally, whether you are citizens of America or citizens of the world, ask of us here the same high standards of strength and sacrifice which we ask of you. With a good conscience our only sure reward, with history the final judge of our deeds, let us go forth to lead the land we love, asking His blessing and His help, but knowing that here on earth God's work must truly be our own.

And, of course, even elementary school children are acquainted with the patriotic conclusion used by Patrick Henry before the Virginia Convention of Delegates in 1775:

> It is in vain, sir, to extenuate the matter. Gentlemen may cry peace, peace—but there is no peace. The war is actually begun! The next gale that sweeps from the north will bring to our ears the clash of resounding arms! Our brethren are already in the field! Why stand we here idle? What is it that gentlemen wish? What would they have? Is life so dear, or peace so sweet, as to be purchased at the price of chains and slavery? Forbid it, Almighty

God! I know not what course other may take; but as for me, give me liberty or give me death!

A speech conclusion presents a final opportunity for a speaker to have an impact on the audience. Such an opportunity must not be wasted by poor preparation. Succinctness, eloquence, and sincerity are the hall-marks of successful conclusions.

If you haven't already noticed the organization of this textbook, take a careful look at the first chapter, the table of contents, and the concluding chapter and see whether the authors have followed the principles of effectively introducing, developing, and concluding their ideas! Look at each chapter and decide whether it has an "attention" step, stresses the importance of the subject, develops a main idea successfully, and summarizes and applies the main idea in the conclusion.

> The sound rhetorical student cannot discard all rules. Eloquent speeches are not the result of momentary inspirations but the product of research, analysis, practice, and application.
> QUINTILIAN

TRANSITIONS

To help the audience follow your ideas as you move from one part of the speech to another, use bridges, internal summaries, and signposts.

Bridges are created when you explain to an audience that we are now moving from point *a* to point *b*. For example, you are explaining that to be an effective speaker, you must start with an attention step, something to capture audience interest. Then you say, "Once we have people listening to us, we must move quickly to showing the audience the importance of our topic in their lives." The audience will now know that you have concluded your discussion of "attention steps" and are now moving on to a discussion of how to create a "need" in the audience to continue to listen because there is something in it for them.

In a speech about the reasons for cheating on examinations that includes poor preparation, unclear testing procedures, and strong competition for high grades, you would use transitions to move between the three main points. "Poor preparation is only one reason for cheating. Let's look now at the misunderstanding that occurs concerning the format and method of testing that causes cheating."

To move between the second and third points, you could say, "Another major cause contributing to the increase of testing dishonesty has to do with the competition created by the need to achieve high grades."

Internal summaries take place when you have finished an important point or group of points. To keep the audience confident and comfortable, we engage in internal summarizing. For example, you can say, "So far, we have learned that to reduce anxiety or stress in our lives, we can engage in a regular exercise routine consisting of stretching, running, and lifting weights. And we can also practice relaxation techniques, such as meditation, deep breathing, and soothing self-talk. But what about the problems and concerns that caused the stress in the first place? What can we do to solve the problems that are still present after exercising and meditating? Our concluding point will explain what is called long-term stress reduction." Internal summarizing is quite effective in helping us to orally organize the speech for our listeners.

Signposts are simple phrases that tell listeners when you are in the speech and where you are headed. A speaker is using signposts when he or she says, "Here are three things that you can do the next time you feel stress." And then he or she says, "First, you could . . . Second, consider . . . and Third, don't forget to. . . ."

A combination of bridges, summaries, and signposts will help keep you and your audience relaxed, confident in what is being explained, and focused on the direction of the speech. It is not enough for a speaker to organize the speech on a piece of paper. The effective speaker must also orally organize the speech for the listeners.

BRINGING IT ALL TOGETHER

Most speakers, after spending time gathering and organizing ideas, make the mistake of assuming that they have a well-organized presentation ready for delivery. They omit a final opportunity to "bring it all together." We have developed the following procedure as a guide to good organization. Try it when you think you have a speech ready to present.

In brief sentences write:

1. The main theme or purpose of your speech.

2. Three or four points that support and develop the main point.

3. a. One thought that gets attention
   b. One thought that shows the importance of listening to your subject.
   c. One thought that would make a great conclusion.

4. Now arrange these sentences so that they follow this sequence:

   a. Attention   d. Three supporting points
   b. Importance   e. Concluding idea
   c. Theme or purpose

5. See whether you have an illustration, some evidence, or an example to support each of your three or four points.

6. Run through in your mind the whole sequence of ideas, and answer these questions:

   a. Do the attention and importance steps lead directly to the thesis idea?
   b. Do the three or four points specifically support the thesis idea?
   c. Does the conclusion directly relate to the thesis and specific purpose of the speech?

Final Check

▨ Does every point direct my audience to the response I want?

▨ Does every point lead to the next one?

▨ Do I make easy transitions, repeat my thesis several times, and summarize so everyone knows where we are at all times?

▨ Am I apologetic, too long, or irrelevant?

▨ Are my ideas exciting and rewarding to my listeners and myself?

What You Now Know

A public speech requires some kind of organization, though the exact steps should be a product of the speaker, the speaker's material, and the audience. There is no standard structure for organizing all speeches, but definite organization is necessary. The basic message unit (point → illustration/proof or proof/illustration → point) is the beginning of organization, even in conversing. This chapter focuses on other organizational patterns, such as Borden's Ho Hum structure and your authors' variation of the traditional introduction, body, and conclusion format.

Within the speech, the main body also needs its own structure. Four basic ways of sequencing main ideas in the body are: chronological or time, space or geographical, topical, and logical.

Attention should also be given to introducing and concluding your speech. Your introduction should get audience attention, demonstrate the importance of the subject, and lead into the main idea of the presentation. Your conclusion should tie the whole speech together. A restatement of the main theme, a summary of the points covered, an appropriate quotation, a personal appeal, or a statement of challenge, among others, can be used to effectively conclude your speech on a high note.

What to Do to Learn More

Reader's Digest

Examine the various articles in an issue of *Reader's Digest*. What purpose does the brief summary statement directly above or below the article's title serve? Skim some of the articles, focusing on topic headings and the first sentence in paragraphs. Note the organizational structure of the content of the articles. Now concentrate on reading just the opening few paragraphs and the closing paragraphs of the articles. What introductory and concluding methods appear to be used the most frequently?

Having looked at the articles in *Reader's Digest*, why do you think many "stolen" or plagiarized student speeches come from *Reader's Digest*?

Vital Speeches

Read or listen to two or three speeches from *Vital Speeches*. Analyze the overall organizational structure. Evaluate how well you like the introductions and conclusions.

6
DELIVERING YOUR IDEAS

The purpose of this chapter is to develop your options for delivering messages. The point is not to tell you what to do but to give you options to consider. You will learn the most frequently used delivery modes, aspects of your voice, and related nonverbal behaviors. We have intentionally kept this chapter basic and short. Your job is to put it into action in interpersonal and public speaking situations.

Chapter Content

■ **Delivery: Focusing Your Energy**
■ **Four Types of Delivery**
   Manuscript Delivery
   Memorized Delivery
   Impromptu Delivery
   Extemporaneous Delivery
   Characteristics of Good and Bad Delivery

■ **Voice**
   Articulation
   Pronunciation
   Voice Qualities
   Vocal Qualifiers
   Pauses and Timing
   Distracting Vocalizations
■ **Language—A Delivery Perspective**
   The Difference between Conversing and Public Speaking
■ **Nonverbal Aspects of Delivery**
   The Importance of Nonverbal Communication
   The Difficulty in Studying Nonverbal Communication
   Managing and Monitoring Our Nonverbal Communication as a Speaker
   Why Rehearse?
■ **What You Now Know**
■ **What to Do to Learn More**

DELIVERY: FOCUSING YOUR ENERGY

One of the most fascinating observations of changes in human behavior can be observed in the classroom. The class members are all sitting in a circle in the room. The instructor directs a question to the whole class: "Let's discuss what the aspects of good delivery are. Does anyone want to start by mentioning a factor you think is related to a good delivery? Be sure to give an example in your comments."

Most of the students are looking at the instructor or at other members of the class. A few students offer their remarks. After four or five students have commented, the instructor says: "Now let's shift gears a minute. Will those of you who haven't said anything yet think about what you'll say when I call on you. Describe a factor that you feel is related to good delivery and give a specific example also."

There is now a noticeable shifting and straightening of posture by those left to speak. Eye contact with the instructor diminishes as the students appear to be thinking. As the next four or five students give their comments as requested, it is obvious that the talkers are more nervous. They tighten up when called on and appear to sigh in relief when their "talk" is over. There are more "ahs" and "uhms" between their words.

The next time the instructor speaks, she says: "For those of you who have not had the opportunity to comment, I would like you to take two minutes to write down on a piece of paper a few key words related to what you want to say. And oh, yes, would you please stand when I call for your comments."

Those class members who have not spoken go into a frenzy of shifting around. They take out a piece of paper, but little writing takes place. Some look at the clock as if they are hoping its hands will get to the end of the hour before they have to speak. Some have a "why me?" look on their faces. The students who have already spoken glance at each other with a look of relief on their faces. As the remaining students stand and attempt to make their comments, it is obvious that they are very nervous—they stare at the door, twist the paper in their hands, and shift from one foot to the other.

What has gone on here? In one respect, very little is different in the three situations. The request for personal comments has remained the same. The second group of students were given a few minutes to think about their remarks and were instructed to speak,

What you are stands over you the while, and thunders so that I cannot hear what you say to the contrary.
RALPH WALDO
EMERSON

rather than asked to volunteer comments. The last group was told to write a few words on a piece of paper and speak from a position about two feet higher than the previous speakers. On the other hand, something quite significant has gone on in the last two groups' minds. They have reacted with increased stage fright the closer the request came to their mental picture of "giving a speech." A similar reaction can also be witnessed when someone is on the way to the dentist or is going to get an injection from the doctor. Our mental picture of what is going to happen is sometimes more difficult to deal with than the event itself.

"Seems a bit nervous."

THE SATURDAY EVENING POST

Much of the beginning speaker's problem is learning to deal with nervousness or anticipation of speaking. The beginner will eventually learn that there will always be nervousness on an important occasion but that this nervousness can be directed to your advantage. The purpose of this chapter is to describe delivery options that can work for you.

How we say something is as important as what we say. Let's move ahead to some items related to the delivery of a presentation that will help channel nervous energy to more constructive use.

FOUR TYPES OF DELIVERY

There are four basic types of delivery—manuscript, memorized, impromptu, and extremporaneous—each with its respective advantages and disadvantages. We will look at each and take the position that extemporaneous delivery is the best type for most general speaking situations.

Manuscript Delivery

Manuscript delivery refers to a presentation that is completely written out in advance. The speech is then read to the audience.

Reasons for Reading from Manuscript

1. The speech is a major policy statement by an official.

2. Technical or legal material is being presented and will be quoted or covered in the news media.

3. A careful choosing of words is crucial to the success of the presentation.

Disadvantages of Reading from Manuscript

1. The sentences may look good on paper but may not sound adequate when read; the speech may sound mechanical.

2. Any spontaneous directness with the audience is lost. The audience feels it is being "talked at."

3. The speaker's eye contact with audience is reduced.

4. Speaker flexibility is reduced. The speaker cannot adapt to changed conditions, cannot lengthen or shorten the speech, and cannot incorporate feedback.

5. Preparation time is longer than that of the extemporaneous speech.

Memorized Delivery

Memorized presentation means the speech is written out, as in the manuscript approach, but rather than being read, it is committed to memory. People who have difficulty "thinking on their feet" and who do not want to read to their audience often attempt to memorize their talks.

Reasons for Memorizing

1. The speaker can present a very precisely worded speech and yet have the freedom to move about and use materials.

2. The speech may contain colorful language or quotations that can be delivered with more impact and expression because the speaker is able, with eye contact and gestures, to direct attention to the audience.

Disadvantages of Memorizing

1. The speaker can forget.

2. Unless there has been considerable rehearsal and practice with vocal variety, the presentation will sound mechanical. (The speech will sound memorized.) Even with considerable practice, few people have the ability to sound conversational.

3. The speaker cannot adapt to special conditions prior to or during the talk.

4. If the speaker does deviate any time during the talk to elaborate or make additional comments that were not part of the memorized speech, the audience will be able to notice the difference in delivery.

5. The audience senses that it is being "talked at."

Impromptu Delivery

An impromptu presentation is a speech given with little, if any, advance preparation. The speaker relies on personal knowledge and speaking skills to get through the situation. The content of the talk depends on what the speaker can think of and express on the spot.

Reasons for Impromptu Speaking

1. A person is called on unexpectedly to speak, as in a meeting.

2. The speaker wishes to appear spontaneous and to talk "to" the listeners, rather than "at" them.

3. The speaker can be extremely flexible in adapting to the listeners and the situation, including questions and comments.

Disadvantages of Impromptu Speaking

1. The speaker can ramble or be repetitive.

2. The speaker may make inappropriate or immature judgments.

3. The speaker may have nonfluent delivery.

Extemporaneous Delivery

An extemporaneous presentation is one in which the speaker has planned the talk thoroughly but has not planned which words will be used to express each point. The desired points and their order are known, but their final form is uncertain. Thus, the extemporaneous speech combines the best of the manuscript and impromptu approaches.

Reasons for Extemporaneous Speaking

1. Direct communication with the audience is encouraged.

2. The artificial manner of the manuscript and memorization presentations is avoided because the speaker must consider the final form when speaking.

3. The speaker can adjust the length of the talk by skipping a subpoint or adding an example or two.

4. The speaker can adjust to the feedback and apparent response from the audience by going into more or less detail.

Meetings such as this one are common forums for impromptu speaking.

Disadvantages of Extemporaneous Speaking

1. The speaker may have poor language choice.

2. The speaker can deviate too far from the speech's outline by developing a point further than was intended in the original outline.

3. If the presentation must be repeated, it will vary each time it is given.

Unless the situation demands otherwise, extemporaneous delivery is the best bet for presenting your ideas in a style that your audience will consider direct, spontaneous, and not distracting.

Characteristics of Good and Bad Delivery

A good style of delivery is like a well-dressed woman or man. The clothes should help to complete the image but should not be so noticeable as to draw attention away from the person wearing them. Whenever the listeners begin to notice how the person is speaking, the delivery is getting in the way of the message. The characteristics of poor delivery are rather obvious to the sensitive listener. Aspects of delivery often considered annoying include:

- Avoidance or lack of eye contact with members of the audience
- Nervous movement and fidgeting
- Monotone voice quality
- Too many "ahs," "uhms," "ers," and "ands"
- Frequent looking at notecards
- Holding and rattling notes
- Failing to smoothly operate equipment and visual aids
- Pacing back and forth
- Lack of energy and enthusiasm

One of your authors conducted a survey of four hundred university students to see what speaking characteristics were associated with "good" college lecturers versus what speaking characteristics were associated with "bad" college lecturers. The results indicated clearly that aspects of the teacher's delivery were by far the most important characteristics associated with "good" and "bad" lectures. The characteristics of the "good" teacher's delivery appeared in the following rank order:

1. Vocal variety

2. Dynamic, enthusiastic; uses gestures and facial expressions

3. Clear voice and articulation

4. Moderate rate of speaking (not slow but not too rapid-fire)

5. Strong, loud voice

6. Eye contact

7. Language and terminology easily understood

8. Neat appearance and good grooming, whether casual or dressed up

9. Conversational delivery

10. Calm and relaxed

11. Smiles

The characteristics of the "bad" teacher's delivery appeared in the following rank order:

1. Monotone voice

2. Speech rate too fast for note taking

3. Lack of expression or enthusiasm in voice

4. Lack of movement; stays behind a podium

5. Reads directly from notes

6. Poor voice quality (harsh, rasping, etc.)

7. Poor eye contact with class (looks at wall, ceiling, or out the window)

8. Uses "big" words, technical terms

9. Uses a lot of "ahs," "uhms," and "dahs"

10. Not loud enough

11. Nervous behaviors with hands and body

12. Sloppy appearance

13. Paces back and forth too much

The results of this study were used in a series of teacher-improvement seminars. Several of the teachers looked at the study and commented that although they did not feel they had those problems, they knew some colleagues who did show the symptoms of the "bad"-delivery teacher.

 **VOICE**

If you have ever heard your voice on a tape recorder, you have experienced the enlightened act of hearing yourself as others hear you. We normally hear ourselves talk through a combination of the air compressions our talking makes on our eardrums and the vibrations of the bones of our head caused by the sounds in the oral and nasal cavities, called bone conduction. As a result of this dual type of hearing, we can never hear ourselves as we sound to others, unless we use a tape recorder. Just as we are unaware of how we sound to others, we may be unaware of the particular voice qualities, defects, or habits we have. Others may recognize them, but we don't. Speech pathologists consistently show that people reported to have minor speech defects (lisps, slurs, sound substitutions, and so on) do not hear these defects in their own speech.

A fascinating example of this was seen when one of your authors recorded a mock job interview with an older student who grew up in Spain. His "accent" was still noticeable, although he was easily understood. After the mock interview, the student was to critique his recording. After about five minutes in the adjoining room, he returned complaining that something must have gone wrong with the taping because the person on the tape had some kind of Hispanic accent, and he couldn't locate on the tape where his interview started. Had his American wife not been in the audience to help add support to our allegation that that *was* his tape—he *did* sound that way—he may never have been convinced.

THE BORN LOSER   **By Art Sansom**

If the voice is important in delivery, and delivery is sometimes a more important message cue than the words spoken, we have good cause to examine the key characteristics of voice. What can we do to go beyond simply living with the way we talk now? In examining voice, we will include: articulation, pronunciation, voice qualities, vocal qualifiers, use of pauses and timing, and distracting vocalizations.

Speaking Excellence

The Beauty Asset You Never Knew You Could Have

■ Do people often ask you, "What did you say?" Do you fade out, especially at the end of phrases? Too soft is as hard on listeners as too loud. I find this often in women who have been programmed from childhood not to put themselves forward. They don't like to speak out and it takes steady practice to overcome the habit. People may constantly ask you to repeat yourself or, worse, may pretend they've heard but tune you out.

■ Do you try for extra-deep tones in an effort to sound breathily sexy? Or does your voice seem tight, as if it were produced by a pressure cooker? Does your throat feel constricted, frequently sore? Do you sound harsh and angry even if you don't actually feel that way? Talk to a mirror to see if the veins on your neck stand out. All these are signs that you are beating up your vocal cords, possibly because you think they are the source of power. They are not. We speak through them, not with them.

■ Does your voice have a little-girl quality? A boy's voice drops about an octave during puberty. Normally, a girl's pitch also descends several notes. If yours didn't, probably no one worried; after all, it didn't matter much in a girl, or so people thought. But today, a childlike intonation seems to contradict firm statements. No one waits long enough to discover the brains and talent beneath the babyish voice.

■ Our nasality has been called "The American Sound," although each area of the country seems to have a different explanation for it. Ralph Waldo Emerson wondered whether the New England twang came about because people feared opening their mouths to let in the cold. Someone else suggested that the vowels of the Midwest flattened to match the Great Plains. Whatever the reason, this unpleasing trait is no cause for pride. Actual "talking through the the nose" is rare—the metallic sound we call nasal comes from tones trapped in a constricted throat. The vowels have a whining sound: "man" becomes "maan," "dance" becomes "deeunce."

■ Then there are monotonous voices. Flat and colorless tone and inflection turn people off. The human voice has unrealized flexibility to stretch both up and down.

■ Talking with runaway speed strains the attention just as inaudible speech does: "The ????? Company, Mr. ????? office. Please leave ????? number ?????." You hang up frustrated.

■ Jagged speech rhythms agitate the very air where many of us live. The pace of the sentences we hear is abrupt, stop-and-go. As our ears sop up the tense beat, we seem to infect each other. It's not easy to close off these jerky sounds, but an attractive speaking voice should have a smooth, flowing rhythm—the speaking equivalent of *legato* in music, which means "without abrupt break in movement and in a manner smooth and connected."

Each of these faulty patterns interferes in some way with your body. To change, you must become sensitized to how the parts of your body feel when they're working properly. Then you will be able to *feel* the tension in your throat, the shallowness of your breathing or the locked-up nasality of your tone. And you master a good speaking voice as you would any other physical activity—through exercise. You don't attack voice production aggressively—the way you would your tennis forehand, for example. It's more like the relaxed, flowing coordination essential to playing a good game.

There are three indispensable components to the proper use of your body that will change the way you sound: (1) releasing the necessary muscles; (2) improving breathing; and (3) learning to use the body's built-in resonators.

To relax muscle tension: First show yourself the worst that muscle tension can do: Tighten your hands at the back of your neck, bunch your tongue toward the back of your throat, fill up your chest with air—and try to count out loud to ten. I dare you.

What concerns us specifically is tension in the head, neck, shoulders, chest—the areas closely related to voice production. By getting rid of unnecessary strains there, you permit the muscles of your voice box the freedom to function the way they were meant to.

Do these exercises on a straight-back chair facing a mirror. Sit tall, legs comfortably apart and parallel, feet flat, hands folded palm-up in your lap. First, rotate your head gently on your neck. "Cut a pie eight ways" by moving your head up and down with graceful, unjerky nods as you rotate. Tilt your head to one side as if you were asleep on an imaginary pillow for the count of ten; repeat on other side, front, back. Next, rotate your head slowly in a small circle, keeping eye contact in the mirror.

Now give your face a light massage. Slide your hands from your hairline down your cheeks until your jaw sags with an idiotic expression. Stick your tongue out, flopping on your lower lip. With a hand on each side of your chin, move your jaw from side to side and up and down. With your fingers under your chin, swallow, feeling the small muscles you use to do so. Soothe and soften them with small circular motions of both hands.

These exercises should leave the muscles of your face, neck, and shoulders relaxed and calm. A dividend: You should see a face without grimaces, quiet cheeks, a calm mouth, and a supple throat. This is an important image to remember. Our faces are frequently far too active—exaggerated gestures of mouth, eyes, eyebrows. Once you become aware of how these muscles feel when they are quiet, you will also begin to sense when they are not, and correct that.

Next we'll deal with the breathing that is essential to a full-bodied voice. We require less air than you probably think. Women tend to breathe too high—what I call "brassiere breathing." As well as making you look insecure, it's a bosomy rise and fall that is incompatible with solid tone (proper breathing is almost invisible).

The best way to feel the breathing you *should* be using is to lie stretched in a swimming position on a rug, flat on your stomach, one arm on the floor above your head, the other at your side with your head turned toward it. Place a small cushion under your head and another between your navel and pelvis. Sink into the floor with a feeling of letting go. Sigh long breaths over and over again, silently inhaling and exhaling, feeling your muscles *expand and contract* against the pillow on the floor. That's where it's at—the muscle girdle of support for speaking and singing. There should be no feeling of ballooning, just a gentle swell of air deep within the body. Now make your sighs audible, to connect that relaxed breathing with sound. Make low, almost moaning sighs from an open, relaxed throat.

To get this same feeling in a more normal speaking position, try this: Sitting on a chair, place hands just under your lower ribs at your sides; feel your breath moving into your fingers. The front of your stomach will be flat. If you feel air ballooning into this or any other part of the chest or stomach area, you are overbreathing (this may happen in the beginning, but with practice it will ebb). The motion against your fingertips should be gentle; it may help to think of it as "side" breathing.

These brief exercises will also help you get a sense of the

muscles you use when breathing properly: (1) Suck in air deeply several times as if sipping through a straw. You will feel a low tug below the waist. (2) With a loose jaw, exhale very slowly as if steaming a glass for cleaning. Then continue breathing in and out, without pushing. (3) Exhale. Then, airless, count down aloud 5–4–3–2–1. At 1, is the reaction below your waist more like an ache? Relieve it by feeding a little air back in, then breathe in and out evenly. If your chest and shoulders do not stay quiet, try placing your hands firmly (not rigidly) beneath the chair seat and then breathe.

These essential routines will help you to build strength, so that you can speak without forcing, and you'll stop fading mid-sentence. Believe me, there is no personality change so telling as a voice that can at last be comfortably, rather than barely, heard.

Resonance is the third component of a good voice. It reinforces the voice like added speakers in a stereo. Taking an easy breath, begin with humming, tongue resting behind lower teeth, jaw relaxed, sustaining the sound of "mmmmmm" at a comfortable pitch. Feel the vibration with your fingers on your lips and cheeks. Hum in your speaking rather than your singing voice. Important: Focus the hum up front on the roof of the mouth (the hard palate) for the clearest possible sound. Once you get a solid feeling of this forward placement, fix it securely in your sense memory—this is where your tones should always be placed.

Imitate a siren, humming in circles of sound. Gradually hum louder, rolling your head to keep loose. Dropping your head and shoulders toward your lap will produce a richer, deeper sound. Put your hand on your forehead and upper chest to feel them vibrate.

Block your ears with your hands and hum up and down the scale—again with your speaking rather than singing voice. Stop at the note that reverberates loudest inside your head. Then change the hum to the word *so*, slaying "so" up and down the spoken scale until you reach that same tonal area. Say a whole sentence there: "So! This sounds pretty good to me." This register is probably the best for your speaking voice—in most women, approximately three notes lower than the one habitually used.

In public, if you feel your voice sliding up to its former high, little-girl pitch or becoming shrill or out of control, stop, breathe out quietly, release your shoulders, and feel yourself literally moving a load off your chest. As a psychological aid, finger a button or necklace as though you were holding down your pitch.

Now, how do you put the proper relaxation, breathing, and resonance together? The best way is by reading aloud, using a cassette recorder. First, tune the instrument: Make sure the proper muscles are relaxed, do a breathing exercise, do a humming exercise, ending with a sentence in the proper register. Then read aloud into your recorder. Pick pieces with varying pace and theme, a mixture of prose and poetry. As you read, speak out as strongly as you can, but avoid pressure. Don't be afraid of overdoing—underdoing is usually the problem.

Reading aloud, playing back, reading again is a necessary, regular routine. It eases the way to a smooth, vital speaking voice. It helps you imprint the right breathing and relaxed muscles and resonating sound, to *know* how your voice is beginning to sound, and to carry over this improved voice more naturally to your everyday speaking. After all, that is what you are ultimately after—raising the performing level of the voice you take with you everywhere in your life.

SOURCE: Reprinted by permission of Curtis Brown Ltd. Copyright ©1977 by Conde Nast Publications Inc.

Articulation

Articulation technically refers to the distinctness of the formation of the speech sounds. The lips, tongue, and jaw are the main components brought into play when vocal sounds are formed. A habit of lazy lips, a sluggish tongue, or a stiff jaw, if not the result of a physical or neurological problem, can be "unlearned" and replaced with new, more acceptable, speech habits. "Hooow nooow brooown cooow" is an articulation exercise.

Pronunciation

Pronunciation is the production of the specific sounds of words in a correct and acceptable manner, as judged by the local or regional speech community. However many times has the accent of a person or the way certain words are pronounced given you immediate cues regarding where the person lives or has lived or how educated that person may be? The following are some examples of accent placements that cue the listener: *genu-iné, dé-vice, ré-fer,* and *ráp-port* instead of the more acceptable *geń-uine, de-vicé, re-feŕ,* and *rap-port.* Deleting sounds results in *li-berry* for *library, guh-mnt* for *government, fur* in place of *for, git* for *get.* Adding additional sounds, such as *ath-a-lete* instead of *athlete,* is common also.

What may be acceptable in social conversation may well be considered objectionable in public speaking. Sloppy articulation and poor pronunciation can produce negative audience judgments.

A fool's mouth is his destruction.
PROVERBS 18:7

Voice Qualities

Voice qualities distinguish one speaker from another. These are the main cues we pick up when we recognize a voice before we actually see a person. It is from these cues that we "get a feeling" about an individual's age, background, social class, and so on. Four specific voice qualities are:

Pitch Range The wide or narrow band of vocal sound

Resonance The rich and full or thin and wispy depth in the sound produced as it "echoes" in the oral and nasal cavities

Rate The speed of sound production

Control How smooth, precise, and rhythmic the sound is

Vocal Qualifiers

Vocal qualifiers are the more temporary characteristics the voice takes on to accomplish momentary expression of feelings. Specific qualifiers are:

Intensity The loudness, softness, or volume of the sound

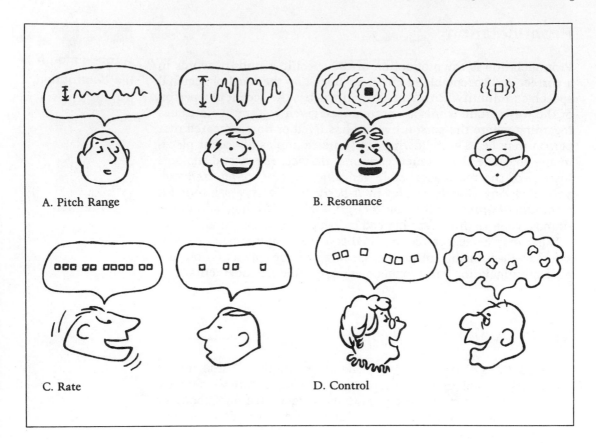

A. Pitch Range

B. Resonance

C. Rate

D. Control

■ **Pitch** The height or depth of the sound as in the musical
scale, "do, re, mi, fa, so, la, ti, do"

■ **Extent** Drawing out or clipping the sound before it is
completed

Pauses and Timing

Pauses (silence between spoken words) can be an effective means
of emphasis, especially if the rate of speaking is rapid-fire. A well-
placed moment of silence will draw the listener's attention because
it is such a contrast. For example: "There is only one way we can

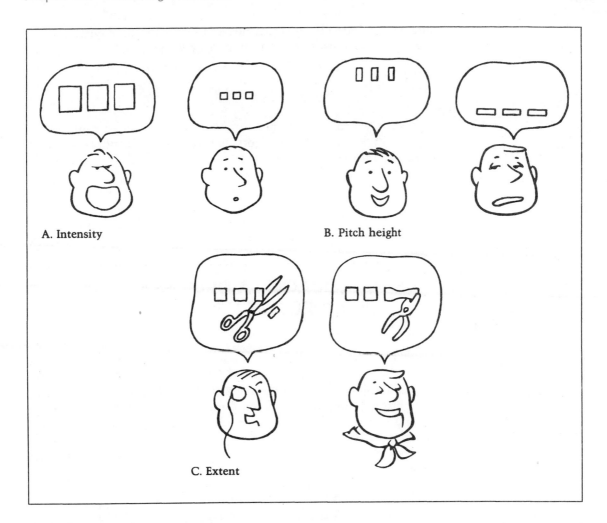

A. Intensity

B. Pitch height

C. Extent

solve this problem. And that one way is . . . [pause] . . . to go directly to the president's office and talk to her personally." The pause builds a few seconds of suspense about what is going to be said.

Timing is changing the tempo (rate) of speaking in conjunction with the use of pauses to produce maximum effects. Johnny Carson is a master of timing in his monologues in the sense that he can lead up to a punch line with a rapid-fire description of the news event of the day, take a long pause, and then deliver the punch line in a slow tempo that appears nonchalant, rather than eager. In order to get a feeling of the acceptable length for a pause and how changing the pacing of the spoken words will sound, you will have to

Vocal qualifiers include (A) intensity, such as overloud or oversoft; (B) pitch height, such as overhigh or overlow; (C) extent, such as clipping or drawing.
(Randall P. Harrison, *Beyond Words*, © 1974, pp. 106–107. Reprinted by permission of Prentice-Hall, Inc., Englewood Cliffs, New Jersey.)

tape-record yourself several times and listen to the playback. Don't expect to use pauses and timing perfectly the first time.

Distracting Vocalizations

Distracting vocalizations are the sounds and words people use to fill the awkward silences between thoughts or phrases of the speech. Examples include "ah," "uhm," "and ah," "so ah," "ya know," and the like.

 LANGUAGE—A DELIVERY PERSPECTIVE

One of the main points a speech-communication teacher must convey in the classroom is that the best language for speaking is the simplest language, short of using slang and clichés. These teachers are fighting a long history of reinforcement that supports the learning and use of "big" words. An adult gives attention to children when they use big words. Sometimes term papers and public speeches that are full of abstract terminology receive misguided praise.

One way to examine the idea of using small instead of big words does not deal with the number of letters in the word, rather it looks at how *concrete* versus how *abstract* the word is. Abstract words or phrasing are those which refer to theoretical ideas that cannot be directly experienced or observed through our senses. *Democracy, justice, capitalism, economy, freedom,* and *evaluation* are abstract. These terms do not create clear mental pictures. Concrete words or phrasing refer to actual objects, events, or experiences in reality. Concrete is the opposite of abstract. We can see, touch, smell, taste, or feel that which is concrete. We can see a "flashing red light," "smell a barbequed steak," "cash a ten-dollar check," and get anxious over "a ten-point quiz."

A second way to look at the idea of big and small words is to examine *specific* versus *general* words. Specific words are those that have a limited meaning. General words refer to a large group of people. "Ted Kennedy, senator from Massachusetts," is more specific. "Speech teachers" is general. "Larry Kraft, the instructor in my speech-communication class," is specific. Language is an inexact tool by which we communicate. Words refer to meanings that are in people and that vary with people. Therefore, the more abstract we get, the more we can expect to be misunderstood by our listeners.

In summary, it is not the magnitude or the banality of the symbol that is significant. Rather it is the specificity of its referent category. (It is not the size or commonness of the word that is important, rather it is how specific and concrete its meaning is.)

The Difference Between Conversing and Public Speaking

Have you ever noticed that national newscasters such as Dan Rather, Tom Brokaw, and Peter Jennings do not have regional accents? They speak what is called the general American dialect, which is the nationally accepted pronunciation for speech. Local or regional television and radio people who are attempting to break into the big time spend hours taking courses or private training to rid themselves of accents that pinpoint their formative years.

We have become so accustomed to hearing general American dialect that even people from the South, New England, or other notorious accent-stereotyped areas do not hear anything "different" when they listen to national newscasters. We have grown to accept two speech standards—our own style and that of the general American dialect. So what does this have to do with language? There is a parallel.

In conversations among close friends, clichés, slang, jargo, poor grammar, habit phrases ("ya know," "right," "see"), vocal fillers ("uhm," "ah"), and even obscenity can be acceptable language forms. However, in public speaking, such language forms are not acceptable. Just as we have learned to speak or at least "hear" general American dialect as appropriate speaking in certain situations, we have also learned to expect "proper" language in public presentations or business conversations.

Cliché
When a phrase or saying is labeled a cliché, it is considered worn out. Phrases such as *burned out, happy as a lark, that's for sure,*

you better believe it, you think that's bad . . ., big deal!, I'm sick and tired of . . . were once uniquely fresh as expressions because they were different. Once a statement is overused, it loses the special meaning it may have had at one time. Clichés used in public-speaking situations are a cue that the speaker lacks originality in thinking and expression and must rely on worn-out phrases.

Slang

Slang terms may ultimately become a part of standard word usage, such as *smog, mob, plane, fresh air,* and *bus,* but until they do, they are considered substandard forms of expression in public-speaking situations. *Rad, chill,* and *dude* are presently considered slang words. Slang words pick up their meaning from the informal atmosphere and situations in which they originated. To frequently transfer this wording to a more formal situation is not considered appropriate.

Jargon

Doctors, teachers, businesspeople, sports fans, military personnel, law officers, computer specialists, lawyers, truckers, and others use jargon in their communication. Jargon is a semiprivate vocabulary used by a specialized group to communicate something the group feels they have in common. Children (and adults) go through stages where jargon becomes very important to their sense of identity. When the general population begins to pick up the use of this jargon, the jargon loses its meaning for those who originally used it.

A good example of this can be heard in the standardization of truckers' CB jargon. Not only have such terms as *handle, ten-four, smokey, on the side,* and *10–36* become popularized among nontruckers, they are being used in everyday conversation. The final blow has been the publication of dictionaries that translate truckers' jargon into standard English.

You may momentarily impress audience members by using jargon they do not regularly use, but you may also alienate them.

Other Problems

Poor grammer, such as *hadn't outta, ain't gonna,* and *they is;* habit phrases, such as *you know* and *ah;* vocal fillers, such as *uhm* and *ah;* and obscenities are considered weak and sometimes offensive substitutes for specific and concrete language.

Speaking Excellence

"You better watch your mouth!"

All of us can remember our mothers saying, "You better watch your mouth young man/young lady!" Of course, she wasn't referring to your mouth at all, she was commenting on your particular choice of words or phrasing.

In a different manner, this advice is very useful in today's speaking situations. The awareness and sensitivity to issues, causes, incidents and laws related to minorities and special interests has increased phenomenally in the last ten years.

Judging by what has happened to scores of politicians and public figures, it is all too easy to speak inappropriately or insensitively to specific members of the audience even when your intentions are honorable.

The following recommendations will help you plan *how* and *what* you *want* to say.

1. Mix He's and She's. Think in both the masculine and the feminine. Attempt to make an equal number of references to female and male examples while avoiding a pattern of having them in stereotyped positions. Interchange the he/she, her/him, and his/her.

This may be awkward or impossible when the specific topic relates to females or males in a particular way . . . as in the case of the success of female prosecutors or the steriod issue in NFL football.

2. Don't Speak at the Expense of Stereotypes. Making reference to generalized stereotypes whether by roles, functions or ethnic groups is not the problem. The problem is when the category (attorneys, police officers, teachers, construction workers, truck drivers, secretaries, Indians, Blacks, bankers, Japanese, teenagers . . .) is a shortcut to recognizing and respecting the individuality of people no matter who they are.

When speakers talk as if they have reached conclusions about individuals, groups, or institutions because of one or more handy generalized categories, they are demonstrating an ignorance of differences.

3. No Lazy Language. Even though certain slang terms, profanities, and euphemisms may be used in everyday conversation, it does not mean that it is appropriate for a speaker to use these same terms and phrases in speaking before a group. Language usage that is below the level your audience considers appropriate just demonstrates a lack of clear and precise thinking on the speaker's part.

There are two reasons for this:

(1) The audience will most often be a mix of individuals with different standards, values and life experiences. "Damn," "hell," "crap," "pissed off," "friggin" will not settle as well with some individuals as well as others.

(2) Always use language that is one or two notches above everyday conversational language when speaking to groups. The more formal or informal the occasion or situation, the

more formal or informal the language to a point. A good guideline is to think of how you change your language choices when
speaking to a religious/church leader, an elderly respected member of the community, or the hiring manager for a company position that is exactly what you are hoping for.

In one or more of these situations, you become a bit more
conscious of word choice and what your behavior and tone of
voice convey. Your whole demeanor is aimed at being appropriate to the person and the situation at hand. This is exactly what
we mean . . . there is no room in speaking for lazy language of
any kind.

In speaking, you don't get a second chance to make a good first
impression.

4. Breaking the Rules. In some specific situations, it is necessary to break the rules of language appropriateness to make a
point. Always demonstrate through your delivery and eye contact
that you are aware of your language . . . it is a choice you are
making, rather than just being asleep at the tongue.

SOURCE: The Noel White Group, June 1991

NONVERBAL ASPECTS OF DELIVERY

Our nonverbal behavior cues the listener how we feel about:

- Ourself
- The message
- The audience or listener
- The situation
- The anticipated outcome of the talk or exchange

Listeners communicate nonverbally as well as speakers. What is this family saying?

Our words represent the idea we wish to express, but our facial expressions, tone of voice, gestures, posture, appearance, and so on express how we feel. Words help us express the **content level** of communication: our thoughts, ideas, and reasoning. Nonverbal behavior helps us express the **relationship level** of communication: our feelings and attitudes and how intense they are.

The Importance of Nonverbal Communication

Early research in the last decade indicated that nonverbal cues may represent from 65 percent to more than 90 percent of the total impact of a message. Specific research by Albert Mehrabian[1] revealed

1. Albert Mehrabian, *Silent Messages*, 2d ed. (Belmont, Calif.: Wadsworth, 1981), p. 76.

that in social, emotional, and first-impression situations, the impact of verbal and nonverbal cues breaks down in this manner:

Percentage of total Impact of Verbal and Nonverbal Cues

Verbal	Nonverbal Face	Voice
7 percent	55 percent	38 percent

Many people are surprised to learn that the voice is considered a nonverbal attribute. It is true that words cannot be separated from how they are vocalized, but, nevertheless, voice quality is a prime nonverbal attribute than can be manipulated to increase message impact. Mehrabian claims we can communicate three major psychological responses with our voice, face, and body movements. These are: degrees of pleasure and displeasure (liking and disliking); arousal and nonarousal; and dominance and submissiveness.

"Born speakers" or "natural speakers" did not inherit the ability to hold an audience. These people are not gifted with something the rest of us do not have. They have simply learned on their own the nonveral behaviors an audience responds to readily and how to combine and manipulate these nonverbal behaviors in the most effective pattern.

Understanding how the brain processes verbal and nonverbal cues is fascinating in itself. The right side (hemisphere) of the brain is responsible for processing nonverbal—nonword—cues. A high percentage of this processing goes on below conscious awareness. The left side (hemisphere) of the brain functions best with words, reasoning, judgments, the sequencing of events, and drawing relationships among thoughts. Often, the left side "thinks" about an event while the right side subconsciously experiences the event. When information from the right and left hemispheres conflicts, the left makes a judgment based on information from both hemispheres. For example, you may have been in a situation where the "vibes" you picked up from a person were "good" or "bad," even though the words were not particularly appealing or distasteful. What you picked up may have been primarily nonverbal cues that you processed at a below-conscious level, while the conscious decision or judgment was rendered by the left hemisphere as it used that information. (See Robert E. Ornstein's *The Psychology of Consciousness*, 2d ed., Penquin Books, 1986, for a further discussion of how we process verbal and nonverbal data.)

Perhaps you have heard a person intently questioning a companion as to why he did not like a specific person he had just been introduced to:

"Why didn't you like him."

"I don't know, I just didn't care for him."

"Is it something he said?"

"Naw. . . ."

"Well, what's wrong with him?"

"Oh, he's just not my type, I guess."

"What is your type?"

"Forget it . . . don't make a federal case out of it."

The Difficulty in Studying Nonverbal Communication

The difficulties in examining nonverbal communication for purposes of increased understanding and better self-control are numerous. The following remarks highlight some of these difficulties.

Nonverbal behavior cannot be separated from verbal behavior in real life. In everyday interactions, hundreds of nonverbal and verbal behaviors blend in complex patterns of message exchanges that are almost beyond analysis. For the lay person to understand and express this complexity would be akin to trying to describe how several hundred separate drops of different-colored dyes disperse and combine in a bucket of water already a mixture of colors from previous dilutions.

Each person's nonverbal behavior is unique and represents different meaning or intent. If you will, each person has a separate body language. In order to "read" that person's body language accurately, you have to study it in many situations and somehow verify what it represents. Noticing differences in a person's behaviors in specific situations does not mean you know what the behavior represents. What you think the behavior stands for may be wrong. In order to be sure, you have to find some way to compare what you think the behavior means with what is actually going on in the head of the other person. Sometimes you can subtly test your guess by asking the person, "Are you feeling a bit upset?"

As soon as we begin to stereotype a person's nonverbal behavior, we are in for trouble. Folding arms across the chest, stepping back, looking away, wringing the hands, and so on can mean different things for people in different contexts. We always need to check out the behavior with the individual to be sure our interpretation is accurate.

Also, it is better to observe a cluster of nonverbal behaviors in interpreting nonverbal communication than to look at one single behavior. Look for consistencies or inconsistencies among several nonverbal behaviors. When many nonverbal cues appear to be consistent in the pattern they form, you are in a better position to infer their meaning. But if inconsistencies appear between, let us say, facial expressions and tension shown by the hands, be careful about drawing conclusions. However, a general observation related to inconsistent cues (when two or more nonverbal cues conflict or when verbal and nonverbal cues conflict) is that the receiver will tend to believe the cue he or she feels is *under the least conscious control* by the speaker.

When a person becomes emotionally involved in a situation or interaction, he or she usually has a heightened awareness of particular nonverbal cues and ignores other nonverbal cues completely. Research also indicates that though there is heightened awareness of some nonverbal cues, the accuracy of their interpretation may be less.

Each individual is capable of an infinite number of combinations of verbal and nonverbal behaviors that are singularly unique to that person. Even though in language there are only so many separate words and in the nonverbal language system there may be a limited number of separate nonverbal cues, when these behaviors are mixed together, completely unique and never before executed combinations are possible.

Managing and Monitoring Our Nonverbal Communication as a Speaker

Our goal is to assist you in raising your nonverbal processing from the below-conscious level to the conscious level. In this way, you will be in greater control of the nonverbal cues you display to others' and better able to interpret the feedback from your listeners (which can be completely nonverbal in many talks). In this examination, we will look at the following nonverbal elements important to the speaker: the face, gestures, posture, body movement, use of space, appearance, and use of time. Just noting these few elements, we hope, will help you become more aware of these nonverbal behaviors in yourself and others.

The Face

The face is one of the richest areas of nonverbal cues. It is capable of more complex cue combinations (for example, by the eyes, mouth, forehead, eyebrows, and so on) than any other area of the body. Though the face has more potential cues, it is also an area people are good at controlling. Facial expressions supply important cues to the audience about how to interpret what the speaker is saying.

The eyes are the primary means for speaker and listeners to establish and maintain interpersonal rapport. The speaker's eye contact can personalize the message to individual listeners in a way that words cannot. The most effective type of eye contact to establish with your listeners is one-to-one. Focus in on an individual in the audience for a few seconds and then move to another individual in the group and so on, randomly having direct eye contact with various listeners.

Gestures

Gestures are the punctuation marks of nonverbal communication (much as commas, question marks, colons, and so on are the punctuation marks of written communication). The accompanying movements of the hands and arms often supplement in a consistent manner what is being said verbally. To be effective, gestures should be full and varied, rather than partial and repetitious. Some people make abbreviated gestures during a talk, with their hands making tiny movements at waist-level. Full gestures require that the arms be raised to chest height so the hands and arms are in full view. The bigger the audience, the more sweeping or large your gestures need to be so the people in the back can pick them up. Some speakers have hand and arm movements that they repeat over and over, no matter what point they are making. For example, some teachers gesture only with their right or left hand and seldom use both; consequently, their hand gestures become repetitive and boring.

Posture

Body posture is usually what listeners mean when they describe a poised speaker. Standing straight, not rigidly, with your weight equally distributed on both feet at once is an appropriate speaking stance. Shifting your weight from one foot to the other, leaning on

a desk or podium, or crossing and uncrossing your legs in some weird balancing act is not appropriate for public speeches. A common saying among speech-communication professionals is that if you want your ideas to stand up, you have to stand up (and stand up appropriately).

Our gestures punctuate our nonverbal conmmunication.

Body Movement

The speaker's body movement that is not included under gestures and posture has to do with movement from one location to another. Such body movement is possible if the speaker is not tied to notes on the podium or lectern. For example, notecards held in the hand make it feasible for the speaker to move periodically, to add variety and life to the delivery. However, listeners, particularly students, do not like it when speakers pace back and forth in a steady pattern.

A speaker should move with a sense of purpose, not just in a random fashion. Poise is the effective use of posture and body movement with gestures and facial expressions. When posture, body movement, gestures, and facial expressions are synchronized with the wording of the speech, the whole delivery is improved dramatically.

Use of Space

Good speakers move with a sense of purpose.

Speakers can put more or less physical space between themselves and the audience depending on where they place themselves when delivering the speech. The closer you stand to your listeners, the more personal you appear to be. Standing behind podiums or desks

can add psychological distance between the speaker and the listeners. The use of a microphone, when it is not necessary for hearing, also adds psychological distance. When you observe a speaker handling questions or comments from the audience, notice whether he or she moves closer when the listener's response is positive or genuinely inquisitive. Notice, as well, whether the speaker takes a couple of steps backward before responding to a negative or critical remark. The speaker's use of space definitely gives many cues about how the speaker feels toward the audience, the situation, and the reception of the message.

Synchronize body movements with word choice.

Appearance

Dressing for a presentation can be important, especially for the speaker who is not known by the listeners. "Dress appropriately" is a better guideline than "Dress up for your speech." Of course, the more formal the speaking situation, the more formal the dress, no matter what the audience wears. But it is also possible to overdress for a presentation. Wearing a tuxedo or an evening dress may be acceptable for an awards banquet but is hardly appropriate for speaking at a professional meeting. Speech-communication teachers usually shake their heads when a student speaking about the survival of our planet stands up in cutoffs, sneakers, and sweatshirt with the sleeves torn off. There is something a little less than believable about the speaker's appearance. The student speaker has forgotten that words are only part of the message.

Use of Time

Starting and ending a presentation on time indicates a professional speaker. This shows respect for the audience and its span of attention. If you haven't made your point with the listeners after the first eight or ten minutes, your listeners will not be around mentally when you do get to your point.

Why Rehearse?

Not rehearsing for a speech situation is like your college football or basketball team learning all the basics, training, diagramming all the plays and moves, but never practicing before the first game. Speakers get nervous enough before presentations without having the added tension of "hoping" everything will go well. A rehearsal is the speaker's way of planning ahead to *ensure* that everything will work out as planned. You may rehearse small parts at a time just to try them out. At some point, however, see the whole presentation in your mind. See it flow from beginning to end in a mental rehearsal. If you are not comfortable imagining the speech presentation, then rehearse it aloud.

The purpose of rehearsing is not to make the speech more and more "canned" so that by the time it is presented to the audience it is all but mechanical. The purpose of rehearsing is to "try out" the speech to see how it will flow together naturally.

What You Now Know

Much of the stage fright about delivering a speech is uncontrolled mental anxiety caused by the anticipation of speaking. Of the four main types of delivery (manuscript, memorized, impromptu, and extemporaneous), extemporaneous is the most preferred.

The voice as a mechanism for transmitting spoken language can be examined in relation to articulation, pronunciation, voice qualities, vocal qualifiers, pauses and timing, and distracting vocalizations. Becoming aware of your voice qualities and speaking characteristics is the first step in improving your overall use of voice in speech delivery.

Language for speaking follows the general principle of KISS (keep it simple, student). Language should be concrete rather than abstract, specific rather than general. The use of transitions and unique wording can add interest to a speech.

An awareness of the nonverbal aspects of delivery can aid the speaker in managing nonverbal cues and interpreting feedback from the listeners.

What to Do to Learn More

Tape-recording

Tape-record the next speech you give in or outside of class. Listen to your delivery. Pay particular attention to your voice control and the following:

- Articulation
- Vocal qualities (range, resonance, tempo)
- Vocal qualifiers (intensity and pitch)
- Use of pauses
- Use of "ahs," "uhms," "ya knows"

After analyzing your delivery, use a new tape or cassette to record your speech again; this time, practice corrective techniques. Now listen to both the first speech and your second attempt.

Arsenio Hall

Tune in the Arsenio show on TV and turn the sound off during his monologue. Record on a sheet of paper all the nonverbal behaviors you observe him using.

Tune in the Arsenio show on a second evening and turn the picture black with the brightness knob and listen to Arsenio's delivery. Record on paper all the aspects of delivery you recognize. What type of delivery is he using during the monologue? What kind of delivery does he use when he is interviewing a guest?

Vocal Impersonators

Obtain a recording of a show-business person who does impersonations, such as Rich Little. Listen to the vocal qualities and qualifiers used to accomplish the impersonation. What aspects of the vocal delivery does the impersonator exaggerate to achieve the imitation effects?

III
SPEAKING WITH A PURPOSE

Every speech ought to be put together like a living creature, with a body of its own, so as to be neither without head or without feet, but to have both a middle and extremities, described proportionately to each other and to the whole.

Plato

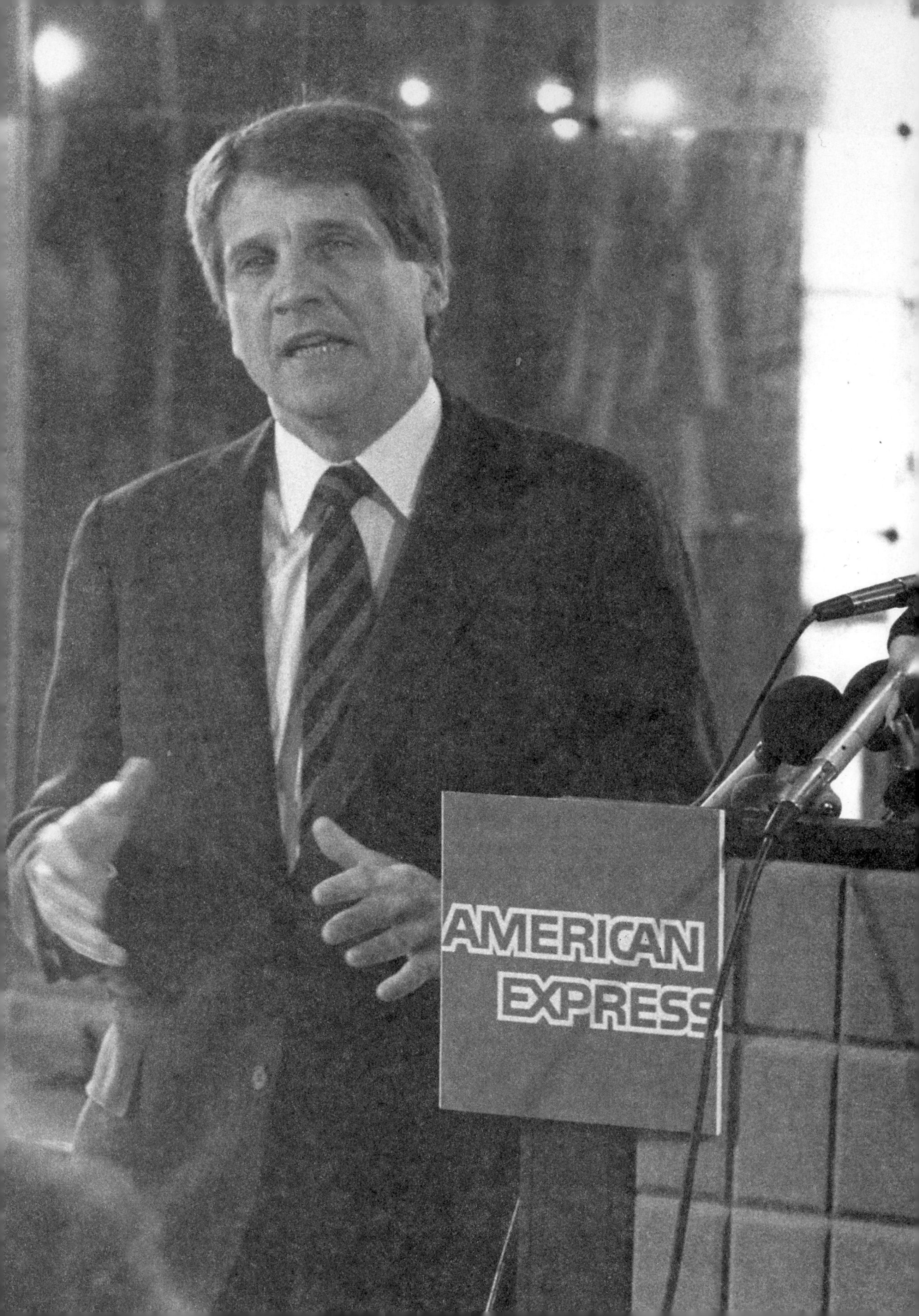
AMERICAN
EXPRESS

7
INFORMATIVE SPEAKING

The goal of the informative speech is to teach and to increase understanding. One of the keys to effective informative speaking is research. The speaker must become knowledgeable regarding the information that is to be presented. This chapter focuses on collecting and organizing information and then putting it together in a speech that will truly inform the listeners.

Chapter Content

ACCURATELY INFORMING OTHERS IS A CHALLENGE

The scene is a speech-communication instructor's office. A student is attempting to clarify her class assignment, which is to prepare and present an informative speech.

STUDENT: I think I see what the difference between an informative speech and a persuasive speech is. The persuasive speech attempts to influence the listener's beliefs, attitudes, feelings, and/or behavior. The informative speech simply furthers the listener's understanding of a topic without attempting to convince.

INSTRUCTOR: Yes, that is generally correct, Karen.

STUDENT: What I am having difficulty doing is finding an interesting topic on which to speak. In my high school speech class, I remember how bored I would get trying to listen to speeches; I don't think I heard one new idea. I don't want that to happen with my speech.

INSTRUCTOR: You have just identified a critical element in the informative speech. If the material does not clarify or give new knowledge to the listener, it is not an informative speech. To inform means to make known, to enlighten, to amplify, to make one aware of something. If the material you were hearing was not new to you, you were not being informed. Maybe someone else in your high school class was being informed, but you were not.

STUDENT: Are you saying my speech has to be on a topic that our class knows nothing about, in order for the speech to be informative?

INSTRUCTOR: Not necessarily. You could clarify or go into depth on a topic with which the class is already familiar. You can extend the listeners' understanding of the topic by relating it to other ideas or to their lives in ways that have not been done before.

STUDENT: So I could talk about safety pins if I could approach the topic in a unique and different way?

INSTRUCTOR: Yes, I suppose you could, although I was hoping for something with a bit more significance.

STUDENT: Now wait a minute, do you mean you know all that is useful to know about safety pins?

INSTRUCTOR: You caught me there. I think I'm about to hear something new about safety pins next Monday at ten. Am I right?

STUDENT: If I can get to the library and pin down some information . . . .

INSTRUCTOR: Ouch! Watch the puns.

◤◢ THE INFORMATIVE SPEECH

The exchange between teacher and student just presented points out the defining aspects of the informative presentation. The key to understanding the purpose of the informative speech lies in the dictionary definition of *inform*. In one way or another, the material must be unknown previously to the listener in order to be considered information. From this perspective, it is possible that an extensive amount of material you hear day in and day out is not informative to you—commercials you have heard before, excuses you have heard before, explanations you have heard before, lectures that repeat the reading assignment verbatim, and so on.

The diagram[1] at the top of page 184 depicts informative and persuasive speaking as falling on a continuum. Up to this point, you may have thought that certain topics are informative and certain topics are persuasive in nature. This is an inaccurate conclusion. It is not the topic that makes the material informative or persuasive; it is the treatment of the material by the speaker and the resulting perception of the intent of the speaker by the listener that determines the informativeness or persuasiveness of the talk. All speeches are informative to the degree that they present new information. However, not all speeches are persuasive unless you view the art of speaking in its broadest sense: When we interact with

---

1. Adapted from a diagram by Paula Michael, Estelle Zannes, and Gerald Goldhaber: *Stand Up, Speak Out.* (Reading, Mass.: Addison-Wesley, 1978) p. 65. Reprinted by permission.

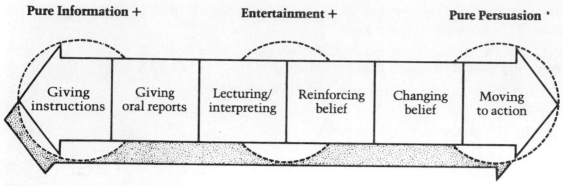

Pure Information +   **Entertainment +**   **Pure Persuasion** *

| Giving instructions | Giving oral reports | Lecturing/ interpreting | Reinforcing belief | Changing belief | Moving to action |

    * *First dimension*
  + *Second dimension*

others, we are attempting to influence others' perceptions of ourselves, even if in the smallest way.

A specific question may have entered your mind by now. "If it is not so much the topic but the treatment of the material that makes a speech informative, how can I give an informative talk on a controversial topic, such as test-tube conception?" For the material to be presented in such a way that the listeners do not believe that the speaker is putting forth a biased position, the information must be:

1. Objective and accurate—the speaker's opinion should not enter into the content either verbally or through nonverbal cues.

2. Balanced and complete—both pros and cons of the material must be given.

Today, Americans are suffering from "information overload." We are bombarded throughout our lives with messages, few of which are objectively presented. The messages come to us from the media, friends, community, and state and from national and international groups and organizations. These messages attempt to influence our hygiene habits, our purchasing preferences, our religious values, our political affiliations, our financial support of nonprofit agencies, our living standards, our recreation preferences, our personal goals, and even our preparations for leaving all these messages behind (death). Undoubtedly, the most controversial aspect of this constant message manipulation is the speculation by communication researchers and psychologists that these messages ultimately affect the devel-

opment and maintenance of our self-concept. We are constantly re-minded that our image is related to our possessions—cars, clothes, homes, deodorants, jewelry, degrees, soft drinks, and on and on.

It seems that we hear and see persuasive messages everywhere that claim they have the way, the product, the service, or the an-swer. (Often the terminology of a persuasive message is subtly de-ceptive in that it implies the intent of the message is to inform. For example, "Did you *know* Sniff deodorant is more effective than . . ."; "We simply want you to *understand* the difference between Pounds Off diet aids and other diet supplements"; and "Are you *aware* that Grub jeans last 50 percent longer?") To counterbalance the scales, wc need to teach people how to be critical listeners, and we also need to teach people the value of presenting material in an informative, balanced manner. From these alternatives, people can make their own decisions. We are not saying that persuasive mes-sages are bad. We are saying that there is an admirable skill to pre-senting information in an open and objective manner.

Few messages are delivered objec-tively, so critical listening is important.

HOW TO INFORM

Whenever you choose to give an informative speech, your major purpose is to gain audience understanding. Your specific purpose is to teach, instruct, clarify, and impart new information about something. The effective informative speech encourages the "I didn't know that!" response from listeners.

An informative speech is necessarily characterized by: (1) accuracy—derived from careful reading, research, and study; (2) completeness—sufficient information to allow understanding of the subject; (3) intelligibility—clarity and organization of ideas, which leads to interest and understanding; and (4) usefulness—related to the audience's needs.

If you speak about how an IBM personal computer functions, the audience expects your presentation to be truthful, accurate, objective, interesting, well-organized, clear, complete, and useful. It would be important for you to see the IBM personal computer demonstrated, read the sales brochures and specifications, listen to a salesperson, compare IBM personal computers with other personal computers, check an electronics consumer guide, look at journals dealing with personal computers, talk to someone who owns an IBM personal computer, and attempt to become an expert yourself before trying to present an effective informative speech on the topic.

In Organizations

In organizational settings and at work, your informative speaking may deal with these topics:

- new employees' orientation
- explaining a promotion
- giving on-the-job instructions
- correcting a procedure that has gone awry
- describing departmental responsibilities to a group of employees

■ reporting on the success of a recent effort to improve productivity

■ implementing a new set of production, training, or reporting procedures

Outside of Organizations

You may also find yourself giving informative speeches to college students, club members, friends, family, and church and civic groups. Topics will range from "How to Buy a House" to "Fat Intake and Running." Included here is a list of possible informative-speech topics in case you do not want to tell us about your hobby or the "best way to succeed at anything you do."

■ the history of acupuncture

■ how to instruct a computer

■ dressing for success

■ why are there so many kinds of diets?

■ what are natural foods?

■ ways to find inner peace

■ the evolution of hang gliders

■ where are the best jobs in the United States

■ what is the purpose of the national debt?

■ can anyone become "physically fit for life?"

■ laser technology in medicine

■ the good and bad side of drugs

All of us are curious yet relatively uninformed about important and exciting things going on around us. Informative speaking gives us the opportunity to increase and enhance understanding, thus closing the gap between the unknown and known for the listeners.

Because the achievement of audience understanding is so important, if at all possible use visual aids like models, pictures, diagrams, and demonstration devices, and follow your informative speech with a question-answer period.

▼◢ THREE STEPS FOR PREPARING AN INFORMATIVE SPEECH

Before you plunge into the detailed development of your informative presentation, you should acquire some background information on your audience, the speaking situation, the topic, and the desired response. Then organize the speech so that it is at once interesting and useful. Finally, you must master the presentation so that you are able to speak directly and spontaneously to the audience.

Step 1: Gathering Essential Information

Begin your preparation by analyzing your listeners, situation, topic, and desired response. Use the following guide:

1. **Analyze your listeners.**
   a. What do they already know about the topic and how often are they exposed to information on the topic?
   b. How interested or disinterested are they in the topic?
   c. What are their attitudes or feelings toward the topic?
   d. What are they likely to know or feel about you as a speaker?
      (1) How much credibility will you have prior to the presentation?
      (2) How much effort will have to be made to build your credibility during the presentation?
      (3) Given your credibility, what balance between your personal thoughts and outside source material will be most effective with this group?
   e. How can you build "thought bridges" between the audience's experiences and attitudes and the materials of your speech?
2. **Consider the situation.**
   a. How large is the room?
   b. How will the seating and speaker's stand be arranged?
   c. Are there any chalkboards, projection screens, microphones?
   d. How many people will attend?

Keep your audience and location in mind when preparing your speech.

    e. What is the purpose of the meeting?
    f. How many speakers will speak?
    g. Will there be any noise or visual distractions?

3. Research the topic.
    a. Examine your own knowledge and experience.
    b. Ask friends and experts.
    c. Use direct observation if possible.
    d. Read printed materials.
    e. Check the library.
    f. Consult newspapers and magazines.
    g. Conduct surveys and interviews.
    h. Examine research materials.
    i. Allow time to think, incubate, and create.

4. Determine the desired response.
   a. Decide on the central idea.
   b. Decide on the specific response desired.
      (1) Understand what about the topic?
      (2) Remember what?
      (3) See how to use what?
      (4) Accept what?
      (5) Reject what?

Step 2: Organizing the Informative Speech

Now that you have analyzed your listeners, considered the speaking situation, researched the topic, and decided on the purpose or desired response, you are ready to organize your presentation. The basic purpose of speech organization is deciding what chunks of information to include and in what order to include them. When we take all the many separate points and lump them into categories, it is easier for us to remember what we want to say, and it is easier for the audience to process the information.

Good organization helps your delivery and helps the audience process the information.

Professional speakers have traditionally limited themselves to three or four ideas in their speaking. Science and tradition are in

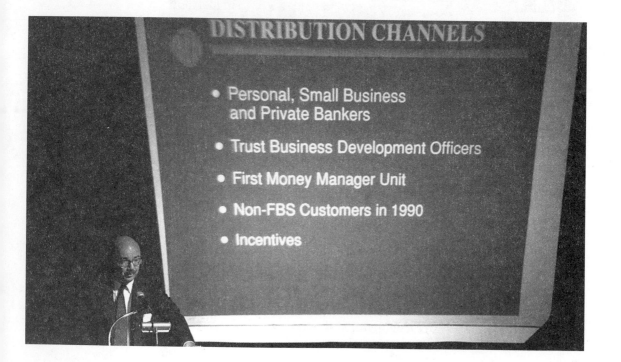

agreement that if a speaker is going to be effective, the number of points covered in any one period of time should be limited. If a speaker has more than four separate pieces of information to cover (say, ten points), then those points will have to be organized into parts that do not exceed three or four.

Select the most important points by going back to the central idea of specific response desired and deciding what main points are needed in order to explain the central idea. Then select enough supportive material, such as facts, statistics, illustrations, quotations, expert testimony, comparisons, visual aids, logical reasoning, and definitions, to prove, clarify, and add interest to each main point.

The following outline may be useful in organizing your informative speech.

Informative-Speaking Outline

		Potential Use
	INTRODUCTION	**of Visual Aids**
I.	Attention	Visual?
II.	Purpose or Importance	
III.	Forecast of Main Points	Visual?
	BODY	
I.	Main Idea	Visual?
	A. Illustrative/Supportive Material	
	B. Illustrative/Supportive Material	
II.	Main Idea	Visual?
	A. Illustrative/Supportive Material	
	B. Illustrative/Supportive Material	
III.	Main Idea	Visual?
	A. Illustrative/Supportive Material	
	B. Illustrative/Supportive Material	
IV.	Main Idea	Visual?
	A. Illustrative/Supportive Material	
	B. Illustrative/Supportive Material	
	CONCLUSION	
I.	Summarize highlights and tie back to introduction	Visual?

When a speaker gets down to the level of simply making a general point and then illustrating that point with a specific example, statistic, personal experience, or whatever, he or she is using the basic message unit for all speaking. If a general point is made and then followed by specific illustrative material, it is called the **deductive** basic message unit. If specific examples are given the followed by a general concluding statement, it is called the **inductive** basic message unit.

The organization of the material in the main body of the speech should fit the topic and purpose of the speech. The following table shows a variety of appropriate ways of structuring the information in the main body of the presentation.

Topic	Information Structure
History of the State of Alaska	Chronological
Staying in College Once You're Accepted	Enumerating the points
How to Study	What, where, when, how why,
The Difference between Credit Unions and Commercial Banks	Comparison/contrast
Our Food-Producing Regions	Spacial sequence
The Cause of AIDS	Cause-effect sequence
Test-Tube Conception	Pros and cons

Let us take a number of ideas about how to recognize a good diamond to purchase and organize those ideas into a speech outline for giving an informative speech.

Recognizing a Good Diamond to Purchase

 Buying diamonds can be hazardous to your health.

 With a little luck and careful examination, you can find a diamond for the right price.

 Carat, the first C, is the weight of the diamond.

 Today, we are going to look at the four Cs of carat, clarity, color, and cutting.

 Before buying a diamond, examine the four Cs of carat, clarity, color, and cutting.

 Color, the third C, is the tint of the diamond.

 A one-carat stone will cost about $3,000.

 A blue tint is most highly prized.

 Clarity, the second C, is the degree of blemish of the diamond.

 A half-carat stone will cost about $600.

 Yellow or brown tints lower the value.

■ Cutting, the final C, is the shaping of the diamond.

■ Virtually no diamond is free of all blemishes.

■ Poor cutting is the biggest factor in reducing the value of a diamond per carat.

■ High-priced diamonds reveal only minor blemishes.

■ Proper sawing, faceting, proportioning, and shaping make a diamond more valuable.

   Organizing these ideas into a meaningful sequence for giving an informative speech is easily done by following the Informative-Speaking Outline.

TITLE: Recognizing a Good Diamond to Purchase
INTRODUCTION
  I. Buying diamonds can be hazardous to your health!
III. With a little luck and careful examination, you can find the right diamond for the right price.
III. Today, we are going to look at the four Cs of carat, clarity, color, and cutting
BODY
III. Carat, the first C, is the weight of the diamond.
    A. A one-carat stone will cost about $3,000.
    B. A half-carat stone is worth about $600.
 II. Clarity, the second C, is the degree of blemish of the diamond.
    A. Virtually no diamond is free of all blemishes.
    B. High-priced diamonds reveal only minor blemishes.
III. Color, the third C. is the tint of the diamond.
    A. A blue tint is most highly prized.
    B. Yellow or brown tints lower the value.
IV. Cutting, the final C, is the shaping of the diamond.
    A. Poor cutting is the biggest factor in reducing the value of the diamond per carat.
    B. Proper sawing, faceting, proportioning, and shaping make a diamond more valuable.
CONCLUSION
  I. Before buying a diamond, examine the four Cs of carat, clarity, color, and cutting.

   If you gather good information, outline it according to the sample outline, and prepare a few visual aids to further clarify your main points, you are ready to mentally practice and "walk through" your presentation.

Step 3: Mastering Your Presentation

Audiences often become interested and respond appropriately when a speech is delivered well. Think about what you would like to say to introduce your main points. Then visualize the order in which you will talk about the main points and the ideas you will use to support them. Finally, imagine how you will conclude your speech on a high note.

If possible, practice using your visual aids. Go to the place where you are to present your speech and walk up to the speaker's spot and look around. How does it feel? Can you imagine giving an enthusiastic presentation?

Above all, think about being very direct with the audience. Be so well prepared that you can look into anyone's eyes without fear. Remember, you know more about the subject than anyone else, so wind up, be spontaneous, and let it rip!

TYPES OF INFORMATIVE SPEAKING

Informative speaking takes many forms. Listeners can be exposed to informative presentations of processes, instructions, and directions. Informative talks can involve demonstrations and descriptions of objects. Informative speeches can also define a term, concept, or value and can offer objective explanations of an idea, a theory, an issue, research, or an event.

The diverse types of informative speeches fall into two practical categories—those where the speaker is personally familiar with the process, procedure, object, and so on and those where the speaker must use outside source materials to give depth to the speech.

As a speaker concerned about your credibility as a message source, you need to establish yourself as a competent and experienced source when presenting an informative speech. You also need to share the range of sources on which you have relied for your information.

Giving Instructions

The key to giving effective instructions is to adapt the material to the learner's perspective (point of view, knowledge, experience, motivation, and so on). The following five steps represent a standard "how to" outline for giving instructions.

1. **The instructor prepares for the presentation:**
   a. Clearly identifies the various goals of the instruction (knowledge, attitude, and behavior).
   b. Determines the knowledge, attitudes, and skills of the learners.
   c. Breaks down the instruction into manageable steps or units.
   d. Arranges the environment where the instruction will take place (materials, equipment, visuals, seating, and so on).
2. **The instructor presents the information:**
   a. Explains the purpose of the instructions and how the learner will benefit. Warns of any difficult areas. (Creates a favorable atmosphere for learning.)
   b. Describes how the results will be measured.
   c. Tells in steps or units.
   d. Proceeds from known to unknown.
   e. Demonstrates.
   f. Reviews, stressing key points.
3. **The learners try out the information:**
   a. The learners participate as the steps are gone through again, or
   b. The learners practice under guidance, or
   c. One of the learners, as a group representative, tries out the instructions while the rest of the learners look on and assist the chosen representative.
4. **The learners practice independently:**
   a. The learners practice independently within an acceptable time frame (minutes, hours, days).
   b. The learners are encouraged to ask questons or ask for assistance (which will only be offered if requested or if the instructor sees a dangerous development or the reinforcing of a negative habit).
5. **Results are measured:**
   a. The learners will be required to demonstrate their knowledge and skills with the following criteria set by the instructor:
      (1) Level of performance or knowledge required (how well).

(2) Time allotted.

(3) Conditions under which performance will be measured.

For briefer, more spontaneous instructions, the following format may prove helpful:

Get the listeners' attention. Tell:

- **What**

- **How**

- **Where**

- **When**

- **Why**

Giving Demonstrations

In the previously described speech, the listeners actually learned how to perform a skill or task themselves through participation. However, not all demonstrations are conducted for the purpose of having listeners learn the task. The objectives of demonstration speeches can also be to get listeners to appreciate, understand, accept, or become enthusiastic about a procedure, process, or piece of equipment. An example of an informative demonstration of this kind is a speech on home fire safety where the speaker actually demonstrates how certain kinds of fires get started. The listeners are not invited to participate by starting the fires. Speeches on life-saving techniques such as CPR (cardiopulmonary resuscitation) can involve either participative or nonparticipative demonstrations. When listeners are observers rather than participants in the demonstration, steps need to be taken to involve and keep the listeners' attention.

1. **Everything hinges on the demonstration.** If it doesn't work, neither will the rest of the speech. Very thorough planning and pretesting needs to take place before the nonparticipative demonstration.

2. **Backup equipment is necessary.** In case a piece of equipment or material fails to perform as expected, you need equipment or

materials in reserve. For example, if a speaker is demonstrating what happens to safety glass on impact, there should be a backup piece of glass in case the first piece doesn't react correctly.

3. **"Skip-ahead" technique can be used.** If the demonstration is a lengthy or complex process, you may want to have parts completed ahead of time so that you can skip the waiting period or lengthy (noninformative) process. You explain what will happen and then display the result already completed prior to the speech. A classic use of this skip-ahead technique is on TV cooking shows, where the host or hostess demonstrates how to prepare

Giving demonstrations requires effective use of visuals and demonstration materials.

the food but the audience does not have to wait for the actual cooking. The host or hostess uses a verbal transition and displays the end product, which was prepared before the show went on the air. The skip-ahead technique is valuable as a time-saver and also allows for better continuity in the presentation.

If you need to demonstrate something that may fail, it is a good idea to have the skip-ahead technique as a backup to save the presentation from total disaster.

When the skip-ahead technique is used, a demonstration that would normally take several minutes, hours, or days can be presented in a short informative speech.

4. **Remind the listener of the purpose of the demonstration.** In the participative demonstration, the listener obviously becomes aware, through direct involvement, of the objective of the demonstration. In the nonparticipative demonstration, the speaker may have to remind the listener of the purpose of the demonstration, what the demonstration is supposed to prove or reveal. For example, in a demonstration dealing with the conditioning of mice in an experimental device, the listeners can get so engrossed in the behavior of the mice that they forget what the demonstration is proving or showing. The speaker will want to take a minute at the end of the demonstration to review the demonstration and relate it to the initial objective of the presentation.

Descriptive Speeches

Descriptive speeches, like the other informative speeches discussed, must meet the principal test of presenting new information, and if the topic is controversial, the information must be presented objectively. Descriptive speeches break down into speeches that describe objects and places; define terms, concepts, and values; or offer explanations of ideas, issues, and events.

Describing Objects and Places
When the purpose of your speech is to describe a city, a sports stadium, a modern recording studio, or the like, you will want to use a spatial organization pattern in presenting the material. Visual aids will be very important in allowing your listeners to "see" what you are talking about. Many slide presentations fall into this category. Aunt Bertha's slide show of her trip to Egypt also falls into this

Above all, the orator should be equipped with a rich store of examples both old and new; and he ought not merely to know those that are recorded in history or are transmitted by oral tradition or occur from day to day, but also fictitious examples invented by great poets.
QUINTILIAN

category. Talking in specific terms about location, size, weight, age, color, shape, and so on is important in this type of informative speech. The speaker's language must be especially vivid in word pictures to assist the listeners in sensing the smells, tastes, sounds, and atmosphere of the place or object described.

Defining Terms, Concepts, and Values

The ability to define terms, concepts, and values clearly is important for the effective speaker. Although the principles of definition can be applied to any type of presentation, we are going to focus on the informative speech. It is rather difficult, but not impossible, to objectively define controversial or emotion-laden concepts, such as birth control, abortion, religious cults, euthanasia, and communism. In a persuasive speech, the speaker may build the whole presentation around an attempt to get the audience to accept the speaker's definition of, let's say, "abortion as murder." The definition of the term in this case is definitely not objective nor representative of all the various accepted meanings.

In an informative speech on definition, there are some methods for defining words (terms, concepts, and the like) that will improve the speaker's effectiveness.

1. **Give the historical derivation or development of the word.** The history of the term may add insight into its present meaning. If the word has a limited historical background, the speaker can connect the word to its original referent. Terms such as *jackass, brown nose, hothead, blabbermouth, slob, dummy,* and the like today have very general meanings whereas they once had singular, specific meanings.

2. **Classify or categorize a word in order to define it.** For example, over the last several years, there has been a considerable attempt to classify alcoholism as a "disease."

3. **Use synonyms** (words that have nearly the same meaning) **and antonyms** (words that have the opposite meaning) **as another way to define.** This is the primary way the dictionary defines words. For example, *verbal* is defined in the dictionary as "spoken, oral, of words." The antonym given for *verbal* is *writing.*

4. **Break a term into its various parts as a way of defining it.** For example, a résumé is defined in the dictionary as "a summary" or a "summing up." For the college-placement director, a résumé is "a brief, clear, and neatly written summary of the key assets of

the applicant with the information organized in order of descending importance." The speech on this topic would develop around explaining what is meant by the terms in the definition. What is *clear*? What is meant by *brief*?

Explaining Ideas, Issues, and Events

Some topics appear to be controversial simply by title. For example:

Pollution of our oceans	Smoking
School financing	Legalized gambling
Advertising appeals	Nuclear power
Pesticides and wildlife	Defense spending

Other topics appear to be more informative by title:

The last Ice Age	Microwave ovens
Silent films	Gravity
The geology of the moon	Einstein's theory of relativity
The music of the Beatles	Weather repeats itself

As an informative speaker, **our goal is to shed new light in an objective and representative manner,** whether the topic of our speech is controversial or noncontroversial. We are not trying to prove a harm, move others to take action, attempt to change attitudes, or stimulate others to renew a commitment to a practice they have become apathetic about. Our goal is to increase understanding. To *inform* an audience about, for example, nuclear power requires that the speaker include both the pros and cons. On the other hand, in an informative speech on alternate sources of power for the world, a speaker could cover nuclear power, solar power, wind power, and wave power *without* covering the pros and cons of each if the speaker's purpose is not to convince the listeners that one of these power sources is better than the others.

To be objective as a speaker, you have to be objective in your analysis of the materials available on the topic and objective in the frame of mind you have while researching the topic. You should not begin your research with the thought, "What can I discover that shows that wind power (or solar power) would be our best alternate energy source for the future?" or "How can I make my audience see that AIDS is a critical problem in the United States today?"

Material on some topics stands a greater chance of being new information to the listener than material on other topics that have been talked about frequently. However, it is not necessarily that the topic of the speech is uninteresting—*it is more likely that the listener's interest has not been aroused.* Presenting new material or a fresh perspective on an overworked topic can be a challenge— just ask ministers, schoolteachers, police officers, mothers and fathers, salespeople, industrial safety directors, and fund-raisers how challenging it is to try to make an old point interesting in a new or unique way.

One of the keys to effective informative speaking is research. The speaker must become thoroughly knowledgeable about all aspects of the topic. The speaker must become a "secondary" expert. During the speech, the speaker can build credibility on the topic by citing the sources of materials in the speech. In a term paper, you use footnotes or endnotes to reference materials and ideas that are not your own. In a speech, you refer to your sources of materials as you are talking. In listening to presentations, you may have heard oral footnotes, such as:

> A recent issue of *Psychology Today* reports that research on eye contact is . . . .
>
> Deaths that occur in the home have gone up 23 percent in the last year. According to the National Safety Council's pamphlet *Accident Facts*, this increase is due to . . . .
>
> The latest Gallup poll reported in *Time* this week states that the American voter is . . . .
>
> I asked ten randomly chosen students on our campus to describe what this picture meant to them. Eight of the ten said essentially the same thing. The picture represented . . . .

Finally, the speaker should be sensitive to the potential bias of the source material. The speaker needs to ask, "How objective or believable will my cited sources seem to my audience?"

> I seem to have been only like a boy playing on the seashore and diverting myself in now and then finding a smooth pebble or a prettier shell than ordinary, whilst the great ocean of truth lay all undiscovered before me.
> **ISAAC NEWTON**

FINAL TIPS FOR INFORMING OTHERS

These final suggestions for effective, informative speaking were developed by a student like yourself who had the chance to hear informative speeches, critique them, and suggest ways to improve informational speaking.

1. **Supply new information.** The purpose of the informative speech includes providing the listeners with information they did not have before, adapting the information in such a way that it will seem important for the listeners to learn, and being clear and meaningful. A speech to inform seeks to analyze, explain, report, describe, or clarify some ideas, object, event, or place.

2. **Establish the significance.** You have sat through enough speeches and discussions to know that sometimes the information the speaker is trying to give you does not sink in. If you do not feel that what is being said is of vital importance to you, you may feel it's not worth the effort to listen. As a speaker, you need to explain early in your talk that your information is of concern to your listeners—these particular listeners.

3. **Establish your authority.** Perhaps you have felt at times that the speaker was no better informed than you. Speakers should, of course, be more informed, and they should in some manner suggest that they are well-informed, through the use of pertinent data or even rhetorical questions or other devices. Often the use of a visual aid, such as the object itself or a series of diagrams or pictures, will help. Sometimes a map or a simple chart can be used not only to clarify a point but also to suggest that you have studied your topic in some detail. This can give you or any other speaker the necessary credibility with the audience.

4. **Explain new ideas through reference to familiar ones.** A speech to inform should relate new ideas to ideas already known. This applies to sentences as well as to the total plan you use for your speech organization. For example, you probably remember a teacher comparing Italy's shape to a boot or noting that Sicily looks like a football about to be kicked.

5. **Avoid unecessary details.** How much detail you should use will depend on how much the listeners already know about the subject. The U.S. Air Force makes these suggestions to its personnel:
   a. Underline the key sentences in your message and then condense these by eliminating "deadhead" words, by making one sentence do the work of two or three, by discarding unneeded illustrations, and by making summaries of exact statistics.

   b. Avoid hasty conclusions, wordiness, repetition, loss expres-
      sions, and mental shortcuts.
6. **Direct yourself to the audience.** During your preparation, think
   of the people who will listen to your presentation. As you
   gather material, try to choose those items that will be most
   easily understood by them. You might try to find examples
   dealing with sports for one audience, but your examples on another occasion might relate to music or family.

   How many examples and illustrations you will need to use
   will depend on how easily you think it will be for your listeners to grasp the ideas. While speaking, you should watch
   the facial expressions of your listeners, and you should be able
   to offer further elaboration of your topic whenever it seems
   necessary.
7. **Use special means to help the listeners remember.** Speakers
   generally want their audience to remember what they say, so
   they use key words, concrete examples, visual aids, and other
   devices they know will help. Sometimes speakers must rely on
   words to develop mental pictures and relationships in the listeners' minds; sometimes they use visible means, such as
   charts graphs, maps and objects themselves.

   If you as a speaker can cause your listeners to see mental
   pictures of the ideas you are presenting just as you can cause
   them to relate your ideas with certain ones they already have,
   they are most likely to remember.

   One way to accomplish this is through **exaggeration.** The
   cartoonist often uses this procedure, especially with carica-
   tures. The cartoonist seeks some prominent feature of the person, such as Teddy Roosevelt's board smile and the big teeth
   of FDR's jutting jaw and his cigarette holder. Jimmie Durante
   built a character around his nose; we still hear John Barrymore
   spoken of as the "Great Profile."

What You Now Know

Speaking to inform requires that the speaker present information
or material that is new to the listener. A unique approach to an old
topic or issue can meet the requirement of being new information

to the listener. In order for a speaker to inform listeners about a controversial topic, the information must be presented in a representative and unbiased manner with both pros and cons given.

Organizing the informative speech in terms of separate points makes it easier for the speaker to cover the information and easier for the listener to process the information.

Speeches dealing with a process, directions, instructions, demonstrations, and descriptions of objects usually require the speaker to be personally familiar with the material. Speeches defining terms, concepts, or values and speeches explaining an idea, theory, issue, research, or event usually require the speaker to use additional reference material outside his or her personal area of experience or expertise.

Speaking to inform is not as easy a task as one might initially suspect. However, the goal of allowing listeners to draw their own conclusions is an admirable one in today's age of mass persuasion. And to increase understanding in a world of complexity and confusion is certainly a noble and eloquent use of speech.

What to Do to Learn More

Find an Informative Presentation

Go to *Vital Speeches* and *Reader's Digest* and locate a speech and an article that you think are informative. Apply the criteria of informative material as presented in the chapter. Do they meet the standards of informative presentation?

My Major

Sometimes it is very difficult for a speaker to inform listeners about knowledge or material he or she (the speaker) is so familiar with that he or she takes it for granted.

Prepare a five-minute talk on your major. If you don't know that much about your major yet, maybe it's time you found out. The challenge here will be to meet the criteria of "newness" or "uniqueness" of material for your listeners. Remember, if your listeners don't learn anything new or don't have an increased understanding of your major, then you failed to inform them—*you simply talked to them.*

Unbiased News Media?

To what degree do you believe the news media's presentation of the news is unbiased? Do you believe investigative reporting, such as that which precipitated Watergate, is objective or unbiased in its intent? Why or why not?

AMOCO

7872

leukem

dwest Triathlon Classic
Bullpucky's

8
PERSUASIVE SPEAKING

The purpose of this chapter is to describe the importance of persuasive communication in today's message-packed environment and the three broad objectives our persuasive messages attempt to accomplish. You will learn several approaches to persuading. Finally, the chapter focuses and elaborates on one of many ways you can organize a persuasive speech.

Chapter Content

**PERSUADING OTHERS:
COMMUNICATING TO GET RESULTS**

The student trying to persuade her teacher that she deserves an A, the schoolteacher trying to convince her class that math is important, the superintendent trying to get his men to work faster, the researcher trying to get her professional association to accept her research, the daughter trying to convince her father that she is old enough to date, and the telemarketer trying to sell you a magazine subscription, are all examples of people involved in the process of persuasive communication.

Persuading people is one of the most common objectives of communicating. As continual senders and receivers (transceivers) of messages, we deal with 3,000 to 4,000 separate messages per day.

Many of these messages are designed to change our thinking, our feelings, and/or our behavior. With this many messages, it is difficult not to have a certain amount of chaos. Some messages conflict or compete with others. Other messages are incongruent or inconsistent with things we already know or believe. Much of this just adds to the existing information and message overload we experience. (For students, this overload can be particularly sensed during final-exam time from papers, tests, reports, projects, and so on.)

A good deal of your speaking, to one or more, will just be another message among the many. To get others to pay attention and then begin to consider (or even change) their thinking, feelings, or behavior will take designed persuasion on your part.

 THE CHALLENGE OF PERSUASIVE COMMUNICATION

The purpose of persuasive speaking is to cause others to believe, to feel, or to act in a way the speaker intends. Full change, or even partial change, usually takes more than a single message. Most people change strongly held thoughts, feelings, or behaviors only after repeated exposure to several messages making the same point from different perspectives. The reason for this is that an individual's thought processes, beliefs, and behaviors are interrelated with numerous other clusters or groupings of thought patterns, beliefs, and behaviors.

It is very difficult to isolate one of these from their intertwined networks and change it. Even if you can cause change in one or two thought processes, beliefs, or behaviors, the connections to others are going to make the others somewhat resistant to change. One way to picture the task of the persuader is to think of beliefs, thought processes, and behaviors as a forest of trees all growing so close together that their root systems are intertwined beneath the surface. It is very difficult to neatly dig up one of the trees, roots intact, and transplant it somewhere else.

Lest you get discouraged, note that not all the change you intend to cause in others will disturb strongly held mental or behavioral systems. Change can be rather easy to achieve for simple messages that receivers do not perceive as a risk, threat, attack, or challenge to their way of thinking and doing things. For example, sometimes getting the car keys or an extra ten dollars or explaining a D grade comes easier than getting the okay to take a co-ed backpacking trip into the grizzly bear habitat of a Northwestern wilderness area.

The point is effective persuasion on topics that people hold dear requires as much research, strategy, planning, and design as it takes to get your peers to give blood at the blood bank against the backdrop of rampant AIDS stories. Though some persuasive speeches can cause dramatic shifts in receivers, most just "open the door" to future change. Opening the door to change is a significant communication result—no small accomplishment when the thoughts, feelings, and behaviors being challenged are firmly established.

PERSUASIVE PURPOSE

To make sure you start off right in preparing a persuasive message, you need to know that there are three broad purposes of persuasive speaking:

to convince: speaking to move people to accept beliefs, feelings and behaviors they are presently (prespeech) opposed to.

to stimulate: speaking to reinforce existing beliefs, feelings, and behaviors that have lost some of their intensity to motivate the individual. (The receiver is not opposed to the message; he or she has just lost some commitment to the topic or issue and needs to be recharged.)

to actuate: speaking primarily to get specific actions from the receivers.

These definitions raise a question. Is the speech to convince or the speech to stimulate that focuses primarily on a call for action or a change in behavior a speech to actuate? Yes. If the primary emphasis is on getting specified actions or behaviors from the receivers, then it is, by definition, a speech to actuate. If the speech meets the definition of convincing or stimulating with no or only incidental references or calls to action, then it is called a speech to convince or a speech to stimulate.

Persuasive speaking is critical in politics.

▰▰ PERSUASION AND THE AUDIENCE

We discussed audience analysis in Chapter Three. But we now need to mention audience analysis as it relates to persuasive speaking.

To bring about changes in beliefs[1], feelings (emotions), or behaviors, the speaker must know, prior to the speech, the listeners' predispositions (sometimes called attitudes), toward the topic. Speakers need to be concerned with these predispositions in relation to the topic for the entire audience, not just a few individuals.

The listeners' predispositions to think, feel, and behave toward the subject can be learned in various ways. One method is to put yourself in their shoes. Try to reverse roles with them and see how you would feel about the matter. Another method is to sample your intended audience. Ask your listeners what they feel about the particular issue and how strongly they feel this. Listen carefully to what they say and you will quickly detect how they feel. The more familiar you become with the audience's attitudes, the better you can adjust your persuasive appeals and organizational pattern.

▰▰ APPROACHES TO PERSUASION

Personality can open doors, but only character can keep them open.
ELMER LETERMAN

When you have selected your persuasive purpose and you understand your audience, you must then become acquainted with approaches for persuading people. Samovar and Mills have this to say about modes or approaches to persuasion:

Twenty-four centuries ago Aristotle in his *Rhetoric* observed that there are three instruments of persuasion: (1) ". . . persuasion is effected by the ARGUMENTS, when we demonstrate the truth, real or apparent, by such means as inhere in particular cases." (2) ". . . persuasion is effected through the audience, when they are brought by the speech into a state of EMOTION; for we give very different decisions under the sway of pain or joy, and liking or hatred." (3) "The CHARACTER of the speaker is a cause of persuasion when the speech is so uttered as to make him worthy of belief; for as a rule we trust men of probity more, and more quickly, about things in general, while on points outside the

---

[1]A legitimate distinction can be made between beliefs, values, and attitudes. For our purposes, we are using the term *beliefs* to stand for all three, though your instructor may wish to separate the three out for distinct understanding and application. These are mental constructs that affect how individuals think and behave about topics and issues.

realm of exact knowledge, where opinion is divided, we trust them absolutely." The durability of Aristotle's classification may be seen by a cursory examination of rhetorical treatises from his day to the present. Perhaps different labels are affixed to the modes of persuasion, and perhaps some of the modes have been subdivided, but all are essentially Aristotelian in their origin.[2]

Based on Aristotle's early approach, we shall briefly discuss arguments or logical appeals, emotions or psychological appeals, and character or personal credibility. Each of these is important for the effective persuasive speaker. Each shall be presented separately. However, in practice, they are inseparable. All the modes work together to effectively influence an audience. The most powerful messages combine logical appeals, psychological appeals, and speaker credibility to persuade.

The Logical Approach

The major aspects of the logical approach are reasoning, testimony, statistics, and factual examples. Each of these was presented in detail in Chapter Four under forms of support. *A brief review of Chapter Four should help you better understand the logical approach, which essentially is the rational approach for persuading others.* Research seems to indicate that the effective use of the logical approach has a more lasting effect on audiences than a comparable use of the other two approaches.

The Psychological or Emotional Approach

The psychological approach reaches out and touches peoples' feelings and emotions. The focus is to draw connections between the point of the message and the needs, values, wants, desires, fears, and so on of the receivers. Psychological appeals provide the motives and the energy for change. If the logical approach provides some of the fuel for the persuasive fire, the psychological approach provides the match, the spark, the ignition.

[2]Samovar, Larry A. and Jack Mills. *Oral Communication: Message and Response.* 7th ed. Dubuque, IA: Wm C. Brown, 1989.

But for the speaker, the task is to decide what, of everything that is possible, should be included. How does the speaker go about deciding which appeals to include and which to leave out? Experience demonstrates that it is best to use a few appeals well than to attempt a shotgun blast of several appeals, hoping one or more small points hit the mark. Taking the analogy a step further, speakers who know their audiences and their targets well may elect to take the risk of using a single appeal, well developed and delivered with force.

Since using psychological appeals requires some reasoning and choosing among options, it is helpful for the speaker to refer to materials that organize the psychological elements into hierarchies or chunks. Maslow's "hierarchy of needs" is one example of this organization of the psychological elements. We will describe Maslow's hierarchy of needs and then indicate how you might use it.

Maslow[3] describes the psychological elements that motivate us to think, feel, and behave as we do. We will describe them as related to a ladder of basic human needs. On the bottom rungs of the ladder are the most basic needs for survival, and on the top rungs of the ladder are the needs related to reaching one's full potential. Beginning at the top of the ladder, these needs are:

■ self-actualization—reaching one's full potential; operating in a optimum mode; feeling competent; feeling authentic and comfortable about one's purpose and value.

■ high self-esteem from reputation and achievement—feeling competent, confident, and in control; feeling good about one's professional development; acceptance of oneself as a growing, changing individual.

■ a feeling of belonging—acceptance by others; perceiving that others approve of and are comfortable with one; the development of meaningful friendships and/or relationships.

■ concern for personal or individual safety—seeking security and freedom from fear or anxiety; needing shelter and physical and psychological protection.

■ concern for life-sustaining functions and processes—needing to avoid life-threatening experiences and conditions; seeking those situations and conditions that help maintain necessary biological functioning.

[3]Abraham, Maslow. *Motivation and Personality* (New York: Harper & Row, 1970).

Maslow's list does not directly include some obvious other needs or values people have, such as power, control, influence, material possessions, choice, independence, relative balance among life forces, fairness to be different from others, and so on.

How does the individual designing a persuasive speech use the ladder or hierarchy of needs? First, realize what it means to describe these needs in a hierarchy like rungs of a ladder. The needs on the bottom rungs need to be somewhat, though not completely, fulfilled before an individual can be appealed to by the next higher level up. Just as in climbing the ladder, you do not reach up for the next rung with one foot until the other foot is secure on the rung below.

Individuals are seldom concerned about belonging when they are experiencing some threat to their job security, family, health, or so on. It would be difficult to find someone who feels he or she is maximizing his or her potential who doesn't also have fairly high self-esteem (the need below self-actualizing).

Needs can be incorporated into persuasive appeals in speaking in very select ways. The idea is not to appeal to all levels of needs at once and hope something works. For example, you may appeal to an individual's concern for a biological healthy life in your persuasive message regarding the ill effects of sun tanning. On the other hand, in a persuasive message to get people to contribute money for skin cancer research, you may be more effective appealing to your receivers' acceptance by others or how well they will be perceived if their organization contributes a significant sum to this cause.

Thinking through what elements you want to incorporate is also needed in the psychological approach. Reasoning is not just the tool of the logical/rational approach. And as we shall see, reasoning also plays a role in the credibility approach.

The Credibility Approach

The message is only as persuasive as the speaker is credible. How you are perceived as the message source is critical in persuasive speaking. Speakers have two kinds of credibility. *Antecedent credibility* is the reputation and character that precedes you before the speech. *Consequent credibility* is the credibility you develop during the speech that makes you more believable to your audience.

Why is the speaker's credibility so important in persuasive speaking? The answer can be seen in what the audience is asked to accept by the speaker without any immediate means (other than experience, prior knowledge, and critical thinking) for confirming or disconfirming what the speaker says.

The receivers have no immediate way of drawing upon additional resources to help them evaluate whether the speaker is in fact being fair, representative, accurate, and so forth. When receivers run out of their own expertise for judging the content of the speech, they compensate for this by making judgments about the value or quality of a speaker's arguments and appeals and by looking at the speaker and deciding whether he or she deserves some degree of credibility as the message source.

By analogy, think of the courtroom situation. Credible witnesses and defendants determine how much weight the jury places on the information. Attorneys expend considerable effort building the antecedent credibility of an "expert witness" in the case. Juries try to determine the consequent credibility of the plaintiff and the defendant by how they act and look and what they say during the trial.

Considerable research since World War II has been conducted to determine the characteristics of credible communicators or message sources. During the war, both sides wanted to know what message sources could best "sell" the messages that needed to be delivered to both friend and foe.

For our purposes, the following is a distilled list of the most recurring characteristics of speaker credibility. These are not the only factors research has discovered, but they are the ones most open to immediate use by a message source who wants some guidelines for making decisions about his or her credibility as a speaker on a given topic.

- expertness, competence, skilled experience
- trustworthiness, reliability
- honesty, sincerity, objectivity
- concern for others, responsiveness to others' needs, goodwill
- dynamic, active, enthusiastic
- friendly, attractive, well-liked

Now that you understand the characteristics of a credible speaker, you need to temper this knowledge with a single practical truth. *The speaker's credibility changes and varies from topic to topic.* What will help you be more credible as a speaker on the topic

of skin cancer may not work in persuading your audience to take responsibility for reporting incidents of animal abuse.

Credibility is essential in persuasion.

The speaker's job is to determine, given the objective of the persuasive message and the audience analysis, what aspects of speaker credibility need to be addressed to help the speaker convey the message the most effectively in that context.

Classroom speakers may feel they have little experience and expertise to build their credibility from on a given topic, but this is not true. Persuasive speakers who lack real-life contact with the topic simply make up for this by demonstrating they are familiar with other sources of expertise through their research.

The composite use of the logical, psychological, and credibility approaches to persuading others will make you a more effective agent of change in your communicative environment.

The Ethics of Persuasion

The ethics of persuasion is of considerable concern today. The power of our message hopefully will be conveyed in the brevity of our comment: **Persuade to create win-win changes, not win-loose changes.** The listener should receive benefits comparable to the speaker's if the intent of the persuasive message is acted upon. If the intent or result of the persuasive message is that the speaker receives all or most of the benefits at the expense of the listeners, then communicative ethics have not been practiced.

 ## ORGANIZING THE PERSUASIVE SPEECH

There are a variety of approaches to organizing a persuasive speech. The problem-solution design, a foreshortening of educational philosopher John Dewey's reflective process, is an organizational structure that includes: a statement of the problem with its nature, extent, and causes; a list of all plausible solutions to the problem; a weighing and evaluating of each solution; the selection of the best solution; and the recommendation of action to implement the solution selected.

The formula for successful advertising, AIDA, suggests the following organizational pattern: Attention, Interest, Desire, and Action.

Douglas Ehninger advances a "motivated sequence" that blends the logical problem-solving approach with the psychological factors of attention, need, satisfaction, visualization, and action.

All these approaches have merit and are good methods for organizing the persuasive speech; however, the approach we shall present is called the **motivating process.**

THE MOTIVATING PROCESS

In 1926, John A. McGee wrote a book entitled *Minimum Essentials of Persuasive Speaking*. This work outlined an approach he called the motivating process. It is an organizational approach for developing a presentation that leads listeners through five steps of problem-solving to motivate them to respond positively to the communicator's goal:

1. **Attention.** Attract favorable interest from listeners and direct their attention toward the main ideas in the presentation.

2. **Need.** Develop a general problem and relate it to the desires of the audience. This is accomplished through the development of the following steps:
   a. State the need.
   b. Illustrate the need.
   c. Develop the need.
   d. Relate the need.

3. **Satisfaction.** Show how the belief or action proposed solves the problem. This is accomplished through development of the following steps:
   a. State the belief or action.
   b. Explain the proposed action.
   c. Show how the action theoretically solves the problem.
   d. Give actual examples showing that the proposed action has worked elsewhere.
   e. Overcome objections that might be raised.

4. **Visualization.** Intensify desire to see the proposed action adopted or carried out. This is accomplished by describing vividly how things will be in the future if the proposal is adopted.

5. **Action.** Translate the desire created into overt behavior. This is accomplished by using specific appeals to secure the desired action.

The emotions that an orator wishes to evoke from his audience dare not be artificial. Nature has assigned special looks and tones to each emotion, and any artifice is quickly discovered. **CRASSUS**

These steps are helpful when developing a presentation designed to motivate listeners to accept and act on an idea. The technique provides a unified approach to developing a persuasive presentation.

When confronted with the necessity of making a decision, people tend to proceed through a fairly uniform sequence of responses. To solve the problem, they must first focus attention on the issues in order to reduce distractions. Second, they must feel a need to change from the current situation, to sense that something about the situation is undesirable or at least could be made better. Third, they must be convinced of the soundness, desirability, and workability of the proposal. Fourth, they must be stimulated to want to act on the recommendation. And last, they must be urged to actually move and do something about the proposal. The motivating process matches each of the steps in problem solving that leads listeners to accept the proposal.

A persuasive speech that uses the motivating process is organized in the following manner:

I. **Attention.** Remember, the attention step is designed to gain the attention of the audience and to create goodwill and respect between the presenter and the audience. This can be accomplished in several different ways, including opening the presentation with any of the following:

A. An example, illustration, or story with a point (the point should be made in a different manner in the need step).

B. A humorous anecdote that makes a point.

C. A quotation from an easily recognized personality or source that expresses a key point to be developed.

D. A striking statement involving some unusual information or unexpected way of phrasing a key point.

E. A rhetorical question that members of the audience can answer mentally and that gets them thinking about a key point of the presentation.

F. A personal greeting, a reference to the subject or occasion.

Unique and humorous tactics can get an audience's attention

II. **Need.** This can be accomplished by following the procedure for developing the need step. Include each of the following forms of support in the order suggested:
   A. A direct statement that describes an undesirable situation that could be improved or strengthened. For example, the statement might be phrased like this: "Just about everyone pays more taxes than they want to"; "Most homes have no fire-warning devices"; or "Dishonesty has resulted in losses in the millions of dollars to average citizens."
   B. An illustration that describes one or more detailed examples showing that the problem stated is actually a fact; tell, for example, about a home fire that killed several members of a family.
   C. Further development that describes additional examples, instances, statistical data, and testimonies that show how serious and widespread the problem is.
   D. A relationship that explains how the problem affects the members of the immediate audience.

III. **Satisfaction.** The objective of this step is to show how the problem can be alleviated. This can be accomplished by making:
   A. A direct statement of the action proposed to meet the need established earlier. Having established the problem that most homes have no fire-warning devices, the statement of satisfaction might be "Although we may not be able to eliminate all fires, we can save lives by providing adequate warning to family members."
   B. An explanation of the proposed action and what is involved in removing the problem by using the method suggested. This should be as clear and as complete an explanation as possible. The use of diagrams and other kinds of visuals should be considered.
   C. A theoretical demonstration that explains how the proposed action should solve the problem. Explain that according to principles involved or the way things usually happen, the proposed action should alleviate the need in this way. Demonstrate that the proposed action is a logical and adequate solution to the problem.
   D. A practical experience that provides support by giving real examples and instances in which such a proposal has solved the problem somewhere else. Add the testimony of experts, data, and the descriptions of real cases to support the proposal.
   E. An effort to forestall objections by explaining how your proposed action solves the problem. Try to answer any major

TRIBUTES

The tribute speech is used to pay tribute to a person's or group's qualities or achievements. At a funeral, a speaker was eulogizing the deceased, a person who enjoyed the reputation of being a great talker, when the congregation began to laugh. The speaker pondered what had caused the audience to laugh in the middle of a serious funeral oration. Then it dawned on him that he had mentioned how great a talker the deceased had been. Almost everyone in the congregation had had experiences with this person's ability to talk unceasingly. Although a bit embarrassed that he had caused laughter at a funeral, the speaker continued his speech. Speeches of tribute should call attention to the qualities and achievements that a person attained. These kinds of speeches need not be without humor, but they should seriously present the person's life.

A tribute should call attention to the qualities and achievements of an individual.

THE NORTHLAND INN

The Purpose

The purpose of a tribute speech is to praise someone's qualities and accomplishments. Tributes take place in a variety of diverse situations, such as funerals, birthday parties, retirements and so on. A special form of the tribute speech is called the eulogy. This is a speech of tribute that is given in memory of a deceased person.

The System

1. **Strive for sincerity.** When giving a tribute, do not overdo it. There is a tendency to say more than the person being praised deserves. When this happens, the audience often questions the sincerity of the speaker and the credibility of the person being spoken about.

2. **Collect as much detail as possible about the person being honored.** Audiences are primarily interested in information they have not heard. This is especially true when the information has to do with a person that the audience cares for. To give an effective tribute, you should collect as many specifics as possible about the person you are going to praise. Focus on laudable characteristics and be willing to mention and discuss special hardships that the person has overcome.

3. **Organize the speech around the subject's accomplishments.** If the subject is well known, you may wish to make the talk more general. If the person is not well known, then you may wish to focus on specific details. Whatever the situation, be certain to organize the speech around a series of the subject's accomplishments.

4. Explain what inspiration or lesson the listeners have gained from the subject's life.

Special Concerns

1. **No one is perfect.** Even though a person is being praised, it is occasionally effective to bring out the person's negative characteristics. As in the funeral eulogy just mentioned, where the deceased had been a ceaseless talker and the speaker mentioned this, the resulting humor will make the person seem more human.

2. **Be objective about the subject.** Tell the truth and say it with sincerity; do not overdo it. It is far better to underpraise than to overpraise.

 NOMINATIONS

Nominating speeches can be heard in small, informal club elections and in the very formal nomination of a presidential candidate. This form of speaking is very similar to the speech of introduction and of tribute. It is very likely that at one time or another, you will have the opportunity to nominate a friend for a position.

The Purpose

The main purpose of a nomination speech is to review the accomplishments of your candidate. You must also cause the audience to move to accept the nomination of your candidate and to actively support the nomination.

The System

1. **Organize as a speech to persuade.** The speech to nominate is essentially a speech to persuade, to get the audience to accept your candidate. The organization for this speech should generally follow that of the speech to persuade.

2. **Get attention.** Create interest by pointing out the problems that must be met by a good nominee.

3. **Emphasize qualities of your candidate.** Tell how he or she can meet the problems that exist with the present system or office. Go into depth about the candidate's qualities. Don't go overboard, but honestly and efficiently enumerate your candidate's qualifications.

4. **Conclude.** Formally place your candidate's name in nomination and ask for the support of the audience.

Introduce the candidate and then place the candidate's name in nomination

Special Concerns

1. **Be positive in your approach.** Do not be sarcastic or ridicule other nominees. Be positive and present your candidate in as positive a manner as you can.

2. **Use conviction and enthusiasm.** Be enthusiastic and speak with all the conviction you have. This will cause the audience to be more enthusiastic. It could have a very positive impact on your audience.

3. **Do not be too lengthy in your presentation.** As in all speaking situations, do not be too windy or take more time than is absolutely necessary to place your candidate's name in nomination.

The orator aims
to instruct, move,
and charm.
QUINTILIAN

 ## SOME GENERAL CONSIDERATIONS

When giving any of these special-occasion speeches, be certain to be brief and to the point. But you should be prepared to be very formal if the occasion calls for it. The best motto for being prepared for these kinds of speaking assignments is to stay flexible and be willing to go with the rules and customs that the situation calls for. One last word of advice is to study the people involved and try to meet their expectations.

What You Now Know

Speeches of introduction, presentation or award, acceptance, welcome, tribute, and nomination are special kinds of speaking. They may be informative, persuasive, or entertaining. They require some homework. The speaker needs to be familiar with the occasion or situation, the audience's expectations, and, in some instances, the person or persons being talked about. Because special-occasion speeches must be brief to be effective, they can be harder to develop than a more complete speech.

What to Do to Learn More

Introducing a Fellow Class Member

Choose someone in the class you do not know very well and interview him or her for the purpose of introducing him or her to the rest of the class. You may find that you will be able to incorporate into this speech ideas from more than one of the special-occaison speeches. For example, you may find ideas from the introductory, tribute, and nomination speeches usable here.

Tribute

Prepare a five-minute speech paying tribute to a person, group, or organization that you personally consider worthy. This person or group may be one of national or international reputation or may simply be someone who has had a meaningful impact on your life.

▼◢ 10
SPEAKING IN SMALL GROUPS AND CONFERENCES

▼◢ ▼◢ ◢ ◢ ◢ ◢ ◢ ◢ ◢ ◢

In business and industry, schools and universities, churches and hospitals, homes and clubs—wherever people work and socialize together—individuals participate in groups. This chapter will focus on giving you an approach to communicate effectively in these various groups. You will learn how to lead as well as to participate in a group.

Chapter Content

■ Groups Are Important in Our Lives
■ Group Discussion versus Group Presentation

■ **The Nature of Groups**
   Group Assets
   Group Size
   Group Accomplishment and Enjoyment
■ **Leading a Discussion**
   Help Prepare the Participants
   Start the Discussion
   Direct the Discussion
■ **Participating in a Discussion**
■ **Discussion Patterns**
   Information-Sharing Patterns
   Problem-Solving Patterns
■ **Large Group Meetings**
■ **Evaluating Group Discussions**
■ **What You Now Know**
■ **What to Do to Learn More**

◤◢ GROUPS ARE IMPORTANT IN OUR LIVES

As you work and participate in society you will find yourself in many situations where you are a member of a group. At your school, you may be part of a class group of five to seven people organized to investigate and report on an assigned subject. At your place of employment, you may be part of a work group that discusses work-related problems. At your home, you may be part of another group that meets frequently and discusses everything from the state of the economy to how to live together comfortably.

A group is defined as a collection of three or more individuals whose interaction is mutually satisfactory. Group satisfaction is usually derived from sharing values and building enjoyable social relations and/or cooperatively solving problems and completing various tasks. And participation in a group means *talking*—as a leader or as a group member. Either we participate as a contributor to reports or discussions or we act as a leader and attempt to organize, direct, and facilitate an effective discussion or conference. And whenever a group or organization grows, institutes new programs, unifies members, and engages in decision making, the members of the organization find themselves in conferences and group meetings of all kinds. How we interact and participate affects our own productivity and happiness, as well as the efficiency and contentment of other members of the group. And, of course, the primary vehicle for successful interaction is effective speaking and listening.

GROUP DISCUSSION VERSUS GROUP PRESENTATION

Notice that when you participate in a small group or conference, either you make an individual presentation or report, usually hoping to persuade or provide special information, or you engage in group discussion with the hope of cooperatively pooling information and arriving at solutions to problems. If you are invited to a meeting or conference to make an individual presentation, we suggest that you carefully review the chapters on informative and persuasive speaking and that you give special consideration to visual appeals and strong evidence.

Remember, there is a difference between an individual presentation to a group and ongoing participation in group discussions. Distinguishing which activity you are engaged in will help you determine the most effective speaking approach to use.

We are assuming here that you are not being invited to a group to make a once-only presentation but that, as a group leader or group member, you will be discussing ideas, questioning information, and making decisions.

Let us now examine the nature of groups and some skills necessary to leading, participating in, and evaluating group discussions. We will also consider the best patterns to use in an information-sharing or problem-solving discussion. Finally, the phenomenon of groupthink and the place of large group meetings will be discussed.

THE NATURE OF GROUPS

Group Assets

Greater Sum Total Knowledge and Information[1]
There is more information in a group than in any of its members.

---

[1]From Norman R. F. Maier, "Assets and Liabilities in Group Problem Solving: The Need for an Integrative Function," *Psychological Review* 74(1967): 239–49. Copyright 1967 by the American Psychological Association. Reprinted by permission.

Thus, problems that require the utilization of knowledge should give groups an advantage over individuals. Even if one member of the group knows much more than anyone else, the limited unique knowledge of lesser-informed individuals could serve to fill in some gaps in knowledge. For example, a skilled machinist might contribute to an engineer's problem solving, and an ordinary worker might supply information on how a new machine might be received by workers.

Greater Number of Approaches to a Problem

It has been shown that individuals get into ruts in their thinking. Many obstacles stand in the way of achieving a goal, and a solution must circumvent these. The individual is handicapped in that he or she tends to persist in an approach and thus fails to find another approach that might solve the problem in a simpler manner. Individuals in a group have the same failing, but their approaches may be different. For example, one researcher may try to prevent the spread of a disease by making humans immune to the germ, another by finding and destroying the carrier of the germ, and still another by altering the environment so as to kill the germ before it reaches us. There is no way of determining which approach will best achieve the desired goal, but undue persistence in any one will stifle new discoveries. Since group members do not have identical approaches, each can contribute by knocking others out of thinking ruts.

Participation in Problem Solving Increases Acceptance

Many problems require solutions that depend on the support of others to be effective. Insofar as group problem solving permits participation and influence, it follows that more individuals accept solutions when a group solves the problem than when one person solves it. When an individual solves a problem, he or she still has the task of persuading others. It follows, therefore, that when groups solve such problems, a greater number of persons accept and feel responsible for making the solution work. A low-quality solution that has good acceptance can be more effective than a higher-quality solution that lacks acceptance.

Better Comprehension of the Decision

Decisions made by an individual, which are to be carried out by others, must be communicated from the decision-maker to the decision-executors. Thus, individual problem solving often requires an additional stage—that of relaying the decision reached. Failure in this communication process detracts from the merits of the decision and can even cause its failure or create a problem of greater magnitude than the initial problem that was solved. Many organizational problems can be traced to inadequate communication of decisions made by superiors and transmitted to subordinates, who have the task of implementing the decisions.

The chances of communication failures are greatly reduced when the individuals who must work together in executing the decision have participated in making it. They not only understand the solution because they saw it develop, but they are also aware of the several other alternatives that were considered and the reasons they were discarded. The common assumption that decisions supplied by superiors are arbitrarily reached therefore disappears. Full knowledge of goals, obstacles, alternatives, and factual information is essential to communication, and this communication is maximized when the total problem-solving process is shared.

Group Size

When groups become too large, some members tend to talk only to the leaders. Other members lose themselves in the group and hardly talk at all. The best size for a problem-solving group seems to be five to seven people. Members of small groups usually speak frequently to one another, and interaction is quite high. Groups with fewer than five people seem to be too small, and groups that have more than seven members usually break down into smaller cliques.

Group Accomplishment and Enjoyment

All groups must work at and accomplish something. If the group is meeting to discuss a problem, members will want to get to the problem. If the group is holding a meeting, members will probably want to get to the agenda and start discussing the items. However, when many people are trying to work together, it is imperative that they feel good about their relationship to the group. In other words, members of a group must enjoy themselves, as well as accomplish work. This means that the group members must have opportunities to joke a bit, to get acquainted with each other, to relax a little, and to pay attention to each other's needs. An atmosphere of fun and trust is vital to a group's being able to enjoy working hard on various tasks. When group members accomplish large amounts of work and at the same time feel a great sense of satisfaction, personal worth, and esprit de corps, the group is successful.

Keeping a group focused on the topic is the leader's responsibility.

◤◢ LEADING A DISCUSSION

Members of a group seem to work best when they feel best. A leader can help by paying attention to the seating arrangements, the heating and lighting, and the general "feel" of the meeting room. The best interaction occurs when members sit in a circle where everyone can visually interact. However, if this is impossible, make certain that it is possible for everyone to see and hear each other comfortably. Make the best accommodation in view of the physical setting. The temperature should be neither too hot nor too cold.

The lighting should be easy on the eyes, and bright glares from sunlight should be avoided. The room's walls, floors, and ceiling should contribute to the kind of mood you desire for your particular group task.

Help Prepare the Participants

The leader is responsible for making sure that group members know ahead of time what the meeting is about. The members need time to think about the subject to be discussed, so that they can arrive at the meeting prepared to contribute ideas. Putting together an agenda or list of items that need to be accomplished, and then giving the agenda to members before the meeting can help prepare the group. In regularly scheduled meetings, the agenda for the next gathering may be partially developed during the present meeting.

Start the Discussion

When the time for the discussion arrives and the members of the group are seated, the leader should introduce any new members and then introduce the topic or objective of the meeting. You may, for example, make a few comments about the topic and its importance and then ask a question in order to start the group discussion. Questions like "What is the specific problem we are trying to solve?" "What seems to be the main cause of the difficulty?" "What is the extent of the problem?" will usually set off a lively discussion. If, however, the questions fail to produce sufficient discussion, you may call on various members to respond.

Direct the Discussion

From start to finish, it is the leader's responsibility to keep the discussion close to the subject at hand. A leader should see to it that key ideas are adequately discussed but that the discussion moves toward a solution or closure. The leader's best tools are questions that move the discussion along and clarify information. For example, if the discussion seems to be drifting away from the topic at hand, you can ask, "Can we relate this to our problem?" or "How does this tie into our last point?"

When time seems to be running out, a leader can often create closure on a matter by asking, "Now, what have we decided?"; "How should we conclude this matter?"; or "Who would like to implement that solution?"

Keep the participation balanced among the members. If someone talks too much, interject by saying, "Yes, we understand your point," and then call on someone who has been rather quiet. Ask participants to keep their contributions brief and to the point so that everyone has time to say something on the topic. Meetings usually gather momentum and become more efficient when individual contributions are brief.

An effective group leader keeps the discussion moving.

If the discussion gets heated, call on more neutral members to contribute ideas, suggest a short break, or get the focus back on information, rather than feelings. For example, ask about the reasoning and evidence on which the disagreement is based. Most conflict can be reduced by retracing the steps leading to the interpretation of the facts. Urge a quick resolution of the disputed point or

delay its consideration until a later time. Be aware, though, that constructive conflict and competition in a group can be good.

Be careful of time limits. You must keep things moving so that group members feel like they are making progress. And you must bring the discussion to a successful ending. Be conscious of obtaining closure or solving a problem. Try to encourage the group to make a decision, delegate an action, or arrive at a conclusion. Nothing is more discouraging than to discuss in circles, lose sight of the subject, and run out of time before reaching a mutually satisfying resolution of a matter.

 ## PARTICIPATING IN A DISCUSSION

In any discussion, the participants must conscientiously prepare and contribute if the discussion is going to have real value. In fact, the more participants are involved, the less the leader has to lead. The best group member is usually one who tries to accomplish the same tasks in the discussion as the leader. A successful group member will:

1. Be aware of the feelings of other group members.

2. Talk briefly and to the point.

3. Help in solving conflicts by focusing on facts.

4. Work toward completing group tasks or agenda items.

5. And, perhaps most important, whenever possible, come to a group discussion with good information and a positive attitude, willing to listen to all ideas and then decide.

 ## DISCUSSION PATTERNS

As you may know, discussion groups most often share information or make decisions. When a family sitting around the supper table talks about new automobile models, for example, it is having a learning, enlightening, information-sharing discussion. If, on the other hand, a group of students meet to decide how to reduce cheating in the classroom, they are having a problem-solving discussion.

Typical Information-Sharing Groups	**Problem-Solving and Decision-Making Groups**
Library study groups	Legislative committees
Hobby workshops	Executive board meetings
Scientific roundtables	Governors' conferences
Professional conferences	Neighborhood action
Convention interest groups	committees
Sales briefing meetings	Employee grievance
Management training groups	committees
Family socials	City councils
	Work supervisors' meetings
	Family help sessions

In most cases, discussion will proceed more efficiently if it follows a specific pattern of organization. The idea is to reduce aimless conversation and yet not force everyone into idea slavery.

Information-Sharing Patterns

For typical information-sharing discussions, patterns used to organize the body of an informative speech can also be helpful for guiding a group discussion.

Time Pattern

Past, present, future.
A group studying hypnosis, for example, might raise the following questions to stimulate and guide the discussion:

1. How, when, and where did hypnosis have its beginning?

2. What are the present uses of hypnosis?

3. What future development can we anticipate?

Spatial Pattern

North, south, east, west.
A group trying to share information on the current state of employment could raise such questions as:

1. What jobs are available in northern states?

2. What kind of employment is needed in the southern states?

3. What kinds of jobs are most advertised in the eastern states?

4. What kind of employment is needed in the western states?

Topical Pattern

Questions drawn from the way a subject is naturally divided. Students trying to become more informed about a university might ask:

1. What are the qualifications of the administrators?

2. What are the characteristics of the faculty?

3. What are the characteristics of the students?

4. What are the strengths and weaknesses of the curriculum?

Or if a camera club was trying to better understand a Polaroid Land camera, it might discuss such questions as:

1. What are the special design features of the Polaroid?

2. How is the picture taken?

3. How does the film develop?

Other information-sharing patterns are cause-effect patterns, advantages-versus-disadvantages patterns, or the problem-solution pattern—how a problem *was* solved in the past.

Problem-Solving Patterns

For problem-solving and decision-making discussions, the most popular patterns used for stimulating and giving direction to a group was popularized in the early 1900s by philosopher and educator John Dewey. Our version of Dewey's approach consists of five steps:

1. Examine the problem or difficulty. Consider the extent and causes of the difficulty. Ask what is happening and why. What is the major concern?

2. Define the problem. Try to frame a *specific* statement of the problem. Avoid generalities. Distinguish between symptoms and causes of the problem. Examples of problems of fact, value and policy and: *fact*—How many students were caught stealing in the bookstore last semester?; *value*—What was the best sports car produced last year?; and *policy*—Should students be punished for dormitory pranks that destroy property?

3. Request all possible solutions to the problem. This is a good place to use brainstorming techniques. Don't try to generate ideas and judge them at the same time.

Brainstorming for many solutions is a good way to solve problems.

4. Select the best solution or combination of solutions. Here is where you can develop criteria for picking the best solution (for example, money, time, and so on), or you can simply make intuitive judgments.

5. Implement the solution. Decide on a course of action, start the action, and plan to evaluate the results. Deciding who is going to do what and when is one way to get started.

Sometimes groups get too cozy. Group loyalty and cohesion are so great that critical thinking is smothered. This leads to a condition called groupthink, elucidated in 1972 by Janis. Read the following article and notice the precautions that are recommended to avoid groupthink and restore quality decision making.

Speaking Excellence

Groupthink

Irving L. Janis

Irving L. Janis, professor of psychology at Yale, teaches courses in attitude change, decision-making, leadership and small-group behavior.

The idea of "groupthink" occurred to me while reading Arthur M. Schlesinger's chapters on the Bay of Pigs in *A Thousand Days*. At first I was puzzled: How could bright men like John F. Kennedy and his advisers be taken in by such a stupid, patchwork plan as the one presented to them by the CIA representatives? I began wondering if some psychological contagion might have interfered with their mental alertness.

I kept thinking about this notion until one day I found myself talking about it in a seminar I was conducting at Yale on the psychology of small groups. I suggested that the poor decision-making performance of those high officials might be akin to the lapses in judgment of ordinary citizens who become more concerned with retaining the approval of the fellow members of their work group than with coming up with good solutions to the tasks at hand.

When I reread Schlesinger's account I was struck by many further observations that fit into exactly the pattern of concurrence-seeking that has impressed me in my research on other face-to-face groups when a "we" feeling of solidarity is running high. I concluded that a group process was subtly at work in Kennedy's team which prevented the members from debating the real issues posed by the CIA's plan and from carefully appraising the serious risks.

By now I was sufficiently fascinated by what I called the "groupthink" hypothesis to start looking into similar historic fiascoes. I selected for intensive analysis three that were made during the administrations of three other American presidents: Fanklin D. Roosevelt (failure to be prepared for Pearl Harbor), Harry S. Truman (the invasion of North Korea) and Lyndon B. Johnson (escalation of the Vietnam war). Each decision was a group product, issuing from a series of meetings held by a small and cohesive group of government officials and advisers. In each case I found the same kind of detrimental group process that was at work in the Bay of Pigs decision. In my earlier research with ordinary citizens I had been impressed by the effects—both unfavorable and favorable—of the social pressures that develop in cohesive groups: in infantry platoons, air crews, therapy groups, seminars and self-study or encounter groups. Members tend to evolve informal objectives to preserve friendly intra-group relations, and this becomes part of the hidden agenda at their meetings. . . .

The term "groupthink" is of the same order as the words in the "newspeak" vocabulary that George Orwell uses in *1984*—a vocabulary with terms such as "doublethink" and "crimethink." By putting "groupthink" with those Orwellian words, I realize that it takes on an invidious connotation. This is international: groupthink refers to a deterioration of mental efficiency, reality testing and moral judgment that results from in-group pressures.

When I investigated the Bay of Pigs invasion and other fiascoes, I found that there were at least six major defects in decision-making which contributed to failures to solve problems adequately.

First, the group's discussions were limited to a few alternatives (often only two) without a survey of the full range of alternatives.

Second, the members failed to reexamine their initial decision from the standpoint of nonobvious drawbacks that had not been originally considered. Third, they neglected courses of action initially evaluated as unsatisfactory; they almost never discussed whether they had overlooked any nonobvious gains.

Fourth, members made little or no attempt to obtain information from experts who could supply sound estimates of losses and gains to be expected from alternative courses. Fifth, selective bias was shown in the way the members reacted to information and judgments from experts, the media and outside critics; they were only interested in facts and opinions that supported their preferred policy. Finally, they spent little time deliberating how the policy might be hindered by bureaucratic inertia, sabotaged by political opponents or derailed by the accidents that happen to the best of well-laid plans. Consequently, they failed to work out contingency plans to cope with foreseeable setbacks that could endanger their success.

I was surprised by the extent to which the group involved in these fiascoes adhered to group norms and pressures toward uniformity, even when their policy was working badly and had unintended consequences that disturbed the conscience of the members. Members consider loyalty to the group the highest form of morality. That loyalty requires each member to avoid raising controversial issues, questioning weak arguments or calling a halt to soft-headed thinking.

Paradoxically, soft-headed groups are likely to be extremely hard-hearted toward out-groups and enemies. In dealing with a rival nation, policy-makers constituting an amiable group find it relatively easy to authorize dehumanizing solutions such as large-scale bombings. An affable group of government officials is unlikely to pursue the difficult issues that arise when alternatives to a harsh military solution come up for discussion. . . .

The leader of a policy-forming group should, for example, assign the role of critical evaluator to each member, encouraging the group to give high priority to airing objections and doubts. He should also be impartial at the outset, instead of stating his own preferences and expectations. He should limit his briefings to unbiased statements about the scope of the problem and the limitations of available resources.

The organization should routinely establish several independent planning and evaluation groups to work on the same policy question, each carrying out its deliberations under a different leader.

One or more qualified colleagues within the organization that are not core members of the policy-making group should be invited to each meeting and encouraged to challenge the views of the core members.

At every meeting, at least one member should be assigned the role of devil's advocate, to function like a good lawyer in challenging the testimony of those who advocate the majority position.

Whenever the policy issue involves relations with a rival nation, a sizable block of time should be spent surveying all warning signals from the rivals and constructing alternative scenarios.

After reaching a preliminary consensus the policy-making group should hold a "second chance" meeting at which all the members are expected to express their residual doubts and to rethink the entire issue. They might take as their model a statement made by Alfred P. Sloan, a former chairman of General Motors, at a meeting of policymakers:

"Gentlemen, I take it we are all in complete agreement on the decision here. Then I propose we postpone further discussion until our next meeting to give ourselves time to develop disagreement and perhaps gain some understanding of what the decision is all about."

It might not be a bad idea for the second-chance meeting to take place in a relaxed atmosphere far from the executive suite, perhaps over drinks. According to a report by Herodotus dating from about 450 B.C., whenever the ancient Persians made a decision following sober deliberations, they would always reconsider the matter under the influence of wine. Tacitus claimed that during Roman times the Germans also had a custom of arriving at each decision twice—once sober, once drunk.

Some institutionalized form of allowing second thoughts to be freely expressed might be remarkably effective for breaking down a false sense of unanimity and related illusions, without endangering anyone's reputation or liver.

LARGE GROUP MEETINGS

The major emphasis in this chapter has been on small group meetings and discussions. There is, however, a place for large group
meetings. In settings where it is necessary to convey information
and receive reactions from several hundred people, a large group
meeting seems to bridge the gap between group discussion and public speaking. The Boeing Aerospace Company's success with this
type of audience participation is described in the following article.
Perhaps Boeing has the answer to the perplexing problem of keeping
massive numbers of people happy and informed through large
meetings.

Speaking Excellence

There's a Place for Large Group Meetings

James R. Douglas
James R. Douglas, ABC,
is internal communication director
for Boeing Aerospace Company
Seattle, Washington

Face-to-face communication—No. 1 on the totem pole of effective communication techniques—often is dismissed as impracti-
cal, time-consuming and too costly when trying to reach large
numbers of people.

Before you reject face-to-face communications on these
grounds, first explore all the possibilities. Boeing Aerospace did,
and one division is giving it a lot of lip-service—literally—in group
employee meetings.

Abraham M. S. Goo, vice-president and manager of the
Boeing Aerospace Company's B-1 Avionics Integration program,

believes in keeping his people informed. And feedback from most of Goo's 800 people indicates his periodic all-employee group meetings are contributing to the program's success and to their performance as individual employees.

Following a recent series of meetings, Boeing Aerospace's internal communication staff conducted a survey of Goo's employees, seeking their evaluation of this type of communication. With an 81 percent response to a questionnaire, 76 percent of the employees said the briefings are definitely contributing to the programs success, 19 percent didn't know if they were contributing and 5 percent said no. When asked if the meetings helped them do a better job, 72 percent said yes, 23 percent didn't know and 5 percent said no.

The meetings, which run 45 to 75 minutes, are given in three sections with 200 to 300 people at each. Meeting in a theater in the Boeing complex, employees may see a movie on the program, charts which relate progress and problems and similar business-oriented material. Goo tells them what's happening in their division, talks about the future, and encourages them to ask questions.

After each meeting, employees are asked to comment on the session. At the next meeting—if not before—Goo responds to any questions asked during the previous get-together. Most of the people in the B-1 Avionics program have commented, "This is the first time a program manager took the time to talk to us."

Meetings are run during working hours on the one-shift program. The three sections are offered on the same day, at about 9 A.M., 10:30 A.M. and 1:30 P.M.

The majority of employees in the Boeing B-1 Avionics program are professionally oriented, with only a small number of production workers. Engineers, business administrative people and supervisors overwhelmingly supported the meetings, with up to 93 percent giving an affirmative answer to the above questions. Clerical employees and production employees were less definite in their support, with "don't know" responses running up to 33 percent.

In open-end questions seeking answers as to how the meetings helped the program, the majority of professional employees stressed the "cooperation promoted between functions" and a

"coordinated effort to meet targets." As for individual performance, the majority of these employees commented on having
"greater incentive to help the program" and a "better understanding of how their jobs tie into the program."

Most clerical and production employees stressed "teamwork"
and "morale."

Management credibility for these meetings rated almost as
pure as Ivory soap. In marking any one of six positive or six negative words regarding credibility, 98.4 percent selected words
such as honest, straightforward, sincere. The remaining 1.6 percent selected words such as evasive or incomplete. No one
chose dishonest, half-truths or lies.

In "open-end" questions asking for pertinent remarks about an
employee's job, the program or the company, high praise was
given to top management and the team spirit management had
developed. Professional employees asked for more detailed information about the business plan and long-range goals. Clerical
and hourly employees asked that the charts used in the briefings
be simplified.

Abe Goo has been conducting all-employee briefings for his
people since taking over management of the B-1 Avionics program three years ago, holding meetings at least on a semiannual
basis. He discusses program performance, cost and schedule
and problem areas needing special attention.

A comment on the success of the Boeing B-1 Avionics Integration program comes from the customers, who evidently think
Goo and his people are on the right track. This is the only Air
Force program ever to receive a 100 percent incentive award fee
for its performance. And like a bowler rolling consecutive perfect
games, Goo and his team have received back-to-back 100 percent incentive award fees.

SOURCE: Reprinted with permission of International Association of Business
Communication's *Journal of Organizational Communication,* Vol. 6, 1976, p.
21–23. James R. Douglas.

◤◢ **EVALUATING GROUP DISCUSSIONS**

Though you may not be called on to professionally evaluate a group discussion, we would like you to notice the following methods of analysis in order to further emphasize and clarify the principles of small group discussion contained in this chapter. If you do have an opportunity to evaluate your discussion group or your own leadership skills, then these tools of analysis should prove beneficial in giving you an opportunity to see whether everything is going well.

Many tools have been developed for evaluating groups, individual participants, and leaders. The forms presented here[2] might even assist you in evaluating classroom group discussions. The first rating scale is for leadership evaluation. The group members as well as the leader can fill it out. The other questionnaires give the participants an opportunity to explain how they felt about the discussion they just completed.

Large group meetings can create effective communication situations.

[2]From John K. Brilhart, *Effective Group Discussion*, 6th ed. (Dubuque, Iowa: Wm. C. Brown Company, 1988).

Leader Rating Scale

Date _____ Leader _____

Time _____ Observer _____

Instructions: Rate the leader on all items which are applicable; draw a line through all items which do not apply. Use the following scale to rate his or her overall performance as a group leader:

     5—superior
     4—above average
     3—average
     2—below average
     1—poor

Leadership Style and Personal Characteristics

To what degree:

_____ Was the leader poised, calm, and self-controlled?

_____ Could the leader be heard and understood easily?

_____ Did the leader show enthusiasm and interest in the group problem?

_____ Did the leader listen well to other participants?

_____ Did the leader show personal warmth and a sense of humor?

_____ Was the leader objective and open-minded to all sides?

_____ Was the leader resourceful and flexible in handling suggestions from members?

_____ Did the leader create a permissive atmosphere?

_____ Did the leader make it easy for all members to share in functional leadership?

_____ To what degree was the leader democratic and group oriented?

continued

Preparation

To what degree:

_____ Were all physical arrangements cared for?

_____ Was the leader's preparation and grasp of the problem thorough?

_____ Were questions prepared to guide the discussion?

_____ Were members notified and given adequate guidance for preparing?

Procedural and Interpersonal Leadership Techniques

To what degree:

_____ Were members introduced and put at ease?

_____ Did the leader introduce the problem and supply necessary background?

_____ Did the leader guide the group to a thorough investigation and understanding of the problem?

_____ Did the leader suggest a suitable organization or pattern for group thinking?

_____ Were members encouraged to modify the leader's plan or agenda?

_____ Did the leader state questions clearly?

_____ Did the leader rebound questions to the group (especially requests for his or her opinion)?

_____ Did the leader make appropriate attempts to clarify communication?

_____ Did the leader keep the discussion on one point at a time, encouraging the group to complete an issue before going to another?

_____ Did the leader provide summaries needed to remind, clarify, and move the group forward?

_____ Was the group encouraged to evaluate critically all evidence and ideas?

_____ Were reticent members encouraged to speak without being coerced to do so?

_____ Did the leader stimulate imagination and creative thinking?

_____ Were aggressive members controlled with skill and tact?

_____ Were misunderstandings, conflicts, and arguments handled promptly and effectively?

_____ Did the leader determine group consensus before moving to each new phase of the discussion?

_____ Were important information, ideas, and agreements recorded accurately?

_____ Were plans made for follow-up and future meetings?

Analyzing its effectiveness can improve a group's performance.

Reaction Questionnaire

Instruction: Circle the number which best indicates your reactions to the following questions about the discussion in which you participated:

1. **Adequacy of communication:** To what extent do you feel members were understanding each others' statements and positions?

0   1   2   3   4   5   6   7   8   9   10

Much talking past each   Communicated directly with
other, misunderstanding   each other, understanding well

2. **Opportunity to speak:** To what extent did you feel free to speak?

0   1   2   3   4   5   6   7   8   9   10

Never had a   All the opportunity to
chance to speak   talk I wanted

3. **Climate of acceptance:** How well did members support each other, show acceptance of individuals:

0   1   2   3   4   5   6   7   8   9   10

Highly critical   Supportive and
and punishing   receptive

4. **Interpersonal relations:** How pleasant and concerned were interpersonal relations?

0   1   2   3   4   5   6   7   8   9   10

Quarrelsome, status   Pleasant, empathic,
differences emphasized   concerned with persons

continued

5. **Leadership:**   How adequate was the leader (or leadership) of the group?

0	1	2	3	4	5	6	7	8	9	10

To weak ( ) or
dominating ( )

Shared, group-centered
and sufficient

6. **Satisfaction with role:**   How satisfied are you with your personal participation in the discussion?

0	1	2	3	4	5	6	7	8	9	10

Very dissatisfied

Very satisfied

7. **Quality of product:**   How satisfied are you with the decisions, solutions, or learnings that came out of this discussion?

0	1	2	3	4	5	6	7	8	9	10

Very displeased

Very satisfied

8. **Overall:**   How do you rate the discussion as a whole apart from any specific aspect of it?

0	1	2	3	4	5	6	7	8	9	10

Awful, waste of time

Superb, time well spent

What You Now Know

This chapter deals with communicating (speaking and listening) in groups. To be productive, group members need to enjoy each other as well as to accomplish tasks. Leaders take direct responsibility for finding a meeting place, preparing participants, starting the discussion, and achieving satisfactory conclusions. Members come to a group discussion with information to contribute and in a mood of inquiry rather than with rigid opinions. By following a meeting agenda and either information-sharing or problem-solving discussion patterns, discussion will proceed efficiently. Checklists for evaluating leader and participant behaviors in groups are used to locate specific strengths and weaknesses so that group discussion and efficiency can be improved. Groupthink and the large group meeting are areas in which discussion could become less effective, depending on whether you plan for quality decision making.

What to Do to Learn More

Observation
Use the leader and group analysis rating scales in this chapter to evaluate the functioning of group meetings at school and in the community, such as in the student government, the history club, the city council, and a faculty or staff meeting.

Your Speech-Communication Course
Reflect back over the functioning of your class as a group. What parts of this chapter apply directly to the classroom? Examine socialization, cliques, group climate, leadership, and so on. In what ways does your class not fit the description of a functioning group? In what ways does it fit the description?

Life-Related Problem Solving
The next time you, your social group, your work group, or your family face the typical problem-solving situation of how, when, and where to get money for the next school term, how to change the work schedule so it is fair to everyone, or how to choose a vacation plan the whole family will like, try using the five-step problem-solving approach (or a modification of it).

Have You Got a Problem?

To what degree is your chosen major going to provide you with the knowledge and skills to solve your present and future life- and work-related problems?

11
LISTENING EFFECTIVELY

Being able to hear and retain the information that is presented to you by a speaker is an important step toward becoming an effective speaker. It is also extremely important to be able to listen effectively when you are asked questions during and following your speech. In this chapter, you will learn some important skills for listening and retaining what you hear.

Chapter Content

285

**Listening is a
learned ability
that takes
concentration.**

◤◣ DEVELOPING THE ABILITY TO LISTEN EFFECTIVELY

How Effective Are You as a Listener?

Becoming an effective listener is an important step to becoming an effective speaker. You have to develop the ability to listen accurately and understand another person's speech. *It is difficult to speak with any more skill than your listening has allowed you to experience.* Dr. Lyman K. Steil, one of the foremost authorities on listening, along with co-workers developed the tests that follow on

page 287–289 to help people rate themselves as listeners. Complete
the tests and see how you compare to others as a listener.

A Personal Listening Profile

Here are three tests in which we'll ask you to rate yourself as a listener. There are no correct or incorrect answers. Your responses,
however, will extend your understanding of yourself as a listener and
highlight areas in which improvement might be welcome . . . to you
and to those around you. When you've completed the tests, please
turn to pages 289–290 to see how your scores compare with those of
thousands of others who've taken the same tests before you.

Quiz 1

A. Circle the term that best describes you as a listener.

Superior   Excellent   Above Average   Average

Below Average   Poor   Terrible

B. On a scale of 0–100 (100 = highest), how would you rate yourself
as a listener?

_____
(0–100)

Quiz 2

How do you think the following people would rate you as a listener?

Your Best Friend   _____

Your Boss   _____

A Business Colleague   _____

A Job Subordinate   _____

Your Spouse   _____

NOTE: This Listening Profile (on pages 287–289) was prepared by Dr.Lyman
K. Steil and appears in a Sperry pamphlet entitled "Your Personal Listening
Profile." Sperry Corporation, © 1980.

Quiz 3

As a listener, how often do you find yourself engaging in these ten bad listening habits? First, check the appropriate columns. Then tabulate your score using the key below.

Listening Habit	Almost Always	Usually	Some-times	Seldom	Almost Never	Score
1. Calling the subject uninteresting	_____	_____	_____	_____	_____	_____
2. Criticizing the speaker's delivery or mannerisms	_____	_____	_____	_____	_____	_____
3. Getting overstimulated by something the speaker says	_____	_____	_____	_____	_____	_____
4. Listening primarily for facts	_____	_____	_____	_____	_____	_____
5. Trying to outline everything	_____	_____	_____	_____	_____	_____
6. Faking attention to the speaker	_____	_____	_____	_____	_____	_____
7. Allowing interfering distractions	_____	_____	_____	_____	_____	_____
8. Avoiding difficult material	_____	_____	_____	_____	_____	_____
9. Letting emotion-laden words arouse personal antagonism	_____	_____	_____	_____	_____	_____

10. Wasting the
    advantage of
    thought speed
    (daydreaming)   _____ _____ _____ _____ _____ _____

                                          Total Score _____

KEY

For every "Almost Always" checked, give yourself a score of 2
For every "Usually" checked, give yourself a score of 4
For every "Sometimes" checked, give yourself a score of 6
For every "Seldom" checked, give yourself a score of 8
For every "Almost Never" checked, give yourself a score of 10

Profile Analysis

This is how other people have responded to the same questions
that you've just answered.

Quiz 1

A. 85 percent of all listeners questioned rated themselves as
   Average or less. Fewer than 5 percent rate themselves as
   Superior or *Excellent.*
B. On the 0–100 scale, the extreme range is 10—90; the general
   range is 35–85; and the *average* rating is 55.

Quiz 2

When comparing the listening self-ratings and projected ratings
of others, most respondents believe that their best friend would
rate them highest as a listener. And that rating would be higher

than the one they gave themselves in Quiz #1 where the average was 55.

How come? We can only guess that best friend status is such an intimate, special kind of relationship that you can't imagine it ever happening unless you *were* a good listener. If you weren't, you and he or she wouldn't be best friends to begin with.

Going down the list, people who take this test usually think their bosses would rate them higher than they rated themselves. Now part of that is probably wishful thinking. And part of it is true. We *do* tend to listen to our bosses better . . . whether it's out of respect or fear or whatever doesn't matter.

The grades for colleague and job subordinate work out to be just about the same as the listener rated himself . . . that 55 figure again.

But when you get to spouse . . . husband or wife . . . something really dramatic happens. The score here is significantly lower than the 55 average that previous profile takers gave themselves. And what's interesting is that the figure goes steadily downhill. While newlyweds tend to rate their spouse at the same high level as their best friend, as the marriage goes on . . . and on . . . the rating falls. So in a household where the couple has been married 50 years, there could be a lot of talk. But maybe nobody is *really* listening.

Quiz 3

The average score is a 62 . . . 7 points higher than the 55 that the average test taker gave himself or herself in Quiz #1. This suggests that when listening is broken down into specific areas of competence, we rate ourselves better than we do when listening is considered only as a generality.

Of course, the best way to discover how well you listen is to ask the people to whom you listen most frequently. Your spouse, boss, best friend, and so on. They'll give you an earful.

We hope you now have a better understanding of yourself as a listener. You should better comprehend the importance of effective listening. This chapter will offer some aids for being more effective.

LISTENING AND RETAINING

In an interview with *U.S. News and World Report,* Lyman K. Steil makes the following points about listening for retention:

1. Because of the listening mistakes of workers (and most make several mistakes each week), letters have to be retyped, appointments rescheduled, and shipments rerouted. Productivity and profits decline.
2. A simple ten-dollar mistake by each of the 100 million workers in the United States would add up to a cost of $1 billion.
3. "Good" or effective listening is more than merely "hearing." Effective listening involves
   a. hearing;
   b. interpreting (which leads to understanding or misunderstanding);
   c. evaluating (weighing the information and deciding how to use it); and
   d. responding (based on what we heard, understood, and evaluated).
4. When all four stages (hearing, interpreting, evaluating, and responding) are considered, people on average listen at an effective rate of 25 percent.
5. The ability to listen is not an inherent trait; it is learned behavior that has to be taught. Unlike reading, writing, speaking, and many other subjects, however, it is not systematically taught in our schools.
6. People have not been taught to listen well. We spend 80 percent of our waking hours communicating and 45 percent of our communication time listening (with speaking, reading, and writing taking up the other 55 percent). Ironically, our schools devote the greatest amount of time to teaching what we do least: writing. The least amount of teaching time is devoted to what we do most: listening.
7. Listening is more complex than reading. If we misread something or are distracted, we can go back and read it again. But listening is transient: "The message is written on the wind. If we don't get it the first time, there usually is no going back."
8. According to a recent study, managers rate listening as the most important competency among the abilities they considered critical for their managerial success. "The higher one advances in

management, the more critical listening ability and skill become." Most problems in business arise because management
fails to listen.

9. Most people recognize the lack of listening skills in others, but
   consider themselves good listeners. Listening exercises usually
   demonstrate that people are not as good at listening as they
   thought they were.

Suggestions for Becoming an Effective Listener

After reviewing a variety of textbooks that deal with listening and
after analyzing the listening process in speaking situations, we have
determined that there are at least ten helps that will enhance your
ability to listen to speeches. Keep in mind that these suggestions
are not sequential and that our order of presentation is random;
however, each one can work to your benefit in a listening situation.

1. **Tune out distractions.** This aid stresses the importance of concentration. Force yourself to pay attention and keep your mind on
   what is being said.

2. **Get what you can get.** Be an opportunist. Do your best to find
   areas of interest between you and the speaker. Ask yourself,
   "What's in this for me? What can I get out of what is being said?"
   Try hard to get a message from each speaker. A good listener will
   always get a message from a speaker.

3. **Don't daydream.** Stay alert. Force yourself to stay alert, even if
   the speaker is slow and boring. If your thoughts run ahead of the
   speaker, don't daydream; instead, anticipate and review what is
   being said.

4. **Identify and understand the speaker's purpose.** What is the
   speaker trying to do? Is the speaker informing, persuading, or entertaining? Whatever the speaker's purpose, identify it and adjust
   to it. Try your best to understand the purpose of the speech.

5. **Report the content of a speech to someone else.** This forces
   you to listen, concentrate, and remember. If you know you must
   report the contents of what you hear, you are more likely to pay
   attention. It is simply a good practice technique.

THE WIZARD OF ID

6. **Become a good note taker.** There are many approaches to note taking. Whichever approach you use, the simple process of writing key points down as you hear them aids in your retaining what you hear, even if you do not read the notes later.

7. **Don't blame the speaker.** As a listener, take primary responsibility for the success of two-way communication. Don't blame the other person for your listening inadequacies. Listening is your responsibility, not the speaker's.

8. Use spare listening time effectively. Research has taught us that we can listen much faster than a speaker can speak. This causes us to be lazy. We find ourselves doodling on a piece of paper, thinking about our evening date, or what to do to pass the course. We can participate in all these activities and many more and still listen to a speaker. However, the danger to effective listening is that when we tune out for any purpose, we might not tune back in. Use the extra time to review and think about the speech.

9. Don't become emotional. There is a tendency to get too involved with a speech that we like or dislike to the extent that we get aroused and miss what is really being said. A good listener remains analytical and does not get caught up in the emotions of the speech.

10. Don't let the speaker's personality and appearance get in your way. Too often we are turned off by the appearance of speakers. Their hair is either too short or too long, their clothes are either too conventional or too unconventional, their makeup is either too heavy or too light, and so on. Don't get caught up in evaluating the speaker's looks and personality and not listening to what the speaker has to say.

These ten aids can be very helpful in your quest to be a better listener. In summary, if you wish to be a good listener, your primary effort must be to *understand* rather than agree, disagree, judge, argue, and so forth. This does not mean that you should not have personal reactions to the speaker and the speech. It does mean that these personal reactions are controlled by you to allow for effective listening.

TEN KEYS TO EFFECTIVE LISTENING

Lyman K. Steil lists these ten keys as a positive guideline to better listening. In fact, they're at the heart of developing better listening habits that could last a lifetime.

Ten Keys to Effective Listening	The Bad Listener	The Good Listener
1. Find areas of interest	Tunes out dry subjects	Is an opportunist, asks, "What's in it for me?"
2. Judge content, not delivery	Tunes out if delivery is poor	Judges content, skips over delivery errors
3. Hold your fire	Tends to enter into argument	Doesn't judge until comprehension is complete
4. Listen for ideas	Listens for facts	Listens for central themes
5. Be flexible	Takes intensive notes using only one system	Takes fewer notes. Uses 4–5 different systems, depending on speaker
6. Work at listening	Shows no energy output Fakes attention	Works hard, exhibits active body state
7. Resist distractions	Is easily distracted	Fights or avoids distractions, tolerates bad habits, knows how to concentrate
8. Exercise your mind	Resists difficult expository material; seeks light, recreational material	Uses heavier material as exercise for the mind
9. Keep your mind open	Reacts to emotional words	Interprets color words; does not get hung up on them
10. Capitalize on the fact that *thought* is faster than *speech*	Tends to daydream with slow speakers	Challenges, anticipates, mentally summarizes, weighs the evidence, listens between the lines to tone of voice

**A good speaker
and a good lis-
tener lead to
shared
communication.**

What You Now Know

You now know how well you listen. It is important that you learn
to be a more effective listener. If you have discovered that you are
a pretty good listener, don't assume that you can't improve. If you
have discovered that you are ineffective or maybe even average, you
obviously need help. Practice the skills that have been presented in
the chapter to help you become more effective.

Lyman K. Steil presented some of the pitfalls of ineffective listening. Be aware of the difficulties that confront you as you try to
be a more effective listener. We have given you a list of ten simple
skills that are easier to discuss than to use; however, we recommend that you do your best to try them and to learn them so that
you will become a more effective listener.

Ric Masten summarizes the need for more effective listening in
the following short poem:

i have just
wandered back
into our conversation
and find
that you
are still
rattling on
about something
or other
i think i must
have been gone
at least
twenty minutes
and you
never missed me
now
this might say
something
about my
acting ability
or it might say
something about
your sensitivity

one thing
troubles me tho
when it
is my turn
to rattle on
for twenty minutes
which i
have been known to do
have you
been missing to?

It is our hope that we may at all times be present in our conversations with others and in public speaking situations. Practice the skills of effective listening, and you will never be missing in listening circumstances.

What to Do to Learn More

1. Effective Listening

Test your listening skills. Select the one best answer among the three given, even though you may feel that all answers may be correct to some degree. See page XX for comments.

1. A person is a good listener only if he/she
   a. Does not think while the other person is talking
   b. Hears everything the other person has to say
   c. Seeks information as listens about his/her own and the other person's assumptions, viewpoints, and feelings

2. To get a clear picture of the other person as we listen
   a. We have to "tune in" on some things that are never actually voiced
   b. We must concentrate on everything she/he says
   c. We must clear our minds of any prejudices or evaluations we may have made in advance

3. The biggest block to interpersonal communications is
   a. One's inability to listen intelligently, understandingly, and skillfully to another person

    b. One's inability to be logical, lucid, and clear in what
      one says
    c. The fact that any statement may have several meanings

4. It is necessary for everyone who must deal with other people
   on important matters to know how to listen with
   understanding because.
    a. In a crucial conversation, false ideas of other people can
      lead to misunderstanding and disagreement
    b. There will be less argument
    c. People usually try to conceal their real feelings

5. You can determine whether you have communicated with the
   other person by
    a. Asking him/her questions
    b. Watching her/his facial expressions
    c. Knowing whether he/she should be interested in what you
      are talking about

6. When we talk to another person, we can assume
    a. That the other person is listening to what we say
    b. That what is important to us may not be important to
      her/him
    c. That he/she knows and shares our unspoken feelings

7. Three factors enter into our daily person-to-person listening.
   Which is most important?
    a. Assumptions
    b. Viewpoints
    c. Feelings

SOURCE: Reprinted from *American Business*. © Geyer-McAllister Publications. Permission to reprint granted by Elliott Service Company, Mount Vernon, New York.

"Effective Listening" Comments

Compare your responses with the following comments about each
question

1. It is not enough to be just a blotter or photographic negative
   that soaks up everything that is said. Good listening requires
   active participation on the part of the listener. The correct
   answer is *c*.

2. It is not enough to concentrate on everything that is said; we
   have to be actively thinking as we listen. It is actually
   impossible to cleanse our minds of our prejudices and

evaluations, but it helps to "know thyself." The correct answer is *a*.

3. No matter how logical, lucid, or clear the transmitter is, unless the receiver is "tuned in," there can be no communication. The fact that one statement may have several meanings complicates the process of interpersonal communication, but good listening habits can overcome this obstacle. The correct answer is *a*.

4. [Answer] *b* is wrong because elimination of arguments in itself does not mean good communication. [Answer] *c* is also wrong because the purpose of listening with understanding is not just to get at hidden feelings, but to be able to communicate with others. The correct answer is *a*.

5. Many times facial expressions can be very deceiving. Just because a person appears interested in a subject does not mean he/she actually understands. The correct answer is *a*.

6. People often think of something else when someone else is speaking, and these unspoken feelings vary with each individual. It is safest to assume that the other person probably has a different set of values from your own. The correct answer is *b*.

7. Feelings are deeply imbedded in people and are not subject to logical argument. Viewpoints and assumptions are more easily changed by new facts and perspectives. The correct answer is *c*.

SOURCE: Reprinted from *American Business.* © Geyer-McAllister Publications. Permission to reprint granted by Elliott Service Company, Mount Vernon, New York.

2. Getting the Point

This is an exercise to help you listen to and understand the main points that a speaker is trying to make. It will also help you determine if you listen for and get the same information as other listeners.

1. Go with a friend to a public speech. It can be a forum on campus, a teacher's lecture, a public meeting, a club meeting, a city council meeting, a student government meeting, a church meeting, or whatever.

2. Listen closely to the speech. Do not take notes. Immediately following the speech, write down the main point of the speech

and then list the three most important subpoints the speaker made.

3. Compare what you have written down with your friend's reviews. See if you both got the same main point and subpoints. Then discuss why you were similar or different.

4. You should be fairly close. However, sometimes if the speaker is not well prepared, it is difficult to determine the main or subpoints of a speech. If you both had different main and/or subpoints, could the speaker have been the problem or were the two of you simply unable to apply the skills of this chapter to be more effective listeners?

12
RESPONDING TO QUESTIONS AND COMMENTS

In everyday conversation, asking questions, making comments, and responding to others are the key ingredients to carrying on a sharing interaction. As the speaking situation becomes more public in nature, the questioning and responding interchanges between speaker and listener become less spontaneous and more planned and controlled by the speaker. In this chapter, you will learn an approach for effectively dealing with questions and comments.

Chapter Content

- The Response Is as Important as the Speech
- Controlling Speaker-Listener Interchanges
- Planning Speaker-Listener Interchanges
- General Guidelines for Handling Question-and-Answer Periods
- Handling Unplanned Interruptions
- Encouraging the Audience to Participate
- What You Now Know
- What to Do to Learn More

**THE RESPONSE IS AS IMPORTANT
AS THE SPEECH**

In the beginning of the book, we developed the point that speaking
is a communicative activity that ranges from everyday conversing
to formal public speaking. The basic elements of talking and listening (including nonverbal behaviors) are present in all speaking. The
pattern or format of this give-and-take is altered to fit the informality or formality of the situation.

In everyday conversation, asking questions, making comments,
and responding to others are the key ingredients to carrying on the
transaction. As the speaking situation becomes more public in nature, the questioning and responding interchanges between speaker
and listener become less spontaneous and more planned and controlled by the speaker. For example, in a problem-solving city council meeting, the mayor can set the interchange rules; each council
member may be allowed five uninterrupted minutes to state his or
her position. A five-minute question-and-answer period may then
follow where other members can probe the individual council
member's position.

The speaker usually has the privilege of setting the constraints
that will keep her or him in control of the talking and listening
segments of the interchanges. Your may know some people on
whom you'd like to impose these constraints when conversing with
them because they do all the talking. (Their idea of conversation is
delivering an impromptu speech.)

 **CONTROLLING SPEAKER-
LISTENER INTERCHANGES**

Common sense seems to tell us that the more we can involve the
listeners throughout our speaking by encouraging their questions

and comments, the more effective we will be. This is not necessarily true. Too much direct audience participation during a speech can interrupt the progression or flow so that the rest of the listeners (and the speaker) lose the feeling for the main point of the presentation. Progressive development and timing are as important building blocks in speaking as in a play or movie. You can put a book down and come back and pick it up later. This is obviously not true with a speech.

   One option the speaker has to control the interchanges with the listeners is to set the "game rules" before the presentation begins. For example, as the speaker, you should tell the listeners that you will:

1. Respond to questions and comments at any time.

2. Respond to comments or questions only at designated points.

3. Respond to comments and questions only after the prepared speech is concluded.

   In summary, we are saying that making public speaking more like a conversation, by allowing or encouraging listener interchange during the speech, does not make for better speaking (although it may make for better teaching). Active speaker-listener interchanges have to be planned and controlled by the speaker.

PLANNING SPEAKER-LISTENER INTERCHANGES

In a one-to-many speaking situation, it may be difficult for you, as the speaker, to anticipate all the obstacles your message will encounter in the case of each individual listener. If you have done your homework on the audience, you have analyzed general characteristics and adapted your material to appeal to the majority or to the average listener. In reality, however, there is no real "average" listener—each listener is a unique individual with unique feelings, attitudes, and views of the world. This makes it difficult for any speaker to satisfactorily "reach" each and every individual in the audience.

Speaker-listener interchanges allow for more accurate information sharing.

Speaker-listener interchange periods allow the speaker an opportunity to take the basic message and further refine it to reach various individuals within the audience more successfully. In responding to individual comments or questions, the speaker can

1. Answer objections or concerns.

2. Clarify a misunderstood point.

3. Illustrate or support a general statement previously made.

4. Go into more depth with the material.

All of this assumes that you have been somewhat effective in communicating with your listeners in the prepared speech. If you have failed to establish yourself and your material during the monologue part of the speech, the audience interchange period will result in:

■ Silence.

■ A few polite questions or comments of a noncommittal nature.

■ A verbal assault on your credibility or your material.

Let's assume that you have been effective during the monologue section of your talk. There are several questioning techniques and specific guidelines that you should then follow in handling an interchange period:

REMEMBER—WHEN YOU STOP TALKING, THE TRANSACTIONAL NATURE OF THE INTERCHANGE WILL CONTINUE.

 GENERAL GUIDELINES FOR HANDLING QUESTION-AND-ANSWER PERIODS

1. **Plan ahead for the exchange.** Anticipate what questions or comments you may receive form the audience. If you find you have difficulty guessing what these will be, you have not done an adequate job of analyzing your audience. As you have prepared

the content of your speaking, you can prepare your responses to potential questions and comments from the listeners.

2. **Understand the general types of questions and comments you are likely to receive, even though you may not know their specific content.** Audience members commonly respond with:

   a. **Agreement:** a statement or specific instance that essentially expresses approval or acceptance of what you have said in your speech.

   b. **Understanding:** a statement that indicates the listener comprehends or appreciates what you have said but doesn't indicate approval or disapproval.

   c. **Request for clarification:** a statement or question that asks for additional information or for another explanation of a particular point or idea.

   d. **Disagreement:** a statement or specific instance that essentially shows disapproval or nonacceptance of what you have said.

   e. **Request for your related opinions:** a statement or question that asks for your opinion on related points, topics, or issues that were not covered in the speech.

   f. **Checking material or sources:** a statement or question that requests additional description or substantiation of your material and the sources of that material.

   g. **Checking reasoning:** a statement or question that attempts to bring to light the logic or rationality of your reasoning in the speech.

3. **Respond to listener comments and questions by maintaining your poise and not overreacting to save face in front of the rest of the audience.** You do not have to know all the answers, put every negative comment down, or match wit with wit. Your job is to keep your reasoning faculties about you and think before you respond. Some techniques for maintaining your poise are:

   a. **Single out one person at a time to respond to if you have several questions or comments at once.**

   b. **Repeat or paraphrase the question or comment.** This ensures that you have understood it correctly. If you have not understood the question, the listener will correct you and you save yourself the embarrassment of answering a question that was not intended. Repeating the question also "buys" you some time for preparing your answer. For example, "Are you asking me if I *personally* agree with the president's position?"

   c. **Rephrase or simplify the question if you feel it is too wordy, too complex, or too technical for the rest of the audience.** You may show respect for the questioner by asking whether your simplification has distorted the intent of the question. If the answer is no, then you proceed to answer the question as you have rephrased it. If the answer is yes, ask for the question to be rephrased. For example, "Is your main question the apparent distortion in the listed miles per gallon for U.S. cars?"

   d. **Postpone the question.** If you feel the question is irrelevant, is too personal, requires too much detailed information, or is not of general interest to the whole audience, you have the option of postponing your response to the end of the whole speaking situation. Thank the person for the question and indicate that you would like the time or freedom of a one-to-one discussion on this question. If he or she would hold the question until the speaking situation has drawn to a close, you will be happy to discuss it personally with him or her.

   e. **Don't cover up.** If you don't know the answer or if you find yourself caught without an appropriate response, simply say so, and respectfully go on to the next question.

   f. **Be sensitive to the time for wrapping up the interchange and officially ending the speaking situation.** You can watch the audience for waning attention and interest cues.

4. **Remember that while you are handling the question-and-answer period, the audience is still judging your credibility.** When you wrap up the question-and-answer interchange, the speech may be finished but the communicative transaction between you and the listeners continues until you leave the setting.

◤◢ HANDLING UNPLANNED INTERRUPTIONS

The single worst problem speakers have in handling unplanned questions, comments, interruptions, and heckling from the audience can be seen in the speaker who responds to save face. We have learned to admire politicians, executives, and media people for their quick, cutting wit. We forget, though, that we do not have the experience they have—hundreds of speaking situations.

The best defense for an unplanned interruption is a good offense. Prior to speaking, indicate when and how you will entertain audience questions and comments. When interrupted, simply remind the person that you will be happy to deal with the comment in the allotted period. The important point is to remain poised. Do not become defensive or condescending in postponing the person's inquiry. How you handle yourself in these situations can be as important for your credibility as what you say.

As a speaker you may be subjected to several types of questions and comments. The following are samples:

▉ **Leading questions:** The desired answer is directly implied in the question. For example, "The rest of the group believes the cost is too great. What do you think?"

▉ **Loaded questions:** Agreement with the questioner is directly asked for, though not expected, by the questioner. This type of question usually has a contraction in it, such as *couldn't, don't,* or *shouldn't*; for example, "Don't you feel that would be too costly right now?" This is really a statement of disagreement or opinion in the disguise of a question.

▉ **Complex, wordy, or multiple questions:** Sometimes a listener will string many questions together. For example, "I understand that your proposal will cost a lot of money . . . I wonder where this money will come from, who is going to administer the program even if we get the money . . . it doesn't seem as if the details have been worked out . . . uhm . . . are you sure this will work? . . . how can we afford it?"

▉ **Statement of open disagreement:** For example, "I don't buy what you are saying one bit."

▉ **Specific contrary example:** A member of the audience gives a specific example in which the point you are making does not hold true. For example, "But your solution is premised on the face that the professional woman has worked out the balance between her career and her family. Not all professional women have done this. I know many professional women who can't decide if they want a family or not."

One of the best ways to prepare yourself to handle such unplanned interruptions is to practice. Practice your speaking with friends or classmates interrupting or at least asking difficult questions during the question-and-answer period. To practice speaking without practicing for the question-and-answer period would be like a basketball player practicing shooting and dribbling without anyone trying to closely guard his or her movement. In a real game, such players would not be ready because their practice would not have helped them develop all the skills needed for the actual event.

There are specific responding techniques for handling interruptions or unplanned interchange periods. The following are some of the more commonly used techniques:

1. Label the questions that are leading, loaded, and multiple for what they are before you attempt to respond.

2. For the leading or loaded questions, you can sometimes respond with your own question or request further information from the listener.

Be prepared for unplanned questions, interruptions, and heckling.

QUESTIONER: But don't you think that would be killing?

SPEAKER: I can see you think it would be; please tell me why you'd call it killing?

3. When asked a multiple question, you can ask which question of all those included the questioner would like you to respond to first.

4. For vague, wordy, complex questions, ask for the main idea behind the question before you attempt to answer it.

SPEAKER: Okay, I understand the general idea of the question. What is the specific point you want me to respond to?

5. For open disagreements, state that there may be a possibility the person is right. You have not agreed by saying this, all you have admitted is that there may be a possibility, however slim, that the person's view is correct. You have reserved the right to stick to your own opinion. After you have indicated the possibility, do not elaborate. Turn to the next question.

SPEAKER: Yes, it is possible that we may find bigger oil fields in the future—not likely enough, though, for me to want to bank on it.

6. For hostile or argumentative statements or questions, begin your response by indicating that you do not appreciate the way the statement was made but that you can understand how the person feels or why he or she thinks that way. For example:

QUESTIONER: That sounds like a bunch of bull to me!

SPEAKER: I'm not sure I like how you put that, but I can see how you would be skeptical, since this project has been discussed for a long time without anything being done.

7. When an audience member has made a valid point that contradicts you or has stated a singular exception to your point of view, give the person credit for the perceptive insight before you attempt to clarify or explain why that statement does not destroy the basis for your point of view. For example:

QUESTIONER: But air bags are only good for head-on accidents and not all accidents in cars are head-on.

SPEAKER: That's a good point you have brought up. It's true that air bags are not as helpful in the side-on collision. However, we are concerned about saving as many lives as possible. Only 12 percent of auto accidents involve side collisions. If more accidents involved side impact, I would have to agree with you more.

◢◤ ENCOURAGING THE AUDIENCE TO PARTICIPATE

In certain speaking situations, one of the goals of the presentation is to get listeners involved actively in controlled interchanges. At times, experienced speakers use these controlled interchanges to further develop ideas with the audience. As a speaker, you need to be familiar with the types of questions you can ask to draw out the audience. After you have the audience members participating, you need to know what types of questions will ensure that listeners begin to see the relationships among the pieces of information as you've intended.

Three basic questions to get listeners involved are:

1. **Open questions.** These ask the audience members for their opinions or reactions, with no restrictions on what the answer does or does not cover. For example: "How do you feel about the plan?" "What is your reaction to legalizing marijuana?" "What do you think we should do?"

2. **Specific or follow-up questions.** These limit or narrow the range of acceptable responses in relation to a previous statement. For example, if a person has just given a description of his teenage years, you could ask that person: "What was *your* high school like?" If a person has indicated that she didn't like the way someone else ran a meeting, you could ask: "Tell us what it is you didn't care for in her approach to running the meeting." And if a person indicates he does not like a proposed plan, you can ask: "What don't you like about the plan?"

   Specific and follow-up questions limit the area in which people can respond. For example, you could ask: "What are some of the advantages?" "Why did you choose to major in communication, rather than business, if you want to go into sales?"

3. **Reflective questions.** These summarize what you understand the person to be saying, in the form of a question that asks the person to indicate how accurate your perceptions of what he or she said are. Sample reflective questions are: "I get the impression you are not sure which field you want to go into?" "You seem to have some doubts about the value of this assignment?" "So

you feel this class forced you to work on some skills you would not have tackled on your own?"

It is important that reflective questions be asked in an open, inquiring, "am I right?" attitude. Sarcasm or implied judgment will destroy their value. Reflective questions accomplish several things for you and the other person in the interchange:

a. The audience member knows you listened to and tried to understand his or her point of view.
b. The audience member can see how well you understand what he or she was attempting to express.
c. The audience member's response to your reflective question shows you how accurately you understand his or her comments.

Do all you can to encourage audience participation.

This chapter has been developed on the premise that speaking exists on a continuum from conversing to formal public speaking. The communication skills that lead to effective conversational interchanges also have a place in public speaking if they are planned and well executed. Not all audience interchanges are as planned or developed as the speaker intends. For these moments, the speaker needs to take steps to control the situation. On the other hand, the speaker may have to encourage or stimulate desired audience interchanges. The bottom line is that an effective speaker in today's environment needs to be skilled in more than talking. She or he must be able to listen, question, and respond to questions and comments in an appropriate manner.

What You Now Know

This chapter points out that the basic speaking and listening of everyday conversing and the formal speaking of public talks come together when the public speaker interacts with his or her audience through question-and-answer interchanges. These speaker-audience interchanges should be controlled by the speaker, and this takes planning. Controlling interchanges may mean handling hostile reactions or encouraging a reluctant group of listeners to ask questions. The speaker needs to anticipate the kinds of questions and comments he or she may get (or the lack of them) and be prepared to handle the interchange with poise.

What to Do to Learn More

Meet the Press/Face the Nation

Make a special effort to observe both the questioning and responding techniques on television programs such as "Firing Line," presidential news conferences, and the like.

Questioning in Class

Focus on asking at least one of the three positive types of questions (open, specific or follow-up, or reflective) in class everyday. You may also wish to observe the types of responses your instructors use in the classroom situation.

Conversation: A Place to Practice

Everyday conversations, especially the more "heated" exchanges in the student center, are useful situations for you to ask questions and respond to others. These conversations will be particularly rich in interruptions, loaded and leading questions, disagreements, and credibility attacks, so you should have ample opportunities to try out your controlling techniques.

13
THE END

Opportunities for speaking surround us. The better prepared we are to speak, the happier we feel during those speaking moments. and the more that we improve our speaking, the more our opportunities for better living increase.

Boldness has
genius, power and
magic in it.
GOETHE

Do not be like the Born Loser! Remember always that public speaking is for listeners. Listeners must be stimulated in order to respond. So, our parting shot (advice) is for you to persuade them, impress them, entertain them, inform them, but do show up and take every opportunity to *speak* with them.

IN CONCLUSION

Speaking never ends, but we are concluding this book. We are concluding the writing of this text and you, the reader, are probably finishing the reading of this text. We feel good about our writing efforts and hope that you too feel good about your speaking success.

As we stated in the beginning of the text, speaking is mainly a matter of getting listeners' attention, keeping listeners interested, and stimulating favorable responses in listeners. (Sounds like we are a little listener-oriented, doesn't it?) We reemphasize that the basic skills for public speaking already exist in our everyday talking and conversing. And that instead of having to learn something new and complex, we simply build upon previously acquired speaking experiences.

Notice how quickly in the following speech the essence of being a "memorable speaker" is summarized.

**Speech is civilization . . . it is silence which isolates.
THOMAS MANN**

The basic skills of public speaking exist in our everyday talking and conversing.

Speaking Excellence

The Speaker and the Ghost:
The Speaker Is the Speech

Carolyn Lomax-Cooke,
Communications Specialist, Cities Service Company

Delivered to the Tulsa Chapter of the
International Association of Business Communicators,
Tulsa, Oklahoma, October 20, 1981

Tonight I want to talk candidly about what makes a good
speech, a good speaker, and a good speechwriter. Please notice
that I am emphasizing "good" in each instance. We have all
heard unimpressive speeches. But what we want to look at tonight is that special quality that makes a speech memorable.

My message is very simple—for the good speech, the good
speaker, and the good speechwriter all center around one understanding of the speech occasion. And that understanding is this:
the speaker IS the speech. The man IS the message. The
woman IS her words. If the speaker and the speechwriter understand this fundamental of a good speech, all will go well. If the
partners fail at this point, so will the speech.

But what do I mean—the speaker IS the speech? I mean that
the listener cannot separate the content of the message from the
character of the speaker. During a speech, the message itself
and the vehicle through which it is delivered (the speaker) are so
integrated that when the audience evaluates one, it automatically
evaluates the other. The speaker and the speech are one and
the same.

Since the audience responds to personality and character, the
good speaker will take care that the speech truly reveals his
character. Personality, life, conviction, excitement, or despair—
these must shine through the speech as a reflection of the
speaker. The audience recognizes such honesty and always re-

sponds to personal stories, anecdotes about the speaker's family, or a reference to a book that the speaker has read. Because let's face it, the audience came to hear the speaker—not to watch a human body mouth the words of a written treatise. . . .

Every truly impressive speech that you can remember is memorable because of the melding of speech content with the speaker's character and life experiences.

Who but Barbara Jordan could have delivered her powerful keynote address at the 1976 Democratic convention? This black congress-woman, with her forceful voice, said: "A lot of years have passed since 1832 (when the first Democratic convention met to nominate a presidential candidate), and during that time it would have been most unusual for any national political party to ask that a Barbara Jordan deliver a keynote address . . . but tonight here I am, and I feel that notwithstanding the past that my presence here is one additional bit of evidence that the American Dream need not forever be deferred."

From that point on, the audience was hers. She was the speech and the message was hers alone No one else could have delivered it.

If you think that you need a fancy platform or an impressive audience to deliver a great speech, you are mistaken. Peter the fisherman stood on an ordinary street in Jerusalem not too long after the crucifixion of Jesus and delivered one of the most effective speeches of all history. He had no podium, no microphone, no notes, not even an invitation to speak. But he spoke from his heart, with the simple honest words of his own experience when he told his fellow Jews that they had killed the Messiah promised by God and foretold by the prophets. His message: "Repent and be baptized." I characterize this speech as a highly effective action-oriented presentation, because 3,000 people were baptized into the Christian faith that day as a result of his word. Now, we have more than our share of ministers on the Tulsa Main Mall—but not one of them is getting this kind of response!

SOURCE: *Vital Speeches of the Day* 48 (December 1, 1981): Reprinted with permission. pg. 125–8.

"Furthermore . . ."

From *The Saturday Evening Post* courtesy of Reg Hider.

APPENDIX A
SAMPLE
INFORMATIVE
AND PERSUASIVE
SPEECHES

Speaking Excellence

Diamonds of Hope
The Value of Our Person

By Paul Henmueller,
Senior, University of Illinois at Chicago
Delivered at Commencement,
University of Illinois,
Chicago, Illinois,
June 11, 1989

President Wolff, President Ikenberry, Chancellor Langenberg,
Members of the Board and of the Faculty, Fellow Graduates and
Honored Guests:

Buried deep within the earth lie vast deposits of diamonds, the
world's most precious gem. Although these stones are tremen-
dously valuable, until they are mined they remain useless—glim-
mering pebbles hidden beneath the surface. Some day these
jewels will be unearthed and the world will marvel at their
brilliance.

Just at there is a great storehouse of wealth hidden in the
vaults of the earth, so is there tremendous wealth buried deep
within the mind and soul and each individual. This wealth may
be in the form of intelligence, personality, honor or a myriad of
other abilities and attributes which comprise the spectrum of the
human spirit.

We graduates of the University of Illinois at Chicago have broken ground and we have lifted our treasures up to the surface—
to sparkle in the sunlight. Just as every diamond offers different
possibilities, so does each of us possess vast potential and
promise which will distinguish us among the accomplished people of the world.

The education which we have received at UIC has been similar to the refinement process which all diamonds must undergo.
Each of us was selected and accepted by this university—just as
diamonds in the rough are chosen when they suggest future

glory. Every course we have taken, every instructor to whom we have listened and every student we have known has added yet another facet to our experience—ultimately increasing the value of our person.

Unlike diamonds, however, our refinement process is never complete. There is no end to the number of facets which may adorn and structure our lives. Some of us will go on to graduate and professional schools, while still others will enter directly into our chosen fields. It is necessary that all of us utilize our individual talents and abilities so that we may preserve the luster and brilliance of our education.

Like diamonds, our education has a certain instrinsic value— that amount which one is willing to sacrifice in order to attain a desired goal. Each of us has contributed vast amounts of time, effort and thought in order to attain the knowledge, the skills and the abilities which we now possess. Today, as we gather together in this auditorium, we emit a striking brilliance—a fiery splendor produced by our many intricate shapes and unique styles.

The decision to retain this luster, this shine, is one that must be made by each one of us—every day in the years to come. The education which we have received at UIC will remain with us forever, both timeless and priceless. Considering the tremendous investments we have made in ourselves, it is only proper that we now exact a fitting yield. Like diamonds, an educated individual can but increase in value.

One of the world's most famous diamonds is not white, but rather, a radiant blue—the very color of the graduation gowns we are wearing today. This diamond is cherished not only for its size and beauty, but also for its uncanny ability to conduct electricity—to energize those objects with which it comes into contact. The jewel I am speaking of is none other than the Hope diamond, the only one of its kind in the world. Looking before me now, I see a room filled with equally unique and powerful blue gems, capable of electrifying the world. I believe that we graduates of the University of Illinois at Chicago are the true "diamonds of hope."

Congratulations graduates, and best wishes for continued success, secure in the knowledge that like diamonds, what we have accomplished here at UIC will last forever.

Speaking Excellence

Cessation of Hostilities
The Challenge of Securing Peace

By George Bush
President of the United States of America
Delivered to the American People
Washington, D.C.
February 27, 1991

Kuwait is liberated. Iraq's army is defeated. Our military objectives are met. Kuwait is once more in the hands of Kuwaitis in control of their own destiny. We share in their joy, a joy tempered only by our compassion for their ordeal.

Tonight, the Kuwaiti flag once again flies above the capital of a free and sovereign nation, and the American flag flies above our embassy.

Seven months ago, America and the world drew a line in the sand. We declare that the aggression against Kuwait would not stand, and tonight America and the world have kept their word. This is not a time of euphoria, certainly not a time to gloat, but it is a time of pride, pride in our troops, pride in the friends who stood with us in the crisis, pride in our nation and the people whose strength and resolve made victory quick, decisive and just.

And soon we will open wide our arms to welcome back home to America our magnificent fighting forces. No one country can claim this victory as its own. It was not only a victory for Kuwait, but a victory for all the coalition partners. This is a victory for the United Nations, for all mankind, for the rule of law, and for what is right.

After consulting with Secretary of Defense Cheney, the Chairman of the Joint Chiefs of Staff, General Powell, and our coalition partners. I am pleased to announce that at midnight tonight,

Eastern standard time, exactly 100 hours since ground operations commenced and 6 weeks since the start of Operation Desert Storm, all United States and coalition forces will suspend offensive combat operations.

It is up to Iraq whether this suspension on the part of the coalition becomes a permanent cease-fire. Coalition, political and military terms for a formal cease-fire include the following requirements:

Iraq must release immediately all coalition prisoners of war, third country nationals and the remains of all who have fallen.

Iraq must release all Kuwaiti detainees.

Iraq also must inform Kuwaiti authorities of the location and nature of all land and sea mines.

Iraq must comply fully with all relevant United Nations Security Council resolutions. This includes a rescinding of Iraq's August decision to annex Kuwait and acceptance in principle of Iraq's responsibility to pay compensation for the loss, damage and injury its aggression has caused.

The coalition calls upon the Iraqi Government to designate military commanders to meet within 48 hours with their coalition counterparts at a place in the theater of operations to be specified to arrange for military aspects of the cease-fire.

Further, I have asked Secretary of State Baker to request that the United Nations Security Council meet to formulate the necessary arrangement for this war to be ended.

This suspension of offensive combat operations is contingent upon Iraq's not firing upon any coalition forces and not launching Scud missiles against any other country. If Iraq violates these terms, coalition forces will be free to resume military operations.

At every opportunity I have said to the people of Iraq that our quarrel was not with them but instead with their leadership and above all with Saddam Hussein. This remains the case. You, the people of Iraq are not our enemy. We do not seek your destruction. We have treated your P.O.W.'s with kindness.

Coalition forces fought this war only as a last resort and look forward to the day when Iraq is led by people prepared to live in peace with their neighbors.

We must now begin to look beyond victory in war. We must meet the challenge of securing the peace. In the future, as before, we will consult with our coalition partners.

We've already done a good deal of thinking and planning for the postwar period and Secretary Baker has already begun to consult with our coalition partners on the region's challenges. There can be and will be no solely American answer to all these challenges, but we can assist and support the countries of the region and be a catalyst for peace.

In this spirit Secretary Baker will go to the region next week to begin a new round of consultations. This war is now behind us. Ahead of us is the difficult task of securing a potentially historic peace. Tonight though, let us be proud to what we have accomplished. Let us give thanks to those who risked their lives. Let us never forget those who gave their lives.

May God bless our valiant military forces and their families and let us all remember them in our prayers.

Good night and may God bless the United States of America.

SOURCE: *Vital Speeches of the Day.* 57 (March 5, 1991).

Speaking Excellence

Speechwriting
The Profession and the Practice

By Charles Parnell
Speechwriter, Nationwide Insurance
Delivered to the International Association of
Business Communicators Conference
Dayton, Ohio
October 9, 1989

Thank you. This is an exciting time to be a speechwriter! With the media putting prominent people under increasing scrutiny, both in government and business, there is going to be an increasing premium placed on the ability to communicate effectively. Ours is going to be a growth industry!

This is also a very convenient time to be a speechwriter—in terms of the technology and tools available.

Two major technical innovations have revolutionized our craft.

The first innovation, word processing, took much of the drudgery out of revision, and made it possible for us to turn out a better product, in less time.

The second innovation, online full text database services, put a megalibrary at our fingertips.

How's the pay for speechwriters?

Last year 150 speechwriters attended the first National Speechwriters Conference in Chicago.

During the conference, a survey was conducted of salaries.

The lowest salary was $18,500. The highest was $100,000. The median salary was $46,000. The average was $49,000.

Now let's talk about the *practice* of speechwriting.

We are talking about an art, not a science, and there is no one single formula for writing a good speech. It is an iterative process.

But there are some guidelines that can give direction to your efforts.

Let's begin our discussion by talking about the *speech triangle.*

The speech triangle refers to the three major elements you must consider before beginning to write any speech:

1. The audience, including the occasion that brings them together (award ceremony, annual meeting, retirement ceremony, political rally, or other occasion).
2. The speaker.
3. The subject matter.

As much as possible, you should tailor the speech to the needs of the *audience,* and the only way you can do that is to have the most detailed possible knowledge about them.

The *second element* is your own *knowledge of the speaker.* Is the speaker a good teller of jokes?

Does the speaker have any background that would build rapport with this audience?

And the *third element* of the speech triangle is the *subject matter.*

If you have done your research well on the audience and know your speaker well, the subject matter will often suggest itself.

Before you start to write the speech, decide exactly what its purpose will be.

I will mention three of the basic purposes of speeches.

1. Speeches can *impart information.* Generally many business reports and briefings are of this nature.

2. Speeches can go beyond merely imparting information. They can *persuade* or *promote* a better *understanding* of important issues, by giving listeners as well-thought out body of facts and analysis.

As Dr. Kenneth McFarland pointed out in his book, *Eloquence in Public Speaking,* we need speeches that can translate information into understanding, and transpose facts into a philosophy.

3. Speeches can *inspire action.* Speeches can cause people to vote for a particular candidate or support a particular cause.

Now, let's assume we have decided on the general purpose of our speech, whether to inform, to persuade, or to rouse to action.

Next, we should arrow down the main point we wish to make, and if possible, reduce it to a single sentence.

That should be the *theme,* and everything else should go to support that point.

Let's talk briefly now about the *outline.*

Use it if it helps, but don't let it become a tyrant.

Feel free to tear it up or revise it as necessary.

Due to the capabilities of my personal computer, I sometimes don't outline at all—on paper.

I often start by jotting down a few ideas on the screen, then move them around as necessary to build some sort of coherent pattern. I then fill in the details as they occur to me.

What that means is that you can really start anywhere and eventually come up with an entire speech, just as you can start with any piece of a puzzle and eventually put it together.

I don't believe that thoughts come to most of us fully formed in logical order.

My favorite composer, Mozart, seemed to work that way as though he were taking dictation.

But for most of us, the mind works by association and stream of consciousness.

We have to impose order on our thoughts and facts after we have gathered them together.

The value of realizing this is that it can take much of the anxiety out of sitting down to a blank sheet of paper or blank computer screen.

Now let's talk more about the actual *writing* of the speech.

In a speech, your organization must at all times be clear to the listener.

Of the many possible methods of organizing and presenting material, I think the *topical* method is one of the most often used.

Usually in a talk, the CEO or other people giving you guidance will offer several ideas they want to include in the speech.

These ideas may not be logically related to each other, so they have to be treated as separate topics and linked by some sort of transitional material.

In some cases you can organize your material in the *chronological* pattern, where you are showing the history of some development. But this will not do for most business speeches.

The *space pattern* could be used if you were giving results by region, such as on the East Coast, the Midwest, and the Pacific Coast.

Another useful pattern that can often be used in a persuasive speech is the *logical pattern,* such as *cause and effect, problem-cause-solution* or other patterns using inductive or deductive logic.

Those are just some of the possible methods of organizing your material, and they may be combined, so long as the overall development is clear to the listener.

While on the subject of organizing your material, let me say a few words about the *beginning* of the speech.

The beginning of a speech is both a challenge and an opportunity.

The first minute or two are critical. During that time the audience will decide whether or not they like the speaker.

Some proven techniques that may be helpful in starting a speech include:

1. Respond to your introduction with humor.
2. Present humor that ties in with the audience or occasion.
3. Get the audience to join in applauding something.
4. Compliment the audience.

5. Ask a question.

6. Capture the attention of the audience with a startling statement.

Whatever technique you use, keep it short, keep it simple, and get off to a *dynamic start.*

In writing the body of the speech, you will want to make your general statement clear and illustrate it with *examples, arguments, quotations, expert testimony*, and anything else your research has found.

Make your examples as specific and concrete as possible.

Try to *humanize* your talk by giving *real stories* about real people.

This was the sort of thing that made Ronald Reagan's speeches so popular, even among people who didn't agree with his political views.

We have talked about beginning the speech and developing the main body.

Now let's talk about the *conclusion* of the speech.

Here your purpose is to leave the listeners in the proper mood.

You want to emphasize the main points in such a way as to ensure that the audience will remember them, agree with them, and if necessary, be prepared to take action based on them.

There are several techniques for ending a speech effectively.

One effective way is to *call for action.* That's assuming your speech had this as its purpose.

This would mean telling the audience to join, telephone, vote, or whatever you want them to do.

But make it something they can do.

Some speakers like to end with a *quotation,* but in most cases it is better to follow the quotation with at least a brief statement of your own to put it in perspective. That way you end the speech with your own words, not some other person's.

In some cases, simply *summarizing* clearly the *main points* of the speech will be an effective ending.

After all, not all speeches are calls for action. Some are simply expositions of an organization's or speaker's views on some subject.

Or they may simply convey interesting information.

All right, so we have researched our topic thoroughly and have written a first draft, with a powerful introduction, as well organized body, and a memorable conclusion.

Are we finished yet? Not by a long shot.

In real estate, the saying is that there are three primary considerations for a good investment: location, location, and location.

I believe that in good writing, the three principles are *revise, revise,* and *revise.*

This takes a lot of extra work. It takes *humility,* to admit that your work was not "taken as dictation from on high."

Break long paragraphs and sentences into small, manageable chunks.

Use *informal language;* use *contractions.*

Read the speech out loud several times. You will hear things that you want to change—that you would never detect if you read silently.

Personalize statistics. Say 1 out of 3, not 33 percent.

In conclusion, let me refer to some words of Dr. E. C. Nance, quoted in *Vital Speeches* more than 30 years ago:

> Words can change the face of a city, build churches, schools, playgrounds, boys' clubs, scout troops, civic forums, civic clubs, little theaters, civic music organizations, garden clubs and better local governments.
>
> We need words that will make us laugh, wonder, work, think, aspire, and hope. We need words that will leap and sing in our souls. We need words that will cause us to face up to life with a fighting faith and contend for those ideals that have made this the greatest nation on earth.

Ladies and gentlemen, with all the problems and challenges facing business, our country and the world, we are going to need words that can inspire us to do all these things.

You, the communicators, are the people who will give us these words.

Good luck to all of you!

SOURCE: *Vital Speeches of the Day* 56 (January 15, 1990): XX.

Minotaurs and Mentors
The Force that Binds Us Together

By Jonathan C. Cutler
Youth Representative to the International Preparatory
Committee for International Youth Service Conference
Delivered at the Second International Youth Services
Conference
Chicago, Illinois
October 4, 1988

GOOD EVENING! I am very excited to be here and very honored to have this chance to share a few thoughts with you. I've been studying Greek philosophy in school recently, and I am amazed at how the writing is still alive and pertinent. I'm slowly learning that we can really benefit from the stories of ancient Greece. I found two Greek characters which might even be helpful in thinking about youth services.

One is the Minotaur and the other is a fellow named Mentor. The Minotaur was a monster that used to eat about seven kids a year. In Homer's *Odyssey,* Mentor was the guardian and teacher Odysseus chose for his son. First let's talk about the Minotaur. This creature lived in a labyrinth on the island of Crete. Theseus, a Greek hero, was given the dangerous task of going down into the labyrinth and slaying the Minotaur. Eventually, Theseus killed the creature, but his work was not finished . . . there was still the labyrinth. With its winding passages, the labyrinth could have kept Theseus wandering eternally in darkness, never to see his way clear to the light. Luckily, he was saved by a woman who left a trail of string showing him how to get out of the labyrinth. I suppose today we might call her a social worker . . . maybe even a mentor. I love that term. As I mentioned, *mentor,* the same term which we use today, originally referred to a teacher and guardian. There are people in my life who fit that description.

Some of my mentors are here tonight. They all possess two qualities in common. First, they all enthusiastically share their experiences with me. This is the teacher part. If life is a journey, then, these teachers have made their travelogues available to me, and have sent me along fascinating roadtrips. The second quality is that they are all guardians to the extent that they care that I am well enough to make the journey. They know that the journey is long and can be dangerous at times, so my physical health and emotional stability are under their guard. The important point here is that their hearts are as open to me as their minds.

These people have various occupations. My parents were the two first mentors I ever had and they still play the role very well. One of my mentors is a student at Brown University, one is a baker, several run youth service agencies. Only three are actually "teachers" professionally. In terms of the story of the labyrinth, these people are constantly leaving me trails of string. Although I still wander in the labyrinth, I am strengthened by the knowledge that I am not the first to do so, and I am not alone on my journey.

Professional youth service providers, whether they be educators, foster parents, agency administrators, or social workers, *must* be mentors. I was lucky in that my parents were my original mentors, but this is becoming a rare phenomenon. The reality is that the family structure is breaking down. Between single parent families and families in which both parents work, I'm not sure who is bringing up the kids. We are learning that more parents are abusive then we ever imagined. If the traditional family is no longer functional and parents are not serving as teachers and guardians, we must expand our concept of family. Youth service providers must take up the slack. This includes youth taking up the slack for their peers. With the declining influence of parents, peers become much more influential. We must encourage youth to look to each other for help. Only when youth feel responsible for each other will they become positive influences on each other's lives. When that day comes, we will see a generation that is not divided between those who are independent and those who are dependent. If we make compassion a part of the education of our young, I believe we will come to see a generation who understands that we are all interdependent.

But a big question remains: How can we, as helpers and care providers, avoid building dependency among our youth? The answer lies back in the labyrinth. Theseus found his way out by following the string left for him. I believe this is a perfect analogy for how Mentors can best be teachers and guardians. It is helping by providing resources, not answers. Opening doors, sparking interest, sharing resources . . . these are the labors of a mentor. They are very different from traditional concepts like training, professing knowledge, and maintaining control . . . these are the labors of the service provider who has lost sight of what makes service effective: love. The difference between "sharing resources" and "professing knowledge" may seem like one of useless semantics, but from the perspective of a youth in need, the difference is love. When love enters the picture, the youth in need can begin to have room to grow. Only a person with an open heart can provide that room to grow.

An open heart will lead to more than a warm hug on a cold night. It is a state of consciousness which will permeate every aspect of service work. For example, it is an open heart which allows the planners of this conference to appreciate the value of youth participation. Many people have worked diligently to get young people to this conference and to find a place for us in the program. There is so much to share and so little time. Hopefully, the youth have enhanced your time here by allowing you to speak with articulate young people who have gone through the system. For the youth, the opportunities made available here have reinforced the belief that our feelings, thoughts, and opinions really do matter. Is that so different than a warm hug on a cold night? . . . I don't think so.

Behind all the problems of my generation, there is really only one problem. It all connects. You want to stop the use of destructive drugs among my peers? You want us to graduate from school? You want us to stop killing ourselves and taking you with us? Then stop for a minute and listen to the Beatles: All you need is love. Now, this doesn't mean that we ought to pretend that everything is coming up roses. I'm not talking about the simplicity of "Just Say No" which is as good as saying "Just Close Your Eyes"! I'm talking about opening your heart to my pain, my joy, my insecurity, my life! Open up so that I know I have a place in you and in your society. Life *is* a labyrinth and it can get really dark and cold. I sure can't face that alone! But there is no stronger a force than the one that binds us together. With the wind of love at our back, no hill is too steep and no day is too dark.

Before I go, I owe you an apology. Obviously, my perspective is purely North American. I have travelled a bit in Europe, but only as a tourist. When I speak of educational deficiencies, I can only refer to those problems which I have seen in the United States. When I speak of the breakdown of the family, I assume universal breakdown. Perhaps the problems are not universal. If not, this is perfect justification for international gatherings. If the teen suicide rate in Egypt is much lower than the rate in Sweden, it is up to us to try to understand why. Hopefully, through intercultural comparisons, we will be able to see more clearly the path to improvements in our own cultures.

The problems facing youth in Peru may be different than the problems facing youth in Germany. However, the answers to the problems are surprisingly similar all over the globe. In 1906, Salvador Mendieta, a Nicaraguan, published a book called *The Sickness of Central America.* In it, he argues that the solution to Central America's problems is a cultural revolution. He pleads with us to "... make (the children) understand that the man or woman isolated from society is helpless; [help them understand] how dependent we are on one another, and how necessary the cooperation of all human beings is if we are to achieve on earth the goals of justice, truth, well-being, love, and beauty ..."

I would only add that it is not enough to *tell* youth that participation and cooperation is necessary. We must *show* that youth have a place to participate. This requires creativity and enthusiasm on the part of mentors. It is not an easy job. It is usually frustrating at first. But if you are a mentor, even if you can be one for only one kid at a time, I promise that you will leave this earth a better place than you found it.

Speaking Excellence

The Right Way
A Matter of Principle

By James E. Perrella
Executive Vice-President
Ingersoll-Rand Company
Delivered at the University of Illinois, Chicago
January 19, 1989

GOOD AFTERNOON. Professor McLimore's invitation to partici-pate in this course with you today stirred a great deal of reflec-tion as to the best subject for discussion. The number and vari-ety of possible subjects seemed endless.

Among the candidates were:

—international business in times of changing currency values;

—product liability and increasing insurance costs;

—business as a societal problem-solver;

—the fact that profit is not a dirty word;

—the South Africa questions, ranging from business-inspired social improvements to complete disinvestment (now, that's a 20th century word for you.)

The list continued. Many subjects. Many ideas. Many possible directions.

In this sea of subjects, one topic surfaced.

It is a topic that touches on every other subject mentioned, a topic much in the news, a topic that affects our attitudes, a topic that touches our lives:

Business ethics.

Think about it for a minute. If you approach the subject, busi-ness ethics, in terms of Ivan Boesky or Dallas's J. R. Ewing, you may believe that "business ethics" is an oxymoron, or, as an ar-ticle in The *Wall Street Journal* suggested, that "business" and "ethics" are mutually exclusive.

Today, we need to ask:

Are they?

Certainly, in fact and fiction, there is much that says business is not ethical, and stories that even suggest that businessmen cannot operate ethically.

Consider the case of Daniel Drew, a New York cattleman of the early 19th century: Stuart Holbrook tells the story in *The Age of the Moguls*: Mr. Drew

> "seems never to have denied his most celebrated piece of knavery, which he used for many years in his cattle business.
>
> "As a big herd of anywhere from six hundred to a thousand head of Ohio beef approached New York City, Drew had his drovers salt them well.
>
> "Then, just before reaching the marketplace, he let them drink their fill.
>
> "Cattle were sold live-weight. Drew's processing with salt and water added many tons to the average herd.
>
> 'Watered stock' soon become a term in Wall Street."

Mr. Drew seemed a follower of a 19th century parody of the Golden Rule:

> "do unto the other feller the way he'd like to do unto you, an' do it fust."

Mr. Drew's motives and actions can fit well with motives and actions prevalent in today's business world, or should I say, in today's world.

We seem to put ourselves first. Or try to. At almost any cost.

The extreme of this "me-first" attitude is the drug addict who will take advantage of anyone and anything to satisfy his insatiable craving.

Think, for a moment, about every-day situations as well:

The driver who tries to move ahead of other cars at every traffic light.

The green grocer who puts the reddest strawberries on the top of the basket.

The person who insists always on having the last word in any domestic argument.

The doctor who prescribes more and more tests, not necessarily for the patient's benefit, but for protection against a possible malpractice claim.

The salesman who thinks more of his commission than of his customer's needs.

The student—certainly not anyone here—who cheats on an exam to gain a higher grade or rank.

The politician who steals another's speech to make himself sound better or wiser.

The individual who pays a tip to the maitre d' to get preferred seating.

In every case, the action is a me-first action.

Me first. A likely, or as many would say, the source of ethics problems.

In your career development, as you become our nation's business leaders, you will face the question:

May business people use any means, fair or foul, to make a sale, to insure success, to take advantage of a customer, or to do a competitor in?

In other words, to put themselves first.

In business, the Ivan Boesky/Drexel Burnham Lambert shenanigans keep reappearing in the nation's headlines.

A recent lawsuit charges that Boeing used bogus misbranded bearings in commercial and military aircraft.

While all sorts of special situations of this type have arisen, many people. I am pleased to say, still do things the old-fashioned way.

In fact, many people still depend on a handshake to seal an agreement. A man's word is his bond. In many negotiations people trust each other completely. Even in complex business transactions.

In today's business world, handshake deals have not disappeared. They are fewer, however, as people depend on written warranties and guarantees and exclusions and warnings in the most confusing language and in the tiniest type.

In fact, "put it in writing" is a common request, accompanying the purchase of anything—from a baby buggy to a used car.

Lawyers love it. They sue people and companies. They defend. They challenge. They appeal. They seem to relish new opportunities in every business transaction. They try to put their clients, and themselves, first.

At the same time, they pose a new question for businessmen.

They replace the question about business activity: "Is it right?" with "Is it legal?"

This trend, developing over years, as attorneys try to protect their clients in an ever more complex business world, has created a division between morality and legality, weakening, if not dissipating, the strength and significance of once-prevalent handshake agreements.

In our Western civilization, laws and morals have strengthened each other since the time of Moses. Until now.

Our question of today should be, what's the right thing to do? The right way to behave? The right way to conduct business? Don't just ask, Is it legal?

Several states have passed laws declaring that companies with investments in South Africa are not acceptable bidders on state purchases and not acceptable as an investment by state pension funds.

My company has investments in South Africa and we provide both our white and black employees with working conditions very close to those in the U.S. and we provide our black employees with financial and growth opportunities not otherwise available.

I personally have sat with our black employees to determine their desires.

We are committed to stay even if we lose some business in the U.S. and our stock is affected by the reduced buying by pension plans.

The law is trying to be detrimental to our South African employees, and that isn't right.

Apartheid itself is another example of a law that isn't right, moral or ethical, and we break that law in our South African factory every day.

Let me be the first to admit that the choice is not always easy.

Consider, for instance, these questions from "Scruples," a Milton Bradley game:

—The garage forgets to charge you for a six-dollar oil filter. You think the labor charge is too high, anyway. Do you mention the undercharge?

—In a parking lot you accidentally dent a car. Do you leave a note?

—You are applying for a job requiring experience you don't

have. Do you claim you do?

Questions of this sort reach beyond legality.

They raise the question of right versus wrong, not legal versus illegal.

The answers require no legal knowledge. They require only common sense and the sense of fair play that we all learned as youngsters.

You remember. I remember. Don't cheat. Don't steal. Don't lie. Don't take advantage of anyone's weakness. The Golden Rule.

Do unto others the way you would have them do unto you.

In other words, treat the other guy fair. That's the way to solve all ethics problems.

You would think that business behavior would reflect that basic groundwork in ethics; that business actions would reflect our generally sound sense of rightness.

You would think that rightness would be an automatic choice—sort of like driving on the right side of the road—for our own benefit.

Have you ever considered what business would be like if we all did it? If every businessman (and businesswoman) followed the Golden Rule?

Ripe, red strawberries would fill a box from top to bottom.

Barrels would not contain a single rotten apple.

My company would not have to file a lawsuit alleging that counterfeit bearings were sold to Boeing Company by a California-based bearing supplier.

My company would not have to file a complaint with the Federal Trade Commission charging dumping of other bearings in United States markets.

Congress would not have to tighten curbs on insider trading.

Companies would not have to require employees to sign codes of conduct or establish strict guidelines for purchasing agents to follow.

The Harvard Business School would not have to require that each entering student take a three-week course on business ethics.

Drexel, Burnham Lambert would not have to pay a $650 million fine.

Many people, including many business leaders, would argue

that such an application of ethics to business would adversely affect bottom-line performance.

I say nay.

The ideas we are considering today go far beyond the bottom line.

If we do things right, because that's the way to do things, just imagine the effect we will have on customers.

Mr. Iacocca showed the beginnings of the possibilities when he led Chrysler in new directions.

Johnson and Johnson set a solid example when it pulled Tylenol off the shelves immediately during the crisis of a few years ago.

H. J. Heinz and Squibb established a high standard of ethical excellence when they supported our nation's pure food and drug laws early in this century.

In these situations, the businesses and their leaders put the public and their customers first.

I ask you to imagine the effect on the bottom lines of tomorrow if business were to follow these examples today.

Good ethics, simply, is good business.

Good ethics will attract investors.

Good ethics will attract good employees.

Moreover, good ethics will attract and retain customers, employees, investors, and build a quality reputation.

As you begin your careers, please remember that you set your own standards.

Your actions can lead to a Chrysler turnaround or to a Wedtech.

In a real sense, the future is up to you. You can change the way things are done. You can make the critical choice.

You can do what's right. Not because of conduct codes. Not because of rules or laws. But because you know what's right.

I will applaud your decision.

SOURCE: *Vital Speeches of the Day* 55 (April 1, 1989):

Speaking Excellence

A Walk on the Demand Side
The Drug Train

By William J. Byron
President of the Catholic University of America
Delivered at Commencement Exercises
St. Thomas University
Miami, Florida
May 14, 1989

COMING TO YOU, as I do, from Washington, D.C., I certainly do not want to appear, to a Miami audience, to be judgmental in reminding you that there is a horrible drug problem in America. Nor do I wash to strike you as excessively grim, on this great Graduation Day, by mixing drugs with diplomas and talking to you graduates about the crisis of drug abuse in America. But that is exactly what I propose to do, and do without apology. For I believe your last class, this final lecture, here at St. Thomas University, could serve you well by reminding you that you are blessed to have missed the assault of drugs during your collegiate years. The fullness of that deadly assault has missed you, obviously; otherwise you would not be here today. I want to challenge you today to do what you can, each one of you, in the years ahead, to reduce the vexing problem which holds such great potential to destroy all that this University has attempted to do for you in the development of your young and promising human potential.

Trust me for the next few minutes. Come with me for a reflective walk on the demand side of the drug problem in America—the drug problem that is there in the America you are stepping into as you leave this campus behind, the drug problem you will find in cities from New York to Los Angeles, from New Orleans to Duluth, and in virtually every town in between. Think about the drug problem confronting families in America—families large and small, rich and poor, black, white, Hispanic, Asian, Protestant, Catholic, Jew, Muslim. Reflect with me on the drug problem bedeviling young and old, educated and ignorant. Think about the problem that awaits a creative remedy from you, the next generation of leaders in this great country of ours. Forget for the moment about the source and supply of illegal drugs in America. Look to the reasons why there is a market for drugs in this nation which awaits your leadership. And then think of how you might reduce that demand in every sphere of your personal influence.

Ask the sixteen-year-old drug abuser from any class, race, or ethnic division why he or she abuses drugs or alcohol and you'll get a mumbled explanation about having "nothing to do" and living in a situation where "everybody else is doing it." Nothing to do. Everyone's doing it.

Deep down on the demand side of the problem of drug abuse in America lie three causal considerations. First is the desire—known to every normal, healthy person—to experience the exhilaration of a "high." Drug-induced highs, however, bring with them a dependency on drugs. Highs resulting from athletic, academic, artistic or other achievements are, of course, unaccompanied by damaging and eventually destructive dependencies. But such highs do not come easily.

The second causal consideration in examining the demand for drugs is the desire to avoid pain—physical or psychological pain. In a culture which cannot tolerate the thought of pain—physical or psychological—it is not surprising that avoidance of all pain, at all times, by all means, should become something of a supreme value. Our cultural denigration of pain, disappointment, discouragement, and monotony encourages escape at any price.

Our collective passivity resulting from a growing preference to have everything ready-made, available on demand and without delay, has left us holding the bag of boredom. "There's nothing to do!" We wait impatiently to be "turned on" and thus render ourselves vulnerable to drug-induced flights not just from humdrum reality, but from the human challenge of transforming reality by the exercise of human creativity. And creativity, even when inborn, does not develop easily.

The third causal consideration in examining the "why" of the human demand for drugs is biological. Babies born of addicted mothers are themselves addicts, right from the start. Other biological predispositions to addiction are possible, but they will not become addictions if addictive substances are never used. The determination to refuse does not come easily, especially when "everyone's doing it." It is not easy to resist peer pressure; it is not easy to swim against the everyone-is-doing-it tide.

There are reasons, of course, why apparently normal people—young people for the most part—will turn to drugs for the experience of a high. Some like to take risks. Risk-takers often fail to measure carefully the consequences. And where addictive substances are involved, risk-takers rarely recognize that there is not risk, but virtual certainty that one experience will lead to the captivity of addiction—not cause it immediately, but lead to it inevitably. Risk-taking is as easy as ignorance, and no less damaging. It is not easy to avoid destructive dependencies.

There are also reasons why normal young people want to avoid pain. Most of them are obvious. Less obvious is the fact that commercial advertisements have instructed them to take pills for the elimination of headache and heartburn long before they knew what these maladies were.

Pain has no redemptive value in the value system of a secular society. And the "no pain, no gain" equation applies only to weightlifters and athletic overachievers, not to normal folks. Pain, in any case, is never easy to bear.

Psychological pain is more often felt than understood by the young. Typically, it is just left unattended and unanalyzed. To the adolescent eye, everyone else is happy, except me. All others feel good about life and about themselves; I'm the only one with the problem. Adolescents appear to take strange delight, we know, in making classmates and other peers feel uncomfortable. They project upon others, more often than not, their own unease, insecurity, and self-depreciation. If only they would open up and talk about the dark view they have of themselves. But it is not easy to open up and drop the mask. It is not easy to admit to one's self-doubt or deficit of self-esteem. Besides, who would want to listen? Who's around to listen or to care? So adolescents are vulnerable to the easy exit, to the seduction of drug-related escapes from psychological pain.

If any of this sounds familiar to you, you may want to consider what you might do in the years ahead—as parents, helping professionals, or just friends—to put yourselves between some adolescents and their problems.

No one of you is an awkward, underconfident adolescent. No one of you is an infant with an addition. Some few of you may have a biological predisposition to addiction (may none of you ever discover it the hard way!).

No one of you is a masochist either, but this is not to say you are already mature enough to manage every pain of body or mind. I would hope you have already grasped something of what your Christian tradition has to tell you about the power of pain for redemptive purposes. No easy lesson to learn, but so well worth the effort!

Every one of you has a healthy appetite for the highs this life has to offer you through legitimate pleasure and honest achieve-ment in balanced and what Edward Bennett Williams used to call "contest living." The contest confronts you every day. The bal-ance is between matter and spirit, soul and body, faith and rea-son. The contest is never an easy victory, nor is the balance ever easy to achieve.

Those of us who have gone before you in the practice of life are not necessarily ahead of you. We have, for the most part, confused the easy life with the happy life. We are quite wrong about that and we hope you will not be condemned to learning that lesson for yourselves.

To those of you—and I hope I'm speaking at the moment to all of you—who have up to now escaped the destructive depen-dency that drug abuse inevitably brings, I want to say simply this. Do not be taken in by the big lie our culture of consumerism perpetuates. Do not believe that to have is to be, that to have more is to be more fully human, and, worst lie of all, to live eas-ily is to live happily.

Life will be painful at times. Bear it, and in the burden you bear you will find happiness.

Life will disappoint you at times, and so will people upon whom you had been counting, and of whom you had expected better. But don't give up on life, or on others, and never give up on yourself.

You are someone regardless of what you do or what you have. Sure, on days like this it is great to be able to celebrate achievement, to receive congratulations for what you have done, for earning the diploma which is yours today. But don't think you always have to do something in order to be someone. You are what you are, and that is saying a lot. You are a person of infinite worth, regardless of what you do or what you have. I hope you realize this. I hope you will communicate this realization by word, action, and the commitment of your concern and time, to others, especially to the young, as your personal contribution to the reduction of the demand side of the drug problem in America. If demand reduces to zero, supply no longer remains a threat.

I chose to speak to you this way today because I care about you and your future. I believe in you and in your ability to rise to the present challenge which is nothing short of a national crisis. I accept *New York Times* columnist A. M. Rosenthal's use of the nightmare metaphor in describing the problem your generation, and mine, must face if America is to be a land of the free, a land free of slavery to drug addiction.

"It is a familiar nightmare;" wrote Rosenthal in the *Times* on February 3, 1989, "we have all had it. The train is coming right down the track at somebody you know, and you scream, 'Get out of the way, get out of the way!' But he doesn't move, and the train comes on and on and you wake up sweating.

"A drug train is coming, but the people standing on the track simply do not seem able to jump out of the way or even hear the screeching whistle."

Well, the train is coming, my friends; not the gravy train but the drug train. And the people on the tracks are not just the addicts. We're there too. On this Graduation Day, your University is quite literally waving your diplomas in front of you not simply to alert you to the danger, but to challenge you this one last time to use your gifts to overcome this crisis and to make your personal contribution to the building of an addiction-free society.

SOURCE: *Vital Speeches of the Day* 55 (August 1, 1989): .

INDEX

CREDITS